I LEARNED ABOUT FLYING FROM THAT!

I LEARNED ABOUT FLYING FROM THAT!

by the Editors of
FLYING®

An Eleanor Friede Book

MACMILLAN PUBLISHING COMPANY

New York

Macmillan Publishing Company
866 Third Avenue, New York, N.Y. 10022
Collier Macmillan Canada, Inc.

Library of Congress Cataloging in Publication Data
Main entry under title:

I learned about flying from that!

Reprint. Originally published: New York: Delacorte Press/Eleanor Friede, c1976.
A collection of articles which appeared previously in **Flying.**
"An Eleanor Friede book."
1. Airplanes—Piloting—Addresses, essays, lectures.
2. Air pilots—Biography.   I. Flying (New York, N.Y.)
TL710.I14   1983   629.13'09'04   83-11304
ISBN 0-02-579340-3

First Macmillan Edition 1983

10 9 8 7 6 5 4 3 2 1

Printed in the United States of America

Substantially all the material in this work was first published in different form in *Flying* magazine.

Grateful acknowledgment is made to *Flying* magazine for permission to use illustrations from the following issues: October 1972, pp. 88-89, Barron Storey; November 1973, p. 63, Jeff Cornell; October 1974, pp. 28-29, Jeff Cornell; November 1974, p. 38, Stu Leuthner; and July 1975, p. 13, Dick Corson.

CONTENTS

    Colby Blodget has this thing about students . . . Morris, Hor-
    ris, what's the difference? Get out there and solo! . . . Flying in
    the shadow of his father . . . Richard Bach finds that he's not
    alone . . . A new pilot discovers her right-of-way . . . Passenger
    in command . . . How a crop duster tried too hard . . . Letter
    from the captain.

●

LIST OF CONTRIBUTORS

Bernard K. Allen *29*
Richard Bach *290*
Colby Blodget *270*
Robert Blodget *211*
James R. Bonde *101*
John F. Bouck *208*
H. Layton Bray *79*
Evelyn Burleson *46*
John Caruso *180*
Sam Chambliss *303*
David C. Cooke *4*
Commander George Cornelius, USN *35*
Bill Cox *218*
Dixon P. Downey *190*
Herbert Ekloh *116*
Devon Francis *92*
Major Wm. R. Fuchs, USAF *71*
Captain Ernest K. Gann *169*
D. Bruch Gardner *135*
Peter Garrison *246*
Ed Gillette *308*
Martin M. Goldsmith *111*
Lew L. Gourley *183*
J. Harvey Gray *263*
Donald Green *246*
Carl J. Grimm, III *159*
Captain William H. Harper *258*
Collingwood J. Harris *282*
Alma Heflin *138*

Clayton E. Henley *200*
Milton W. Horowitz *73*
Ensign Seymour Kail, USN *15*
Jack Katzenstein *124*
John A. Kent, Wing Commander, RAF *98*
Paul R. Kingston *119*
James Lemmart *187*
Guernsey Le Pelley *265*
Mel Lewis *174*
Garland Lincoln *203*
Lieutenant Colonel John M. Lowery *198*
David Lowrey *64*
James G. McCary *7*
Major H. James McConnell *236*
Paul Mantz *43*
Robert J. Martin *83*
Keith R. Matzinger *214*
Robert F. Meckoll *108*
Lieutenant Commander Franklin Metz-ner, USN *238*
N. R. de Mille *221*
Jeffrey Miller *142*
F. Robert Morrison *177*
Dee Mosteller *20*
Gary L. Nelson *154*
Wm. R. Novak *76*
David Petersen *24*
Robert Peterson *250*

viii

PREFACE

Experienced pilots like to observe that flying is unremitting boredom occasionally interrupted by moments of sheer terror. This appraisal is, of course, not quite accurate, and both experienced and inexperienced pilots know it. It is true, however, that the times when things go wrong in an airplane are considerably more exciting than when things are normal. It is also true that pilots tend to remember and to talk about the experiences that they had when things did not go as planned.

That's why pilots like to congregate in corners at social events, harangue each other in hangars and make swooping motions with their hands as they talk excitedly about harrowing adventures they've experienced.

The "I Learned About Flying from That" series is a way for pilots to address a considerably broader audience, bringing the benefits that other pilots accrue from hearing about misadventures, and serving as the expiation of their errors.

The feature started in May 1939 and has since run without major interruption in *Flying* Magazine, establishing a record of sorts.

With well over 400 individual articles to choose from, the selection, grouping and editing was clearly a monumental task. Here great credit is due *Flying* Senior Editor George C. Larson for his editing and Associate Editor Norbert Slepyan for his original culling.

While we sought to introduce as many different situations as possible in this collection, we were also influenced by each writer's style and the drama brought to the telling of his tale. Nonetheless, it is interesting to note how many of the incidents do involve weather problems. There are, of course, a number of mechanical malfunctions and just plain oversights on the part of the pilot, but unforeseen weather seems to be the stand-out villain in most cases.

We might add that as this series continues in *Flying,* the number of weather-related incidents seems to be decreasing. Doubtless, this is due in part to an improvement in weather forecasting and hopefully to a greater degree of proficiency and understanding of weather by modern pilots. There is, however, no dearth of submissions of "I Learned About Flying from That" experiences to *Flying.* The average holds at about 10 per day.

—ROBERT B. PARKE
Editor and Publisher, *Flying*

1/BEGINNER'S LUCK

Students of flying are unlike students in any other realm of endeavor; what sets them apart is their habit of plunging gaily ahead into situations that would turn a veteran of the trade ashen white. There is nothing inherently dangerous in most of these situations—given adequate training on the students' part. What makes these adventures hair-curling is the blissful unawareness with which the young pilots charge ahead. To the knowing, it is somewhat akin to watching a blindfolded person walking briskly toward the rim of a cliff. In some cases, one can only wonder if these near-victims' innocence is what protects them from the harm that seems sure to follow their failure to realize that they have missed their only chance to turn back.

Is it any easier for the student and the low-time pilot to confess their lapses than it is for the veteran? Sometimes yes, sometimes no. On the one hand, the beginner is *expected* to make mistakes and to run into situations that are new and unrecognizable, to him, as being dangerous. That is an inescapable part of learning to fly. For most pilots, that first encounter with hazard, alone, with only one's judgment to match against the wiles of nature and machinery, eclipses any and all close shaves that follow. This naturally leads to the reason why it is sometimes more difficult for the students to tell their story than it is for the advanced pilot: Students know that the outcome of the story is frequently entirely out of their hands, that there is reliance only on luck and none on self. The veteran can at least reasonably argue, if only with himself, that his skills helped to determine the outcome.

To begin with the beginning, here is a tale of a student with only two hours' solo experience tackling a weather situation far beyond his ability to cope. The story betrays not only the innocence of a new pilot but the innocence of the era—1937, when such bravado as this writer displayed was often admired.

●

I knew all there was to know about flying and aviation. According to my logbook, I had less than two hours' solo on Cubs under my belt. Of course, it would have been more if my instructor had let me go when I thought he should have.

Regardless of my "long" experience, he still tried to keep me under his wing, and on that 1937 Sunday morning he cautioned me to stay near Roosevelt Field. One of those typical Long Island fogs was slowly rolling in from the east. But I had different ideas; I wanted to fly out to the Seversky field at Farmingdale, Long Island, and shoot landings. It was only a few miles and a very few minutes by Cub, so I didn't believe I would have any difficulty.

Once in the air, it was a different problem. Although the fog was moving along ever so slowly down below, there was plenty of crosswind upstairs, and I battled and bucked all the way to Farmingdale, following a wide highway.

And then suddenly it got worse. The little drifting wisps of fog that I had encountered around Roosevelt were a lot different here. The fog was almost a solid mass, with small holes appearing occasionally. Still I wasn't worried. I knew the Seversky field and the surrounding territory well because of formerly having flown from there. With this wind, I figured I could come in smoothly over a cement-pipe plant, the location of which I had firmly fixed in my mind, and touch down easily about the middle of the field, rolling all the way to the hangar at the far end if necessary. The field was plenty large, and with a Cub it should be a cinch.

The approach worked out exactly as I had planned. When I eventually saw the dye plant on the left and the cement-pipe plant on the right, I knew I was almost on the field. I cut the throttle, just keeping enough power so that I would not be blown back to Roosevelt Field by the ever-increasing wind, and I started to ease forward on the stick to approach over the wires. It wasn't quite so bad close to the ground, and the Cub settled as smoothly as could be expected. I yanked the stick back to my stomach and held.

All three points touched in reasonable proximity, and the ship came to a sudden halt. There had been plenty of rain the past few days, and I had been unfortunate enough to hit a bare spot on the field's otherwise-smooth grass surface. The wheels were in hub-high mud!

I had enough presence of mind to cut the switch as the tail started to point skyward, and I tried to haul back even farther on the stick. Luckily, though, the Cub didn't go up on its nose, probably because of the stiff wind, not because of my efforts, and the tail settled back with a jarring crash.

After a cursory examination of the ship, I discovered that there was no apparent damage. I started the engine, but it was impossible to blast the Cub from the mud. I had to get out and prop the tail up on my shoulder in the approved manner and lug and pull and twist to get the wheels free and on solid ground.

I've often wondered why I didn't just stay there until the fog blew over. I lived in Farmingdale and could easily have gotten help to anchor the plane down, but at the moment I didn't realize the possible danger of the return trip. I took off even though visibility couldn't have been more than 100 yards at the outside. After leaving Farmingdale, however, visibility was much worse and the highway I was following disappeared completely.

After a reasonable length of time, I thought that I should be near Roosevelt and started to look for it. But there were no holes in the fog, and even the huge water tower at Mitchell Field was completely hidden. Then, for the first time, worry dew began to gather on my forehead. I started to come down through, hoping to find the field by beginner's dumb luck, but the thought of trying to push that checkered water tower out of the way was none too inviting. There was also the menace of trees near the edge of the field—and the high-tension wires didn't make me feel any better.

Instead of trying to make it blind, I cruised around, praying that some kind divinity would blow a hole through the soup and let this inexperienced one at least see a hangar below. But the fog seemed to close up even tighter, holding the ground below in a death shroud.

The gas tank had been full when I left Roosevelt, and the bob up front was slowly lowering. I just had to do something, and quickly—then I dimly saw a toothpick in the ocean of cloud.

That toothpick was the steeple of a Garden City church jutting up through the fog. It was the only structure in the area high enough to push through the overcast. At last I knew exactly where I was. I had often used that steeple as a landmark for judging turns and approaches. Trying to visualize the entire layout of the field and estimate the distances, I made my turn into the wind and ducked as cautiously as possible into the fog.

I was immediately swallowed up and practically digested by the fog. The windscreen up front became a mass of white nothing and I really couldn't tell whether I was level or upside down, turning or flying straight, climbing or diving. I prayed that I was doing the right things at the right times.

The throttle was back as far as was feasible, and I was trying to keep the nose down just enough so that there would still be room to pull up and away in case high-tension wires or other obstructions loomed in my path by some error in judgment.

Then I saw a bridge dimly. "That must be the Old Country Road," I said aloud, and I raised my nose slightly and advanced the throttle to stretch out the approach. Sure enough, the field fence passed beneath me and I could see the Air Associates' building off to the right a bit.

In at last—and right on the button!

I landed safely without further ado and taxied up to Hangar 7. My instructor was standing there by the fence when I climbed out. I was somewhat dejected and thoroughly beaten. He probably realized what I had gone through, although it didn't dawn on me at that time that he had undoubtedly suffered even more than I. He didn't say a word about the flight —not then. Later, though, I got hell aplenty from him.

I know enough about the aerial poker game now to realize that, with weather, sometimes it's a better idea to sit one out and wait for a new deal.

●

He may have caught hell, but heaven certainly appeared to have had a hand in his making it through that one unscathed. Here's another one-chance-in-a-million story of intercession on behalf of an Army Air Corps cadet who, like the student on Long Island, got stuck on top and had to find a way down.

●

It was a warm August evening at Maxwell Field, Alabama, when the cadets of Flight D fell out in their blue coveralls and marched to the flight line. We were to make our first solo night cross-country flight—in fact, our first night cross-country flight of any kind. Those were the days before all cadets were given the first night cross-country flight in a loose formation, accompanied by an instructor in a lead plane.

One of the wiseacres left behind remarked loudly as we marched away, "Count 'em now; there won't be that many when they get back."

At the hangar, we were dismissed from formation and sent inside for a briefing by the squadron commander. At the back of the briefing room stood a blackboard showing the route, altitude, bearings, radio frequencies and other data for the flight.

The squadron commander announced that the flight would be a round robin from Maxwell Field at Montgomery to Mobile, Alabama, and return. The entire flight was on beacon-lighted airways. After emphasizing the data on the blackboard, he dismissed us to our individual instructors. From them we received help in preparing maps and flight logs and were given last-minute advice. The words of my instructor stayed in my mind as I lugged my parachute toward the T-6: "If you can't maintain the recommended altitude due to clouds, don't go on top; stay underneath and in visual contact so you can see those beacons."

He didn't say what to do if the clouds came down to the treetops—and an inexperienced cadet didn't think to ask such a question.

The takeoff was uneventful, and as I climbed south to pick up the first beacon I could see that the weather was indeed CAVU, as promised by the forecaster. All the way to Mobile everything went smoothly as planned. Over Mobile, as I checked in by radio with the squadron control plane, the T-6 began to pass through cloud. Big, fluffy clouds were forming fast, rolling in over the city lights and gradually obscuring them.

I descended to the recommended altitude—2,000 feet—and set course for Maxwell. I now found myself flying through solid cloud, so I pulled up to 3,000 feet, and thereby put myself about 500 feet on top. There was no comforting flash from a beacon to be seen anywhere. I grimly held my course and stared through the darkness ahead, hoping to see a break.

After several minutes, I recalled my instructor's parting words and realized that I was flying on top, just as he had told me not to do. In my mind, there was nothing to do but let down until I could fly VFR under the clouds. I set up a letdown at 120 mph, 500-fpm rate of descent, and eased the T-6 into the clouds.

Looking up, I saw the last star disappear. In my concentration on the instrument panel, I could not afford to dwell on the thought that this was my first time to be flying entirely by instruments. Before this, instrument flying had consisted of being under a hood, with a fellow student or instructor in the other cockpit as observer. Now I was alone, flying on instruments in bad weather on my first night cross-country flight.

The letdown was only slightly erratic, for the air was fairly smooth. The altimeter slowly wound down. At an indicated 1,200 feet, I decided I had gone far enough. The highest point along this route was 700 feet, which theoretically left me 500 feet of clearance. I moved the throttle forward and changed the descent to a climb. This time I had to go to 4,000 feet to get on top of the cloud mass. For about 20 minutes I flew on course and waited for a break in the overcast.

There was none. Gradually my desire to see the friendly lights of towns and beacons overcame my better judgment. Once again I began a letdown. This time there was no decision to level off at 1,200 feet. Surely, I thought, these clouds must be well above the trees.

Everything was under control, and the altimeter was passing through 900 feet, when suddenly the T-6 broke into the clear, heading straight for an automobile moving along a backwoods road. I was almost blinded by the sudden sight of its headlights. Straight ahead lay a row of trees, and treetops were passing in a blur beneath the wings.

In a flash, I laid on full throttle, pulled up across the car and was immediately in cloud again. The sudden burst of engine power and the accompanying torque made all the instruments seem to go crazy. In a cold sweat I fought to settle them down again, but in my fright it seemed that I could only straighten out one instrument at a time. I kept reciting to myself, "Rate of climb, up for sure; watch that airspeed, already back to 100; level the wings on the artificial horizon; get back to that compass heading."

After long minutes, everything was under control and I had

the T-6 back on top. There I resolved to stay, until I sighted Maxwell or the fuel gave out.

Before long, as I was tuning in the Maxwell radio range, the solid clouds became broken and the beacon lights came into view about 10 miles to my left. They led me into the home field and to a safe landing.

My sleep that night was broken many times as I dreamed over and over again of that sudden pull-up from a near-crash. Each time, the sight of those car lights saved me from going down a few more feet, into the trees. Then and there I resolved never to let down on instruments to get under a low ceiling unless I was making the prescribed radio-range letdown and low approach to an airport.

●

Presumably, the reason the Army changed its procedures later on and put instructors up in lead planes at night was that what happened to this cadet was no isolated incident. That was during World War II, a time when you were on your own if you got stuck on top without instruments or the training to use them. Air traffic control was then a new idea, and pilots worried more about hitting the terrain than they did about hitting each other. With the growth of air activity, both civilian and military, the sheer volume of traffic demanded a better way: radar—and behind the radarscope, a controller.

Here's what happened when a 70-hour pilot got stuck on top because he was anxious to put his new license to use and do a favor for a friend. The difference between this story and that of the cadet is that the 1973 pilot had a helping hand when he got into trouble.

●

Saturday dawned clear and cold. It would be chilly for the preflight, but it looked like a nice day for flying. We expected the cold, since it was the last weekend in January, but the sun was a surprise: New Yorkers hadn't seen the sun in over a week, due to a storm that had deposited eight inches of snow and ice over most of the East Coast. I had promised to take a friend and his sister-in-law to Syracuse so she could be back at college on Monday. Flight service confirmed that the outlook for the day was good until late that afternoon. Our departure was set for 10 A.M., so I figured we'd be back before the weather turned bad.

Our first indication that the day wouldn't go according to plan came when I arrived at the airport and found the Cherokee all but buried under a snowdrift and held firmly in place by a solid sheet of ice. The only way to get it cleaned off was to move it into the hangar and hose it down. Unfortunately, five other pilots had the same idea, and they had gotten there first. By the time we lifted off, it was after one o'clock, but the forecast hadn't changed, and I was still confident that we'd have plenty of time to make the flight and return before either nightfall or weather would cause any concern.

The initial portion of the trip was uneventful, and I settled down to explain some of the mysteries of aviation to my two nonpilot passengers. Class was cut short, however, about the time we passed over the Huguenot Vortac, for the horizon to the north and west was slowly disappearing. Nothing to worry about, folks, but I was wondering what had happened to the 12,000-foot ceiling I'd heard about in the morning.

I didn't have to wonder long. Ceilings were dropping all around me, and I started running into snow showers and decreasing visibility. A call to Wilkes-Barre Flight Service prompted a decision to head south and try to skirt this fairly localized disturbance. The weather soon cleared, and I started to swing west and head toward Binghamton. So far, it was nothing I couldn't handle, but I was beginning to think that maybe a 70-hour pilot like myself shouldn't promise to deliver someone at a prescribed time. Not in the heart of winter.

Suddenly, there were strange grinding noises from somewhere behind the panel. A quick scan showed that the tachometer needle was bouncing all over the face of the instrument. I told my passengers that there was nothing to be concerned about, and I hoped I sounded convincing. At least the engine sounded all right.

Ten miles north of Binghamton, we were no longer bothered by noise from behind the panel: The tach needle convulsed once more and finally died. To make things worse, we seemed to be working our way back into the snowstorms and low ceilings we had seen earlier. A classic 180-degree turn put us back in the area of the Broome County Airport, but in the three or four minutes since we had seen the field, it had gone below minimums. All we could do now was to remain VFR over Binghamton, but the tower advised they had an American Airlines 727 on final and could we please give way. After 30 minutes of waiting, Tri-Cities Airport opened up and we landed to stretch our legs, check the weather and look for someone who might know the right things to say to motionless tachometers. We had now been flying for nearly three hours; my passengers were wondering what they'd gotten into.

As the skies continued to clear over the field, our hopes for a successful finish to the trip rose. I had already decided that we would spend the night in Syracuse, if we could just get there. Flight service reported that Syracuse was showing 2,000 broken and seven-plus miles, so we went back out to the plane. Trying to find run-up rpm and the proper cruise settings by ear was a whole new experience for me, but fortunately the Six was equipped with a fuel-flow gauge and EGT, and the 1973 fuel crisis had made me more aware of appropriate fuel readings at cruise.

Ahead of me lay the now-familiar clouds. This time, I decided not to try to poke around, under or through them; I climbed to get on top. This was more like it! Sunshine, clear air, unlimited visibility and no sweaty palms. Why didn't I think of this before? My passengers seemed much more at ease, and one of them even managed to fall asleep. The one disadvantage to

VFR on top is the absence of landmarks to confirm your radio navigation. It seemed a small price to pay, and besides, the DME was reassuringly counting down the miles to Hancock International, just outside Syracuse. All seemed right with the world.

I kept thinking 2,000 broken, but it sure looked solid from where I sat. I tuned in the ATIS, and the numbers I got were the same ones I had heard earlier. My companions were asking if we had to go through that stuff. I called approach control, and when the voice said, "Go ahead," I explained the situation. "One-One November is 23 DME southeast of Hancock, level at 8,500 VFR on top, squawking 1200. We've got just over one hour of fuel remaining and cloud cover appears to be solid. Oh, by the way, we have a minor equipment malfunction. Our tach's dead."

"Roger, One-One November, radar contact. Can you accept an instrument approach?"

"Negative."

"What does your license say?"

"Private pilot, aircraft, single-engine land."

"Say your type aircraft, number of hours you've logged and number of hours in type."

"Sir, the aircraft is a Cherokee Six. I've logged 70 hours total, with about 12 hours in type."

I could almost see him grab for the operating manual, and he quickly started asking questions and giving directions.

"One-One November, is your pitot heat on?"

"Affirmative."

"If you are straight and level, set your directional gyro against your compass and turn to a heading of 320 degrees."

By stages (approach control suggesting and pilot complying), we managed to get to within four miles of Hancock, where the snow-covered ground became distantly visible. I advised radar that I could barely see the ground and asked if they had any traffic in the area. When the answer was negative (who else would be slogging around in this mess?), I pulled the power back and started a spiraling descent through the misty hole. When I advised that I was down to 1,000 feet indicated, they gave me radar vectors, which brought me right over the end of Runway 32, and I got my first glimpse of a nearly socked-in field. I made a wide circle to the right to get set up for the landing, and the last thing approach control said before I touched down was, "Relax, you've got over 9,000 feet of runway in front of you."

After touchdown, ground control requested that I call the tower and discuss with them the circumstances that had led to my making a landing at a field which was, by then, down to 600 and one mile in blowing snow. I thought about it then, and I've thought about it often since, for I've realized that I had all the elements of a serious problem: a low-time, VFR pilot in a relatively unknown airplane faced with mechanical problems, rapidly deteriorating weather and low fuel, but because of a mental commitment, refusing to take the really smart step of turning back. Any one or two of these problems could be handled, and were. But the problem that turned out to be potentially the most dangerous, and the hardest to handle, was plain old stubbornness. I hope I never forget when to say, "We can't make it today. It's time to turn back."

●

What a difference three decades of progress make when you compare that tale with the two that preceded it. Being lost on top had less of a sting to it in 1973 than it did back in the '40s. For this pilot, there was a valuable lesson in the forecast that failed to come true, a lesson that he might not have learned if he had not attempted the flight at all. Having encountered those surprise snow showers and having successfully landed at one airport, he made his judgmental error when he took off the second time.

Still, one cannot fault the new pilot for wanting to use what he has worked for. There is the natural urge in everyone to move onward and upward, to probe, to try bigger things. Trainers are for training, after all, and with that license fresh in hand, the new pilot feels rightly entitled to fly "real" airplanes on "real" missions.

Here's what happened to a Navy cadet who was so eager to make the big step up to a serious flying machine that he couldn't hear some good advice when it was given.

●

When a budding Navy pilot has gone through five months of stunts, precision landings, formation work and general maneuvers in the faithful old NY primary seaplanes and yellow Stearman NS-1 landplane trainers at Pensacola, he's likely to fancy himself with very few peers in the flying realm.

That's just how I felt the day they moved me up from Squadron Two to Squadron Three, where you climb into the cockpit of a silver service-type Chance-Vought SU-1 for the first time in what is probably the most exacting military aviation training school in the world. Cockiness is a mild word for it. I just had what it took, that's all. Uncle Sam was indeed a fortunate gent when I decided to get my wings.

In Squadron Three, cadets are indoctrinated into the whys and wherefores of service flying—close 9- and 18-plane formation, navigation flights, machine gunnery from the rear cockpit with a swivel gun, radio and wireless procedure, circle shooting with the faster and heavier military-type craft. Up to that point in his course, the student has had all of 130 hours, hence the likelihood of exalted ego in a fellow who a few short months back didn't know an aileron from a rudder.

But that is kindergarten, and suddenly you go into the higher education of flying. Altogether some 80 hours are spent in Squadron Three, each student part of an 18-plane formation. These same 18 cadets go through Squadron Four, the advanced seaplane outfit in which are imparted the mysteries of catapulting, torpedo planes and the big twin-engined flying boats. Then comes the senior course in Squadron Five—the fighting-plane unit. All this should have given me at least an inkling that Squadron Three was still far from the goal of a finished, fully trained pilot.

Before handling a plane on his own in Squadron Three, a cadet must be checked out, sometimes by a hard-bitten veteran chief aviation-machinist's mate who has many years of flying behind him and has packed into his noggin a full payload of useful, life-saving information. My check-out pilot was methodical, conscientious, and so thorough about his instructions I became bored, and I committed the inexcusable blunder of allowing the information that penetrated one ear to slip blithely out of the other.

He explained the numerous gadgets and gauges in the unfamiliar cockpit, launched into a lengthy dissertation on engines in general and this supercharged one in particular. My brain was numb and unreceptive, my attitude one of "hurry up and finish your lecture, which I hope you're enjoying, but let me at that plane." The know-it-all with five months of flying experience was being merely condescending to the teacher, who was following a routine that seemed ludicrously secondary to the actual operation of the plane.

As I comb the cobwebs away and look back at that morning, I vaguely recall an earnestly uttered appeal that had to do with the yellow-and-red squares painted on the exhaust stacks, denoting a supercharged, high-pressure Pratt & Whitney engine. There were five minutes or so of how to treat this 450-hp gem while I gazed fondly at the dull-gray fuselage and tail section, imagining this thing of power in a loop. Of course, loops were forbidden, but there was no harm in dreaming, was there?

The oration having ended, we climbed in and practiced landings at a small field about 15 miles from Pensacola. My instructor apparently was satisfied. The plane was a revelation to one accustomed to the slower training craft, but I adjusted myself rapidly to its idiosyncrasies and proceeded to show Age in the back seat how Youth was handling a situation of this sort these days.

The following morning, my name appeared on the blackboard—"one hour familiarization." That meant I had 60 minutes to practice landings in any of several fields near Pensacola and thoroughly acquaint myself with the ship before entering into 18-plane formation tactics. With joy in my heart, I drew a parachute—number 13. I'm not superstitious, you see, and besides, that plane was really my baby. Only 15 minutes at the controls had proved that to me yesterday.

I inspected the craft from wingtip to tail, scrutinized closely each flying wire and turnbuckle, checked the oleos and peered with traditional suspicion at all the control wires. As for the engine, the mechanics in the squadron were experts, gave it as perfect a grooming as Seabiscuit would have gotten at peak racing glory, and there was nothing I could do either to aid its efficiency or to assure its future as part of the plane.

As I examine my reasoning of that particular moment, I wonder if that isn't the unfortunate attitude of many another military or commercial transport pilot who has a corps of highly trained grease monkeys continually toiling over his plane's engine to guarantee its perfect performance.

Don't take anything for granted!

I feebly tried to recall what the chief aviation-machinist's mate, my instructor of the day before, had said about the engine, but it simply hadn't registered. I took off easily, headed into the morning sun and circled left toward the traffic lane to Veterans Field, about one mile north of the Pensacola Municipal Airport and 15 miles from my takeoff point.

I approached the small field at 1,500 feet, saw the 100-foot white circle and decided to practice circle shots, made by flying either downwind at 800 feet or upwind at 1,200 feet, cutting the engine to idle and maneuvering the ship to a landing.

Down I came, S-turning and slipping off excess altitude to drop smack in the middle on the first attempt. This was child's play. With the plane still rolling, I slammed the throttle forward. The resultant backfire momentarily startled me. The engine caught with a roar of smooth power and back up I went, noting with some amazement that I had barely cleared a forest of tall trees at the end.

Say, this was a tight field! Hardly two city blocks long, and the circle in the middle. With a heavy military plane I had to clear 50-foot trees in a stunningly small area. Musing over this, I remembered the backfire, wondering for a moment what had caused it. Then it slipped just as quickly from my thoughts.

I was at 1,200 feet directly over the field and heading upwind. There was the circle just emerging from under my left wingtip. Back came the throttle and forward the nose. I maneuvered to keep the circle just off my wingtip until I was heading downwind. Then I allowed the plane to go a short distance beyond the field, but within gliding distance of the circle. At the correct moment I banked and headed for the landing sphere, slipping off the excess height, easing back on the stick slowly until it fell out from under me just as all three points were in landing position inside the near edge of the circle. Another beauty!

Then I plunged the throttle forward again. Alarm replaced bravado. The motor was spitting and popping convulsively. My speed was easily 60 knots, but a quick glance at the tachometer revealed 1,350 rpm with the hand waving wildly between 1,100 and 1,500. Neither would pull me off the ground soon enough to avoid a terrific head-on crash into that wall of trees ahead. The sputtering engine pulled the plane over the ground swiftly, but just under takeoff speed. I did the only thing I could in such an emergency.

I desperately yanked the throttle back as far as it would go. The trees were only 100 feet in front of me. I eased on the brakes at first, then literally stood on the right one to ground-loop me in that direction and away from a stone wall that now arose to add to the horror of the impending crash.

The next few seconds were a blur. With the sickening realization that I was turning over, I threw my hands in front of my face to ward off a blow from the cockpit edge or instrument panel. Up and on its back went the plane, its churning prop chewing up Florida real estate in huge, ravenous bites. As the tail went over in a sweeping arc, it seemed the ground was rushing at me like the Twentieth Century Limited.

By a stroke of good fortune, the upper wing did not collapse, or my neck would have been garlanded with an inextricable wreath of fabric and metal. While my head remained foolishly suspended only a few inches from gravel and dirt, sounds of wings cracking and buckling, control surfaces shooting in various directions and the engine shuddering a painful farewell to the mounts drifted to my burning ears. Dejectedly the plane itself seemed to settle—*slump* probably would be a better word. Silence reigned, but not for long.

A trickling sound claimed my dulled attention. Leaking gasoline! I snapped open the safety belt in what was probably my speediest and best-timed move of that day. Parachute and all, I was dumped from the seat. I scurried out from under the ship like a sand crab and stood panting 20 feet away. Gasoline was pouring all over the plane from the tanks on the side of the fuselage. Luckily the fuel from the split containers had not ignited. Later, as I sat in the crash truck amid a litter of accusing wreckage, my good, good friend the chief machinist's mate told me what had occurred. It seems that on the previous day he had given me explicit instructions on how to treat this engine. A supercharged engine, he had said, will not take a sudden slapping forward of the throttle. It will either cut entirely or perform as mine did when a load of too much raw gasoline is forced into the cylinders. There was a 50–50 chance it might catch, as it had on the first circle shot, but don't remind me of the second.

My mistake had been to take for granted that an engine was just an engine and not the concern of the pilot. It was my capital error to ignore the fact that a powerplant has a personality of its own, with definite reactions to certain treatment, just like the aviator himself. I took my engine for granted. I regarded as unimportant and dull routine the instructions of an older and far wiser head.

Flying over water day after day in landplanes as Navy pilots do, we are supposed to cherish the value of a perfectly functioning engine. Every fact and figure on the engine is available to him who wishes to read as well as run. Exhaustive factory tests and men's sweat and blood have made the present-day engine the acme of perfection. But one fool behind a throttle can jimmy years of painstaking development. I know from personal experience.

●

If the step from a normally aspirated engine to a supercharged one looms large in retrospect to that pilot, the move from a trainer to a four-seat Cherokee turned out to be an equal challenge to this young woman, who was as anxious as the cadet to move up to what she calls "Big Iron." The catch that nearly tripped her up was something she hardly expected.

●

This has got to be the dumbest thing a pilot ever did. (But we all say that every time, don't we?) The day I logged my seventy-first hour, I reached the second plateau of overconfidence that comes in most normal flying lifetimes. The first had occurred, as it does to all self-respecting pilots, on the third solo flight, and was immediately hollered away by a tough old instructor. Now, holding a 20-hour-old private license, I decided that I was ready for new challenges.

I wanted to be free of the confines of my heretofore-limited flying area, which consisted of about 100,000 square miles of Texas flat. Give me Big Iron, I cried. Get me out of those dinky two-seaters and put me into something fast and furious, something that can scale mountains.

The mountains lay 250 miles to the northwest, jagged, thorny and twisting they were, like the encrusted tail of a dragon. The Sangre de Cristo Mountains whipped their angry peaks 10,000, even 12,000 feet into the New Mexico sky, forming an awesome end for the great Rockies. There's where I wanted to wander.

I had heard fearsome tales about mountain flying, about instant thunderstorms with rocks in the clouds, giant down-drafts that crush little airplanes, insidious creeping hypoxia, aircraft performance that went *kaput* just when you needed it most. But I had studied the ways of mountain flying in books, and I was prepared.

Oh yeah, I was very well prepared. Two weeks before my proposed three-hour flight to Sante Fe, I was calling daily for weather between Abilene and SFE, seeking winds aloft, dew points, forecasts, pireps, any news of the atmosphere that holds the Sangre de Cristos in place. My route was ruled in indelible red on a new sectional, checkpoints heavily cross-hatched every 10 miles, the few en-route VORs circled. My flight plan was written; a new friend in Santa Fe was apprised of my ETD and ETA; my traveling clothes had been selected and now hung isolated in the closet.

My chosen airplane was a slightly careworn but nonetheless beautiful Cherokee with a masterful 160 Lycoming, the prede-cessor of the efficient Cherokee 180. Now, the 160-hp Cherokee wasn't exactly a four-place airplane—more like three and a half —but it had four seats and an alleged cruise speed of something like 117 knots. To me, that was Big Iron.

Of course, I had never flown a Cherokee in my life, and all but 20 minutes of my 71 hours had been in high-wings; those other 20 minutes had been in a Mooney. But what did I care about particulars? I had read and memorized the performance figures. I knew in theory at what speed it would stall, how many feet per minute it ought to climb, and all that other jazz. And after all, didn't I have a license to take people into the sky and do with them what I willed? Besides, the guy who was renting me the Cherokee swore I'd have no trouble with this easy-flying, easy-handling airplane once he'd given me a thorough check-out.

Somehow, he didn't get around to the check-out until the day before I was to leave; but when he did, I was superb. I fit into the left seat like I was born there, took off straight and true, and climbed out right on the numbers, marveling at the terrific rate of climb—all the way up to 2,500 feet. We drove out west a couple of miles, did two low-level stalls (he was in a hurry to get back to a ground-school class waiting in the hangar) and came home. I did one touch-and-go, and on the second approach he called for full stop, congratulating me on becoming a Cherokee pilot.

I departed on a glorious day when you could see practically all the way to Sante Fe. I climbed up 12,500 feet, into the thin-oxygen zone, long before I needed to. A little more than two hours into the flight, I was over the Sangre de Cristo Mountains with my nose pressed to the window, gawking at the overpowering beauty. I don't think I ever looked at the instrument panel from the moment I reached the first molehill—until my engine quit. Even then I didn't look at the panel. Instead, I looked at the propeller, which seemed to be slowing down considerably, at the blue sky, where I figured I'd soon be meeting my Maker, at the peaks below, which instantly changed from wonderland to inferno. Where does one land on a Rocky Mountain? Was I within gliding distance of some smooth, green valley? Gliding distance? What the heck was the glide ratio of this sonofagun? How should I know? I didn't know a thing about the airplane.

I didn't look at the panel until after I had picked out the least offensive-looking spot to land, or until I had wasted some time worrying that if I pranged the Cherokee no one would let me rent a plane again. This silly stuff was roaring through my head, keeping out the practicalities that should have been there—like what made the engine stop and what would make it start again.

I still had about a thousand feet between me and my emergency landing field when I finally looked at the panel. Naturally, everything was out of place. I found the airspeed and rate-of-climb indicators first, which made me not want to look at the panel anymore.

Slowly a smidgen of early training lumbered back into mind. What was that old checklist anagram? CIGAR! Maybe that would help. C for controls: Forget it. I for instruments: The flight instruments all looked terrible, but that wasn't the cause, it was the effect. The engine instruments looked okay, except for the fuel pressure. Fuel pressure? G for gas: Ohmygod.

Where's the bloody gas gauge? Was I surprised to see *two* of them, one reading "F" and the other "E." All those hours in high-wingers hadn't taught me a thing about balancing a fuel load or switching tanks. Here I was with all the gas gone from the left wing, but a gloriously full right tank, and I didn't know how to switch. At that moment I sheepishly realized that this was why the airplane had kept trying to turn right.

If I hadn't flown that Mooney with an instructor who was conscientious enough to explain the airplane, including its fuel system, even for a 20-minute flight, I might have tried that mountain landing. As my entire flying life flashed through my mind, somewhere in there was a vivid picture of the Mooney fuel selector, hunched down between the pilot's legs. Naturally, I stared at my feet, only to see the bare floor. In those days, the Cherokee's fuel switch was on the pilot's-side wall slightly farther back than it is today. And being five-foot-three, I had the seat jammed as far forward as possible. My body was inched even closer to the pedals by pillows placed behind my back, so that most of the selector was hidden. The portion of it that might have been visible was obscured by the crumpled sectional in my lap and my stylishly baggy culottes.

Willing to try anything, I released the seat, frantically looking in the back for the fuel selector, and when I turned around, what to my wondering walleyes did appear but the precious item. I lunged, and so did the Cherokee. I didn't even turn the fuel pump on, but the fuel system was reliable enough without it. Within a few seconds the engine was singing the Hallelujah Chorus.

I crept into Santa Fe, did a terrible nosewheel landing, taxied the wrong way, climbed out on shaky underpinnings, fell off the wing walk and scratched my shin on the step. Thankfully, my friend was late to the airport and missed my entrance. My second plateau of overconfidence was past, and I had learned a big lesson: *Never trust a stranger.* Airplanes are enough like people so that you must be well acquainted with them to establish a meaningful relationship; you must understand their ways so as not to get hurt by them.

●

Anyone might think from reading that story that high-wing air-planes, in which both fuel tanks supply fuel if the pilot chooses, would eliminate any fuel-management problem. But the odds say that a student would figure out some way to run out of fuel, even with a Stone-Age-simple fuel system like that in a Cessna 150. And that's exactly what happened here.

●

Being a student pilot with exactly six hours of solo cross-country time and enthralled by my first two solo excursions, I decided to get my ten needed hours by flying four hours in one trip. With that out of the way, my private license seemed close enough to touch.

Two hundred miles would be a good distance. A Cessna 150 usually ended up getting a little less than 100 mph over the ground, and that would give me a certain four hours of flight time. I pulled the string of the wall map out of the 200-mile mark and moved it in a circle around Chicago. La Crosse, Wisconsin, caught my eye, and I wove the string over the VORs. Two hundred and ten miles. That's well within the range allowed student pilots, I thought. Mentally calculating my cash, I decided to go before the next weekend, at which time my wife and I would be driving to La Crosse to hunt. Not only would it wrap up my cross-country time, but I'd be able to scan the landscape for suitable hunting territory. Suddenly the $72 it would cost for the four hours shrank to the size of a bargain basement special.

Three days later I showed up at the airport laden with a detailed en-route flight log and a set of sectionals. I called flight service: Scattered at 5,000, nothing coming. Winds aloft, not much—between six and eight knots, westerly, at 3,000 and 6,000. I collared an instructor and laid out my flight plan for him. After asking the routine questions—weather, what radial are you going to be dialing here, how long will it take, when is legal sunset (this last seemed silly since it was only 11 A.M.)— he signed my log and watched as I filed my flight plan. That done, I headed for the plane.

I had no reason to worry. Navigation was easy, and I had more than four hours' fuel for a two-hour 19-minute flight. The weather was good, the shortest runway at La Crosse was a mile long, and the plane was new, with full gyros. It would be fun.

I noticed the fuel truck just moving away from my plane as I neared it, but I snapped on the master and checked the gauges anyway. Full. I checked the plane and was reaching up on top of the wing to be certain the fuel caps were on tightly, when a lineman good-naturedly yelled, "I never see *anybody* do that."

Waving back to him, I was confident my fuel tanks weren't going to be sucked dry suddenly by a missing fuel cap. I shouted, "Clear prop," locked the window and taxied out of the parking area. After the completely normal run-up and a silent unicom frequency, I scanned the pattern, turned onto the active and was off.

I crossed the Northbrook VOR a few minutes later and tapped my chronograph into activity. In another minute I was on the radial. I called Chicago Radio and activated my flight plan for 1700 Zulu, with arrival 1930 Zulu, then got down to the business of flying.

It wasn't a particularly bumpy day, and once trimmed, the 150 required little attention. I decided the Fox River, 17 miles out, would be an excellent checkpoint for my groundspeed. I was flying over the student practice area and really didn't need a map, but when the Fox River was slow in turning up I got out the Chicago Local to have a look. I checked the radial on the VOR and the compass heading. Yes, I was flying in the right direction. The Fox River finally appeared; I pressed my watch, noted the time and started the watch again. Thirteen minutes. I manipulated my computer and was stunned when it read 79 mph. That isn't possible, I thought, checking the settings. But I had the outer 17 by the inner 13 and there it was. Well, I thought, that includes climb, I'm probably getting 90 now, and that will do.

But checkpoints were not coming up as they should have, and my next groundspeed check showed 74 mph. I got out the cruise performance chart and looked up 2,500 rpm at 2,500 feet. One hundred and eight TAS at 68 percent power. That was correct, and I'd been warned about running it over 2,500 rpm —be kind to your engine. I wondered if I was caught in a freak headwind. I thought about that awhile and then went lower, watching the trees and lakes as I did. They didn't appear to be ruffled much.

Probably I'd mistaken my place on the map. Maybe I was much farther along than I had thought. A sign painted on the roof of a lumberyard deflated that delusion.

Twenty minutes at 1,000 feet off the ground netted me 76 mph. Oh well, so what, it's just more solo time. Then I computed the total hours to La Crosse. Two hours and 45 minutes. That's okay. Except that the farther I went, the slower it got. An hour and 25 minutes from Chicago found me just approaching a sharp bend in Victor Airway 97—90 miles out of Chicago! I tuned in the Lone Rock VOR and was gratified when I made the turn on my single VOR so perfectly that, as I rolled out on my new heading, the needle settled on dead center.

My confidence renewed, I spent the next 15 minutes feeling good. Then I happened to glance at the fuel gauges. It was incredible! They were half empty after only 1.4 hours! I tried to remember the gallons per hour and the endurance hours and couldn't. I *knew* the endurance had to be over 4 hours; it just *had* to be. The book reassured me with 4.4 hours at 2,500 feet and 4.7 at 5,000 feet. Even though I was at 4,500 feet, I relied on the lower figure. I got out my computer again. So far I was making 67 mph over the ground. Then I computed the gallons. I should have used 8.5 gallons according to my computations, but the gauges showed over 11 gone. According to the gauges, I was burning it up at the rate of 7 gallons an hour! Impossible, I thought; I had it leaned out. I decided to wait and see.

Maybe the wind wouldn't be so bad on a more northerly heading. Actually, I didn't believe the wind was that bad. It must be the plane. A friend had been discussing how these planes would never do what the book said. I vaguely considered landing for gas and looked over the airport guide. Gonstead: fuel available, unattended. How do you get fuel when it's unattended? I could see myself acting like a fool at a strange airport, so I tried looking up New Glarus, a little behind me now. Not listed on the back of the map. Dodgeville? That was quite a way off my route; besides, the computer said I'd make it to La Crosse.

I listened to the weather on the VOR and then called to have them let La Crosse know I'd be late arriving on my filed flight plan. What presence of mind! I was well on my way to being later than I knew.

I finally became certain the gas gauges were entirely incorrect, and that knowledge kept me flying for another hour until the needles were dangerously close to empty, showing much less than a quarter tank on each gauge. This got me to wondering just exactly where "empty" was on the scale. I began looking over the terrain with a different eye from before. Trees, big hills, sharply sloping farms. But La Crosse was so close now, only 21 miles away. So it went that one moment I'd be sure I'd make it, but then the next moment I'd think I'd do better choosing a place to land while I vacillated.

I thought about landing at Viroqua. That was a grass strip, however, and I once spent 15 minutes circling a town looking for a grass strip. Once again La Crosse came up as the safest bet.

I was still at 4,500 feet when I spotted the break in the hills that I knew must be the Mississippi. It seemed to inch toward the plane ever so slowly. I wasn't fooling with the computer anymore, just watching that line of hills creep toward me. Three hours and five minutes. I had 4.4 hours of gas at worst; at least that's what I thought, I wasn't sure about anything anymore. The gauges showed nearly empty.

Listen to La Crosse (at least they had an FSS on the field); they'll be giving runways and wind. Which way is the wind from? Three hundred degrees? Land into the west then. But everything west looks uphill. How do you land going uphill? I had an immediate vision of smashing into a slope. Try to explain that. How about landing somewhere that isn't a field?

Then I spotted the point of land running out into the river with a bay on the east side of it. Water around the airport. Just what I needed.

The needles aren't *really* on empty—are they? Thank goodness I'm high enough to glide. If you can glide ten miles from 6,000, I reasoned, then you can glide six miles from 4,000. In another few minutes I can make it. Gliding.

Trying to call La Crosse, I dialed the wrong frequency twice. Once I got them, though, they gave me Runway 13. One-Three? That's over the water. I'd better stay high in the pattern.

Then I was there; high by nearly a thousand feet until final, when I bravely dumped it off with a slip and sat down on that wonderful, long runway. My eyesight being somewhat narrow-visioned at the moment, I immediately spotted Shell signs and did everything except taxi straight across the grass between the runways to get there. I had made it.

I stood around as the plane was being filled. A lineman asked, "How much *does* a 150 hold?" The gas meter had stopped at 22.9 gallons. Fumbling for the owner's manual, I stammered, "22.5 usable . . . I think."

All of the things I had worried over—faulty gauges, excessive fuel consumption, unreported high winds resulting in too long a flight for the fuel on board—could have been cured by landing and topping off. However, the lesson I learned was that when in doubt, land. Getting aggravated in an anxious situation while in the air only produces a very poor environment for cool thinking.

●

How did it keep flying after all its usable fuel was gone? Only the airplane could answer that one, and it's not talking. That little white-knuckle saga illustrates how strong is the urge to reach one's destination no matter what forces are working against the completion of the trip.

At least that fellow knew where he was. The winds may have conspired against him, but he didn't get lost. More than you can say for our next beginner, who thought all he had to do to get home was to execute the magical 180-degree turn. Who cares about wind correction angles anyway?

●

I wanted to log as many hours as possible toward the 160 needed for a commercial ticket. Just flying around the airport can get boring. So I planned a cross-country flight to Bakersfield, California. I worked out every detail carefully—maps, checkpoints, flight plan. I was to leave Cable-Claremont Airport at Claremont, California, fly through Cajon Pass, over the desert, then beyond the ridge to Bakersfield. The round trip was to take less than five hours.

The day was clear, and all stations reported VFR conditions. It was a bit cool, but the Cessna 120 had a good heater, so that was no problem. I made my preflight check and took off at 1 P.M.

Five minutes later I found that what had seemed a beautiful day on the ground was a terror in the air. Cajon Pass is quite an experience even flying at 6,000 feet in ordinary weather, but on a clear, cold day it's like shooting the rapids on a raft. When I finally came out on the desert side of the pass, I was considerably shaken. I was ready to turn back, but I didn't relish taking another beating in the invisible hands of the turbulent air. Besides, the thought of logging that five hours was mighty good. So I continued into the desert. The rest of the flight was easy. My checkpoints came up and fell behind, and I landed at Bakersfield right on schedule.

Fearing that darkness would overtake me before I arrived back in familiar territory, I took off in a hurry, clawed for altitude and headed back. Then I looked for my flight plan to get the compass heading—and discovered my first mistake: I had left the flight plan at Bakersfield. If I had checked my compass heading before taking off, as I should have, I would have discovered the lapse.

Right there, a novice pilot in my position should have returned to the field and worked out a new plan; but that would have meant losing a half hour or so. Instead, I hit on a foolish idea. My incoming compass heading had been 305 degrees; by subtracting 180 degrees from this, I figured I would be turned around and headed back toward Palmdale, a checkpoint en route. It seemed brilliant.

My checkpoints were marked on the map, and I searched for the first one. It didn't appear, but I'd missed one or two in previous flights without any disastrous results. I waited for the second—Double Mountain—which should appear about 20 minutes later. That, I thought, I just couldn't miss. But when I looked off my left wing, the mountain wasn't there. Nor was it anywhere in sight. There were plenty of mountains out there, but no double ones. Something was wrong.

I started to think carefully. Just where had I pulled a boner? I had reasoned that by subtracting 180 degrees from my incoming heading, I would be headed back toward Palmdale. But wait a minute. What about wind? Could it have changed direction? Not very likely, I thought. I had been in these same skies not long before and no drastic weather changes had occurred. And then it hit me! The wind had been on my left going into Bakersfield. Therefore, it would now be on my right. In order to get a reverse compass heading, the correct procedure would have been first to *add* the incoming wind correction (since I had subtracted for left wind on the flight down), *then* subtract the 180 degrees, and add another correction for the wind now coming from my right. For the past 20 or 30 minutes I had been flying just 20 degrees off my correct compass heading.

Now I was straight on that, but where was I? By carefully comparing the map and the formidable-looking terrain below, I was able to set a new course. Constant checking and careful inching along finally brought me within sight of Double Mountain. I tuned in Palmdale Radio and waited until I caught the range-course signal. With my map and the steady hum of the beam, it was simple to reach Palmdale, where I landed and worked out a new flight plan.

I flew home through San Fernando Pass, a quicker and smoother route than Cajon Pass, and arrived just as it started to get dark. From that day on, locating my flight plan became a part of my preflight check on all cross-countries.

●

Oh well. Better late than never. Whoever coined the phrase "learn by doing" must have had that young pilot in mind, for he

*seems to have learned all about wind correction on that flight—
and for the first time. That he was able to find himself after
realizing his error says that someone had obviously taught him
the elements of pilotage and how to read a chart.*

*Try as they may, instructors can't equip students for each and
every contingency; the real airman's world is made up of too
many contingencies, and reality often confronts the student with
combinations of them all at once. So many tales end as narrow
escapes instead of as tragedies because a student is able to recall
just a phrase or two of advice. In this near-misadventure, a
student's recall of some vague terms from the classroom prevented his being totally unprepared for an encounter that is
hardly a planned part of most students' first solo flight.*

●

I learned a lesson early in my flying career, on my first solo
flight, first landing—you can't get much earlier than that.

It was a calm, late afternoon in May. The sun was low in the
sky, and if you tried, you couldn't have found a bump in the
air around the Birmingham, Alabama, airport. We stayed in the
pattern, making touch-and-goes, and things seemed to be going
pretty well, when my instructor said, "Tell the tower that this
landing will be a full stop." I glanced at the clock and noticed
that we had been flying only about 30 minutes. Since the lesson
usually lasted about an hour, this could mean just one thing—
my solo.

I cleared the active and was just about to switch to ground
control when he said, "Well, do you think you're ready to take
it around by yourself?" I replied, "I think so." He took the mike
and said, "Birmingham Tower, this is Colt Niner-One Zulu. I
have a student who is going to make his first solo, and I would
appreciate your looking out for him."

"Roger, Niner-One Zulu, we'll keep an eye on him."

He stepped out of the plane, then stuck his head back in the
door and said, "I want you to make two touch-and-goes, then

a full-stop landing and come back and pick me up. The plane will seem a little peppier and get off the ground quicker with you in it by yourself, but other than that, it will fly just as if I were sitting there with you. Remember to use your carburetor heat and watch airspeed on final." Then he closed the door and I was on my own.

As I taxied out after the tower had cleared me, I was very careful to use every available inch of runway, as I had been taught. I eased the throttle open, held a little right rudder, and just as I was really concentrating on holding it on the centerline, I had flying speed and up I went. When I reached about 1,000 feet, I started a gentle left turn, being careful to keep the airspeed right on 80. While in this turn, the full impact of what I was doing hit me: Here I am, flying this plane by myself—I'm really the pilot in command, the sole operator of the controls, the master of my fate. I looked at the empty seat beside me, and even sneaked a glance over it into the baggage area. Sure enough, I *was* alone—as alone as I had ever been.

"Birmingham Tower, Colt Niner-One Zulu, downwind for touch-and-go."

"Colt Niner-One Zulu, you're number two to land, Runway 5, wind calm. Your traffic is a KB-50 on a two-mile final."

"Uhhh . . . Roger, I have him in sight, Niner-One Zulu." There he was, a big silver four-engine monster, low and slow. Now, what was it I'd been told about prop wash? Let's see, my instructor had said something about staying 100 feet behind a big plane on the warm-up pad—or was it 1,000? I couldn't remember exactly, but he did say to stay away from them. And then there was that night at ground school when we talked about those whirlwinds formed by the wingtips of large planes —vortices, they called them—and I was supposed to stay away from those, too. Guess I'd better extend my downwind leg and not get too close behind him—but then, my instructor *did* ask the tower to watch out for me. Certainly they wouldn't let me get too close behind him.

When I was even with the KB-50, I called the tower: "Birmingham Tower, Colt Niner-One Zulu turning base."

"Niner-One Zulu, cleared for touch-and-go," came the familiar reply. I turned base, then final. Lined up pretty well, hold that 80 mph, use the trim tab; easy now, you're looking good, just hold it like you have it. Everything was going fine until I got to within 50 feet above the runway. A few sharp bumps at first, just enough to make the word "vortex" flash through my mind. I applied full power, pushed the carburetor heat closed and attempted to establish a climb. By this time, I had the nose level and was about 20 feet over the runway. Then I caught the full force of the wingtip vortices of the KB-50. It carried me to the right at almost a right angle to the runway and all the way over the grass. I knew I was over the grass because I was in at least a 60-degree bank to the left and could see nothing but green out the left window. As I was trying to get the wings level, I was wrenched back over the runway to the left. By the time I was back over the centerline of the runway, I had the wings level and had climbed to about 50 feet, which got me back into smooth air. Looking down, I saw my instructor on the grass beside the taxiway, his hands over his eyes. I'm sure he thought his student and his airplane had just given up flying.

On the way around the pattern, I decided that my experience was much like that of falling off a horse: Get right back on again before you lose your nerve. I made one touch-and-go before making a full-stop landing, figuring that I'd gained enough experience during my first approach to count that as one of my touch-and-goes.

I remember vividly that the KB-50 had rolled all the way to the other end of the runway and turned off on the taxiway before I hit its wake turbulence. It left enough of an impression on me that today I try to land at least five minutes behind large aircraft in calm air; even in a crosswind, I wait two or three minutes and then try to land at a point past where the other plane touched down, and on the upwind side of the runway. If you ever see an extra-long space between a large aircraft on final and the lightplane behind him, it's a good bet that I am the pilot in that lightplane.

●

It's easy to understand his reluctance to tangle with heavies after having been exposed to their bite so early in his flying career. That instructor was probably very thankful that his student had at least heard of wake turbulence before he experienced it firsthand.

To save the hairiest for last, here is a classic encounter between a young Navy cadet and an aerobatic maneuver that no 30-hour pilot would be expected to handle. Again, a canny instructor who foresaw the possibility of his student's blundering into trouble enabled the young cadet to work his way out—of an inverted spin.

●

It was the kind of day that brought the Naval Air Training Command to Texas. The sky was that bright azure the Dallas Chamber of Commerce would have you believe prevails there all year round, and only here and there did a cotton-puff of fair-weather cumulus wisp above a flat landscape. On the line at NAS Grand Prairie sat row on row of "Yellow Perils," rugged Navy Stearman N2S biplane trainers. Thirty-odd hours along toward my Navy wings of gold, the world was my oyster that morning before the hop.

Aerobatics! C stage of primary. My instructor had been so encouraged by my favorable reaction to his antics that he had seen fit to give me early check-outs in a few maneuvers. One of these was the inverted spin. "Students are not permitted to execute inverted spins," explained the instructor through the gosport tube connecting his mouth to my ears. "We teach them by demonstration only, to provide insurance against your ever getting into one. The most probable causes are either getting too slow at the top of a loop or getting too slow at the top of an Immelmann during the roll-out recovery."

With this statement, he proceeded to pull up into a loop, keeping the stick back until he hit the top, inverted. At this point, he shoved the stick forward, then tapped right rudder. My eyeballs bounced off the instrument panel as the safety belt bit into my legs. I felt centrifugal force trying to throw me clear of the cockpit, and the earth and sky seemed to be going by in opposite directions.

"Recovery is easier than from a normal spin," calmly stated the voice in the gosport. While I strove frantically to cage my eyeballs, it went on, "Opposite rudder until rotation stops, then *back* stick, the opposite of corrective stick action, for a normal spin. Regain flying speed, then pull through. If you are too low to pull through, roll out smoothly instead."

I felt my buttocks settle back into place on the seat pack as the instructor concluded, "Just don't go on spinning too long, as an inverted flat spin might result. In a flat spin, there is less air flowing over the control surfaces, and it's harder to recover."

But I wasn't thinking of these words of wisdom as I found my scheduled airplane that hot June day in 1946. With a list of the aerobatic maneuvers I was to practice that period, I could hardly wait to become airborne. I leveled off at altitude and flew S-turns along a road en route to the aerobatic area. Once in the area, I fished the list of scheduled practice maneuvers out of my pocket and began clearing the area for other aircraft. A 180 to the left, another to the right; all clear. I was ready to begin. A couple of slow rolls to the right, then some loops and I was ready for the Immelmann turn.

The first one wasn't bad; on the other hand, it wasn't good. As I had done on the first slow roll, I scooped out. The looping portion went okay, but as I tried to roll out to the left at the top of the loop and resume level flight, I did not hold the nose up and the airplane lost altitude. I decided to try another, this time rolling to the right.

Again, the loop went well. At the top, in an effort to apply sufficient forward stick to keep the nose on the point as I rolled out to the right, I held that forward stick too long.

The world went crazy. The sky was in the wrong place. Somebody had moved it up where the ground was supposed to be. Where was the ground? It was gone altogether. A weird feeling of complete disorientation overcame any ability to think logically. The wind sounds in the airplane rigging were new. The earth appeared again, but in the wrong place. And it was turning!

Control pressure was gone; my hands and feet moved, but the familiar resistance was not there. Why was this?

Inverted spin! My flying speed had been lost at the top of the Immelmann when I held the stick too far forward for too long a time. I must have kicked a rudder early, starting a roll, and that started the inverted spin.

My eyes managed to focus on the altimeter. Four thousand feet. The spin had begun around 7,000. What had I been doing all this time? Got to stop the spin. "Check the rotation," says the manual. Full opposite rudder, that ought to do it, but nothing's happening. Kick it hard, again. Still nothing!

What was it that instructor said? Inverted flat spin, less air over control surfaces, this is it!

As the airplane continued to wind up, I worked frantically with the controls, kicking full rudder with, then full against, the spin. Nothing. The stick felt mushy, unreal. It could see the trees now, big cottonwoods that seemed to grow, getting larger and larger as I spun toward the ground. I was going in.

For no reason I could give, I let go of the controls, removing hands and feet from stick and rudder pedals, and cut the power. Instantly, the spin stopped. The nose dropped toward me and the wild gyrations ceased. As in the last part of a loop, I grasped the stick again and drew it gently but firmly toward my lap. As docile as a canary, the N2S swept gracefully through the nose-down position and resumed level flight. The altimeter read 500 feet.

It occurred to me on the return flight to base that I had never even thought of bailing out. If the airplane hadn't stopped spinning, I would probably have ridden it in. From then on, I resolved to hold a mental drill on bailout procedure periodically, so that the thought would occur to me when necessary, and so that I would be prepared mentally to react.

Keeping current on the latest dope on flying techniques pays off. I had read about "letting go" as a recovery technique in a Navy tech order. It had also been covered in preflight once or twice, as had cutting the power in spin recovery.

I don't believe I acted consciously in taking my hands off the controls; rather some previous knowledge must have taken over in the absence of conscious effort.

Back at the base, the mirror showed me one older and colder *student* pilot who had an awful lot more to learn than he had realized. Just when you are beginning to think you have flying by the tail, the beautiful, ugly vixen turns her head and bites you.

Look at her, boys. Ain't she a beauty?

2/TALK
ABOUT
THE
WEATHER

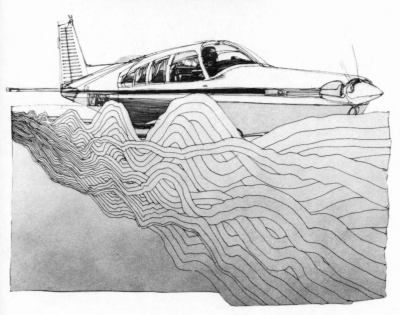

O f all the forces a pilot must live with, weather is the one over which he has the least control. In the pioneering days of aviation, weather was a threat often outweighed by the vagaries of the machines themselves. One had so much to think about just getting airborne and down again safely that there was little concern left to give to the condition of the air through which one hoped to fly.

Improving the airplane's reliability turned out to be a relatively easy task compared to that of taming the weather. Within a remarkably short time, the pilot could reasonably expect safe, steady performance out of an airplane. That left only the weather. It is probably fair to observe that almost all of the major developments in aviation within the past 20 years have been aimed at conquering the obstinate elements. The word "schedule" used to be a euphemism coming from the airlines, but now it has meaning. Light, single-engine airplanes now fly routinely in instrument conditions with solid assurance of success. Such an accomplishment was not at all common even in sophisticated aircraft back in the early days, when so-called "blind flying" made headlines.

With improvements in the aircraft, in the instruments and in the navigation aids, there was a seemingly contradictory change in pilots' attitudes toward the weather. It seems that the older the pilot, the more casually he or she tended to regard the danger posed by weather. That's odd, because in the beginning, very few pilots were trained or equipped to keep an airplane right side up without visual references outside the cockpit. Entering cloud was something instructors forbade their students to do (often frightening them more than was necessary and causing panic when the inevitable encounter happened), although if pressed, most would have had to admit they'd done it themselves; a curious hypocrisy. There existed, side by side, two ideas: If one entered cloud, one would be lucky indeed to emerge alive; on the other hand, to be in the flying business meant to dare. As a consequence, many pilots seemed to get into IFR situations with an alacrity that shocks their modern brothers and sisters.

Today's pilot, despite his exposure to instrument techniques throughout his training, regards violation of the weather rules as the sin with the direst consequences. As aviation has matured to become a legitimate form of transportation, whereas it once was an adventure, the spirit of daring has diminished; some might say good riddance to it. With instrument flying now routine, a pilot's flying into weather ill-equipped for it looms as a greater threat than it did earlier.

Training in basic instrument flying is meant to enable the private pilot to extricate himself from the weather trap, yet a large number fail to escape it. Then there are the regulations, which now spell out grim consequences for the airman who plunges into cloud intentionally and without being qualified. If there was ever any doubt about the wisdom of daring, the law has cleared it up forever. Despite the shift in attitude and the writing of law, there seems to be no shortage of weather-related emergencies today. The effort to subdue nature will continue and probably even gain some ground, but no betting person would ever pay good money to back an aviator thrown against the weather at its worst.

One pioneer who had to deal with the weather in an era when the aircraft were rudimentary and the rules were vague was Paul Mantz, a well-known stunt pilot who appeared in flight in many feature films about aviation. In this episode plucked from his experiences, he frankly expressed many attitudes about the weather, some of them typical of his time.

●

Theory is all right in a nice, comfortable classroom. Theory is all right, too, when you're flying on a bright, sunny day over the flat fields of Texas. But when the time comes to get out over the California mountains on a cross-country trip of 350 miles from Los Angeles to San Francisco, it's a darned good idea to have a little practical knowledge mixed in with your theories. In other words, ground training is swell—but it's also swell to have a dash of that Boy Scout motto, "Be prepared," thrown in.

The year was 1928. It was spring. I was feeling pretty good about myself and my flying. I was riding in the saddle of a nice, shiny Stearman biplane, which I had purchased used from Cliff Durant. I had signed the papers in Los Angeles, had the plane at Metropolitan Airport, and I was going to take off for San Francisco, which at that time was my base of operations.

I was supposed to be a trained pilot. I'd taken my first flying lessons in 1919. I'd been in and out of flying until 1927, when I'd applied for a year's course at the Army Air School at Kelly Field, San Antonio, and had been accepted. I'd been with the Army for the past year.

Yes, I'd had everything from class work to aerobatics, and from military duty to cross-country flying over those nice, flat fields around San Antonio, where they don't even know how to *spell* fog. Nobody could tell me anything.

"Plot a compass course. Fly in a straight line from takeoff to destination."

That's what they'd told me out there in the sunshine, so that is what I did. There were a couple of things I didn't think about, didn't bother to ask about. They're the things I learned on this day in 1928, when low clouds hung like the bottom of a plate over the San Fernando Valley and I wheeled out the winged chariot to go places.

I poured on the coal, got off the field and went into the soup, right on up through it to make an over-the-top flight. I had my map all laid out and I swung the ship until it was heading on course. All I had to do when I got on top was to stick to the compass and I'd be flying right up Market Street in San Francisco.

The first rude shock I got was when I came out of the overcast. About half a mile from the point where I broke through, a mountain had also broken through. It suddenly occurred to me that the mountain was more permanent than I was, that it would win an argument with me, and that the only reason I hadn't plowed into it while climbing up through the soup was simply that I hadn't headed in that direction. No science, all luck.

I shook off the picture of $8,000 worth of biplane stacked on the mountainside, got my bearings and went onward over the top with less assurance. It was swell, though, it really was. Except that I was getting cold. I was still grabbing altitude, the soup wasn't far below me—and I *had* to stay up there, because I didn't know where the clouds left off, visibility began and altitude ended. So I hung on for a while.

I was bucking a jolly little headwind. It prevails at that time of year. I didn't know it then, but I know it now. Still, I stuck with the compass, until I got too cold.

I went down, down and still down through the muck. Imagine my surprise when I found I was over Coalinga. Just over Coalinga. In fact, hardly over Coalinga at all, if you know what I mean. And Coalinga is surrounded by mountains.

So I went up again. I flew along, getting numb, when I saw a beautiful cumulus cloud up higher. I was tired of watching the compass, so I checked myself against the cloud. I did some fine navigating, using that cloud for a bearing. What I didn't stop to realize was that, while it looked very permanent from where I sat, there wasn't any anchor on it. It was drifting, and so was I. By the time I realized this, I was far off my course. I corrected about 30 degrees because I was practically among the trees on a mountain. Of course, I overcorrected and swung far off my course once more.

I got a hole, went down and found out where I was. Then I went up again. I'd figured on a short flight and the wind was making it a long one. The wind certainly lengthens out a flight in a 100-mph ship. I hung on doggedly, wishing that I'd never taken up flying for a living in the first place.

After a long time I figured that I must be somewhere near the San Francisco Bay region—if not right over Market Street. I went down through the soup and found out that I was right —generally. I was in California, all right. I had about 500 feet of altitude, and I was flirting with the Oakland side of the San Mateo Bridge. I got my bearings right away only because I was so familiar with the area.

From that point, it was easy. A short time later I had to return to Los Angeles. I threw theory into the wastebasket. I asked a lot of questions and found out that it would take me 10 minutes longer to go via Lebec and Sandberg, which is a sort of pass, than it would to go the way I had come—practically smack into Frazier Mountain and over the Matau flats, which is very, very tough country.

I asked more questions and found other little detours I could make, thus adding a few minutes to my flying time, but giving me peace of mind. I also added another little innovation to my flight. I took the trouble to check the weather along the route and at my destination.

These two things—(1) checking the route over which I was going to fly, and (2) checking the weather at destination— became inviolable rules to me from that time on. I never have made a flight since without knowing exactly what I was going to encounter.

●

You have to hand it to the man for being courageous. Try not to be too harsh on his judgment, though, because his flight into instrument conditions only seems foolhardy in the hindsight afforded by the intervening years. Of course, even today's beginner could have educated that veteran of his age long before he took off and learned it for himself.

In a way, it fell to the oldest, boldest pilots to discover all that the weather could do and to report their experiences to the newcomers—a grim duty that the veterans never sought but rather had thrust upon them. Paul Mantz had the advantage of experience—knowledge of the area in which he flew and a sensitivity to the machine. Just how terrifying it was to blunder into cloud at night for the first time was detailed beautifully by Evelyn Burleson, who encountered bad weather while on a flight in her Taylorcraft, Miss Liberty, in 1941. She, too, emerged safely because her wealth of experience helped direct her actions. And her contemporaries benefited from her observations.

•

When you hear a pilot friend discuss an unusual flying experience or difficult situation that stands out in his memory, you are interested and entertained for the time being. But soon his story is crowded from your mind by newer subjects. You forget it. While the incident may have been the highlight of your friend's flying career, it's just another story to you. That is the case with all of us. How many times have you heard this or that pilot tell of being lost in a fog or snowstorm, of making a forced landing in a difficult place or of bailing out? Quite often, no doubt. Somehow, those things don't seem to apply until they happen to you. Then those stories come back with a rush and you begin comparing notes. You find that the other pilots' reactions to a situation were the same as your own. That happened to me. I have since compared the experience of which I am writing with those of pilots who have been in a similar predicament, and have learned that theirs differed only slightly from mine.

On October 1, 1941, I took off from Sea Island Airport in Vancouver, British Columbia, in my Taylorcraft, *Miss Liberty,*

on a nonstop good-will flight to Tijuana, Mexico. The takeoff
had been delayed a day, due to bad weather in various places
along the proposed route. I was anxious to start. October 1
dawned bright and clear in Vancouver. The weather reports
looked favorable all the way with the exception of scattered
showers over the Cascades and Siskiyous. I thought it over. To
go or not to go? The weatherman wouldn't advise me either
way. I couldn't blame him. After all, why should he assume the
responsibility for sending someone on such a long trip, on a
word from him? He did say that a front had just passed and
another was on the way, which would possibly reach Vancouver in a day or two. If I were to leave that day, I would miss
both of them. As for the scattered showers, it was still early in
the day. By night, when I would be over the mountains, the
condition could be changed considerably. At night, the temperatures would be more uniform and there was a possibility that
the showers would be cleared out by then. The weatherman's
attitude indicated that he would have preferred me to stay over
to wait for better weather, no matter how long the delay. Regardless, I decided to go. I reasoned that you can't hand-pick
your weather in the fall of the year, especially near the coast,
and that I had best take advantage of what I had.

The departure was at 2:30 that afternoon. *Miss Liberty* got
off in an easy 1,000-foot run, despite a 315-pound overload of 80
gallons of gasoline, extra tanks, extra oil, incidentals, parachute
and pilot. By the time I reached Blaine, Washington, about 25
miles out of Vancouver, I had climbed 2,000 feet.

There was a high overcast in Washington that extended to
southern Oregon. The visibility was good. It was grand, flying
along and watching Bellingham, Everett, Seattle, Tacoma and
Kelso pass under me. Then a half hour's flight down the beautiful Columbia River to Portland. There, it was nearly sundown.
By the time I reached Albany, it was pitch dark and I could see
several beacons ahead. Near Eugene, there were large breaks in
the overcast and the moon was shining through.

The trip over the Cascades was uneventful except for a large cloud bank near Roseburg. By the light of the moon, I could see that it was only local, so I flew around it. At Grants Pass, the overcast had disappeared and it was clear all the way to Medford. Well, I thought, this looks like clear sailing from now on, I think the worst is over. But I was mistaken. If I could have foreseen what was ahead, I would have opened the dump valve to dispose of the gas load and landed at Medford.

South of Medford, in the vicinity of Ashland, I encountered another overcast. I was flying at 8,000 feet by that time, to clear the 5,000- and 6,000-foot Siskiyous, which start immediately south of Ashland. The overcast appeared to be about 1,000 feet above me, and as far as I could ascertain, there was nothing ragged on the bottom. Feeling somewhat uneasy with this turn of events, I shoved in under it. It was black as the ace of spades under there and all I had to go by were the lights on the ground. Ashland passed behind and I could see the first and second beacons to the south. By that, I judged that the visibility was at least 10 miles and there didn't seem to be anything to worry about. I looked back for my final sight of the lights of Ashland. One beacon was below me and the other ahead. I glanced forward and began watching for a third beacon. Just then, the farthest beacon disappeared. I sat there, staring at the place where I had last seen it, waiting for it to reappear. I thought, Either there's a high hill between that beacon and me, or there are some low-hanging clouds. I made up my mind to turn back, but a moment too late. Suddenly, I realized that the beacon below me and the one at Ashland had disappeared, too. I turned on the cabin light. Cloud was all around the windows. I was right in the soup.

My only thought was to get back out of it, back to Medford. It was an eerie, all-alone feeling. I was totally unfamiliar with blind flying and almost as totally unprepared for it with what instruments I had. Friends who had felt concern for me on this flight had warned me to turn back at the first sign of bad weather, and I had promised faithfully that I would. Now here I was, right in the thick of it, and I had flown into it without knowing it was there. The lighted airport at Medford would have looked like heaven just then!

My first reaction was one not of panic but an urge to remedy the situation in a hurry. That's where I made my first mistake: I acted too hastily. Perhaps I was mentally fatigued by the seven or eight hours of flying I had already put in that day. Perhaps it was just plain ignorance. At any rate, I acted before I thought. If I had taken into consideration the rarity of the air at 8,000 feet and the effect a steep bank would have on an overloaded airplane at this altitude, I might successfully have made a gentle 180-degree turn. There is a chance, although a slim one, that I would have come out headed north. But in my anxiety to turn back, I banked too steeply. I may have applied too much rudder. I didn't know that anything was wrong until I noticed the engine was racing. I felt the airspeed pick up and saw the compass whirl around rapidly. This was a complete surprise, and for a second it didn't seem possible. "This must be a spiral or a spin," I said to myself, and throttled back the engine. Then I decided that it was a spiral and that the ship would be spiraling in the direction that I had turned. In trying to recover from the spiral, I only made matters worse. The compass was still whirling and the airspeed indicator was showing an alarming rate of speed. I decided on a spin recovery. There was no time to lose. I neutralized the controls, waited for about a second, then I pulled back on the wheel. I could feel the ship respond, and I knew instinctively that I had done the right thing. Soon, the engine was running normally once more and the airspeed stayed at 80. I glanced at the altimeter. My hair almost stood on end when I saw that it read only 5,000 feet! How quickly I had lost 3,000 feet of altitude!

The surrounding hills were shown on the chart to be 5,000 and 6,000 feet high. I expected any moment to fly into a mountain. The fog was still around the windows. I learned later that

I was somewhere near a valley, which was at 3,000 or 4,000 feet. A couple of guardian angels must have been working overtime that night.

It occurred to me to bail out. But I figured that my best chance was in staying with the ship, that I was probably too low to jump anyway. Perhaps I would step right out into a tree.

With the airspeed at 80, the ship should have felt normal, but it didn't. I was positive that it was diving, so I pulled back on the wheel and watched the airspeed indicator drop toward the stalling speed. While the airspeed indicator showed a loss of speed, the nose of the ship seemed to be going farther down. Then for a moment, I'd believe the airspeed indicator and let the wheel go forward.

On information from other pilots and from books, I had learned that your sensations will fool you when you are flying blind. Truer words were never spoken. My senses really got the better of me. I imagined that the airspeed indicator had gone haywire in the spiral; how else could a ship feel so different?

I did a series of these climbs and dives before I came to my senses. In a flash I remembered something: "When in doubt, let the ship fly itself." This I did, and the airspeed came back to 80 and stayed there. Then I set the stabilizer back until the airspeed read 70 and I let the ship climb. The main thing was to get higher than the mountaintops. That was my only chance. Slowly—it seemed a long time—the ship climbed to 7,000 feet. What a relief! In the meantime, I was trying to keep the ship level laterally and to keep headed north to Medford and safety.

There was a bank indicator in the ship, thank goodness. Without it, I'd have been sunk. The compass slowly went round and round, north, east, south and west. Then back the other way, north, west, south and east. I knew the ship was in a gentle turn, first in one direction, then the other, and I was trying very hard to keep the ball in the center; but somehow, I couldn't. It was maddening. You become angry with yourself at a time like that. You are failing the ship, you are failing yourself. You blame only yourself.

Finally, it dawned on me that I was trying *too* hard to keep the wings level. I was fighting it. "Take it easy," I said to myself, "keep your head." After a while, I managed to head the ship north. Frequently the ball would roll off center, to left or right, and the compass would veer slightly to west or east.

I flew this way for a long time. It seemed hours. It may have been only a few minutes. I became impatient, thinking that I should have come out of it before this, never considering that I was bucking a north wind. The north wind must have drifted the ship south, and in heading north there was also a reduced groundspeed. I evidently didn't allow enough time.

Feeling that I was getting nowhere fast, I decided to head south instead, that there was as much chance in that direction as there was heading north. Very carefully, and fearful of getting into another spiral, I made a gentle turn and was able to bring it out headed south with no further difficulties. The oscillation of the compass was something to cope with, and I got my best results by making every move very slowly.

Miss Liberty continued to climb steadily. My next worry was Mount Shasta, which stands higher than 14,000 feet and which was only a little east of the course. Now and then I altered my course slightly to the west. Better to be off course than to hit a mountain!

I thought of a lot of things as I sat there climbing in the cloud. I thought of the Ninety-Nines and the Associated Women Pilots in Seattle, who had so confidently given me a lovely send-off dinner. I thought of the swell people up in Canada who had graciously put forth their best to entertain a neighbor from the United States. I thought of the people who had spent evening after evening preparing *Miss Liberty* for this flight. I thought of my mother and was glad that she didn't know where I was at the moment. Mostly, I mentally kicked myself for being a nitwit.

Finally, at around 8,000 feet, I had my first indication that I was coming out of the stuff. I saw a tiny round white thing about the size of a pea. It was the moon, shining through the fog. It got bigger and bigger, and soon I popped out into the clear moonlight. Approximately five miles ahead and five miles to the right was majestic Mount Shasta. Never have I seen a more welcome sight. A little farther on, I picked up the beacons once more. I had come out nearly on course.

At Redding, California, where the Siskiyous end, I descended to 2,000 feet and followed the beacons, mile after mile, through the Sacramento Valley, the San Joaquin Valley, over Fresno, Bakersfield, the Tehachapi Mountains and Los Angeles. I landed in Tijuana, Mexico, at 7 A.M., just 16 1/2 hours out of Vancouver.

On the return trip, I had *Miss Liberty* checked for possible damage resulting from the strain of pulling out of the spiral. They didn't find a thing wrong.

In looking back over this flight, I try to analyze it: Would anyone else have bailed out during the spiral, instead of trying to right the ship? Would anyone else have gone under this overcast the way I did, not knowing what was under there, instead of turning back to Medford at the first sight of it? Someone with more experience can answer these questions.

After an episode of this kind, one realizes how easily a pilot inexperienced in blind flying can get into trouble and how quickly a fatal accident would result. Those instrument ratings of yours are nothing to be sneezed at; they're precious.

Suppose I had had less altitude when I started over the Siskiyous; suppose I hadn't been able to recover the ship from her spiral in time; suppose I hadn't been over a valley. I'd be pushing up daisies right now, and a possibly fruitless search might have been made for one more missing airplane.

There's no use kidding myself. Lady Luck was riding with

me that night. Believe you me, that won't happen to this gal again—once bitten, twice shy.

●

Evelyn Burleson's description of her feelings that night shows how novel was the idea of managing an airplane without visual reference. At least she didn't have to worry about running out of fuel, with all that auxiliary tankage on board. She was able to find her way back, slip underneath and continue the flight.

Most pilots who are not rated to fly instruments do keep going —one reason why so many of them have accidents. Although a new pilot's instruction urges a precautionary landing when confronted by weather beyond his or her ability to cope, it is hard to find anyone who has ever landed off the airport. This next description of just such a landing, and the consequences of it, is therefore of great value to anyone who has ever faced the need to put it down before reaching the destination. Most people resist and press on; here's one who didn't.

●

I was working for the McKenzie Flying Service when this happened. I had checked out in a Beech Bonanza and had one hour's flying time in this aircraft, plus a little over 800 hours in various others. We figured that we would fly the Bonanza and really go in style to spend Thanksgiving in eastern Colorado. The airplane had gone to San Diego and returned as far as Klamath Falls, Oregon, where the pilot had left it because of the weather over the hills.

We decided to drive as far as Klamath Falls, pick up the Bonanza and fly on to Colorado. We reached the top of Willamette Pass just at daybreak. The solid overcast was changing to broken, and as we proceeded down the east side of the mountains, it became scattered. When we reached Klamath Falls, we had to wait about an hour for a local fog to rise enough to meet VFR minimums. The weather office was reporting partly cloudy, with scattered snow showers over most of eastern Oregon, Nevada and Utah; Colorado was wide open. A few miles south of the field, we could see the edge of the local overcast, so we filed a flight plan to Ogden, Utah, estimating arrival there at 2 P.M.

We headed south to get out from under the local overcast. For about 30 minutes we flew under the broken overcast, but because the air was rough and the clouds were thinning, I decided to go on top. At 10,000 feet the air was smooth, and I could see an occasional checkpoint through the holes.

About an hour out of Klamath Falls, we ran into cumulus that appeared to go up to about 16,000 feet. I couldn't see going over that, so I decided to take a look underneath. We went down through a large hole, and on leveling out, looked around and found that the cumulus was shedding a moderate snow shower. Mountains prevented going around it, but it didn't look bad. The ground was flat, with an occasional mountain rising sharply, so onward we went. Twenty minutes later it was still snowing, and the visibility extremely limited. I figured that I had better get back the way I had come in. I dropped the gear and slowed down to 90 mph—there were some steep hills sticking out. The plane wasn't picking up ice, and I should have climbed to a safe altitude and headed out of the snow shower. I had about 50 hours of hood time, no actual instrument time, and this ship was different from those with which I was familiar, so I rejected the idea of climbing out and continued to sneak along at about 200 feet.

About then my wife said, "It's flat under us; let's land." It sounded like a good idea, so after considerable maneuvering to find the right spot, and to check it for holes, I landed and came to a bouncing stop. The quiet and the firmness of the ground felt good. We had landed about 30 miles northwest of Lovelock, Nevada, in one of the most desolate parts of the state.

As soon as my nerves quieted down, I tried the radio. I could hear Reno and tried to call them. They answered: "Aircraft calling Reno Radio, say again." I tried over and over again, but without response. Apparently they could not read me. I tried calling blind, giving my position, but no one heard me. I gave up on the radio and got out to look around. We couldn't go very far from the ship without losing track of it. I had put a pair of heavy shoes and an extra jacket in the baggage compartment that morning just in case, and it was beginning to look as if I might need them.

I didn't have any idea which way to go for help, so I decided to stick with the aircraft. While in the air, we hadn't seen a building or a road for a good many miles; however, since we were on a flight plan and were on course, it would not be too long before Air Rescue or the Civil Air Patrol would find us.

About an hour later it quit snowing, and I could see 20 miles to the west and north. I began to toy with the idea of taking off. After inspecting the ground for about a half mile, we began weighing the possibilities. In our favor, the ground was fairly smooth and very hard. It sloped slightly to the northwest, and there was a light breeze from that direction. Looking back now, I know that I didn't realize just how many negative conditions existed, or I probably would not have tried to take off. The altimeter read just a mile above sea level, and there was about three-quarters of an inch of snow on the ground. The sagebrush was two to three feet high, though somewhat scattered. The gas tanks were about three-quarters full, and with our baggage, we were not far under gross weight.

After standing and shivering for a while, I was sure that we didn't want to spend the night there; it was going to be down-right cold. We had enough clothes to keep from freezing, but it wouldn't be very comfortable. The only way to keep from staying there was to take off.

That Bonanza moved as if it were dragging an anchor. I thought that it would be in the air within the half mile that I had paced off; but it wasn't! Every time a bump bounced us into the air, the plane would fall off on the left wing, and I would have to set it back down. The prop was throwing sagebrush, and I knew that if I stopped now, I would never have nerve enough to try again. After about a mile of this, a shallow wash showed up in front, and I knew that it was then or never. I hauled clear back on the wheel, and that good old Bonanza sailed over the wash, bounced twice on the other side and stayed in the air. The prop was shaking badly from the beating it had taken in the sage, but after getting it in the air, I vowed to keep it there, if possible. I flipped up the gear switch as soon as I knew that we would stay in the air, but nothing happened. I looked at the airspeed indicator, and it showed 10 miles per hour. It was still snowing to the south and east, so I decided to try to get back to Alturas, California. I tried to call every radio that I could hear, but I couldn't get an answer. I think the radio was damaged during takeoff. About 20 miles south of Alturas, we ran into another snow shower. I had had my fill of snow for the day, so did a 180 and headed south. There was a small field at Ravendale, a few miles to the south. The snow on the ground there looked too deep, so I tried for a CAA emergency field shown on the chart a little farther down the line. When I found it, it was evident that it had been abandoned and that it was unusable. The only field within range of the remaining daylight was Susanville, so I headed for it.

There was a low overcast near Susanville, and I switched to the left tank, which indicated three-quarters full. That should have been about right, for I had flown on the left tank for about 30 minutes after I left Klamath Falls. We were doing fine, and could almost see the airport, when the engine quit cold.

I turned about 30 degrees to the left to line up with a wheat field, at the same time trying to figure out why the engine had quit. I knew that it couldn't be out of gas because I had just switched to a tank with lots of gas in it. Nevertheless, the fuel pressure gauge indicated zero. I switched back to the right tank, turned on the electric fuel pump, and just as I was beginning to flare out for the landing, the engine started with a roar. We headed for the airport. It really looked good; no snow and two nice, long runways. On final approach, I am in the habit of pushing on the brake pedals to test them. This time the right pedal went clear down without resistance, and it didn't do any good to pump it. My first thought was that the right gear was gone; that last bounce before takeoff had been especially severe. Pouring on the coal, I pulled up and around the pattern again, trying to catch a glimpse of the gear, but in a Bonanza it is not possible. The next time I brought it in slower and with a little power. The airspeed still read 10 miles per hour. I eased it down, and it sure felt good to get those wheels rolling on the ground, all three of them—one of the smoothest landings I ever made.

When we taxied up to the gas pump, the airport manager stood there with his hands on his hips, shaking his head. When I got out, he said, "Where in heaven's name have you been?" When I looked under the ship, I saw what he meant. Each main landing gear leg had about a bushel of sagebrush and snow wrapped around it. After wrestling with the party-line phone for about 15 minutes, with the help of the airport operator, we got the flight plan turned off. It was two and a half hours overdue. Rescue was in the process of starting the search.

On making a close inspection, we found the reasons for the various reactions of the ship. The pitot tube was full of snow, hence, no airspeed indication. A piece of sage had wedged between the skin and the quick-drain plug on the bottom of the left tank; this let the gasoline out, causing the engine to quit on the left tank. The tips of the prop were pretty well beat, causing it to vibrate. The plug on the bottom of the right brake housing had come unscrewed, or had been stripped by the sagebrush. It let all the brake fluid out on that side, so we had no right brake. The right shock strut broke in the struggle and fouled in the compressed position. It couldn't drop down and trip the safety switch that keeps the gear from being accidentally raised when the ship is on the ground. That was very fortunate, because if the gear had retracted, it would have fouled in the housing and not gone back down when it was needed.

The next morning, after temporary repairs, we flew to Klamath Falls, where my wife picked up the car and drove it back over the mountains to Springfield. My daughter and I went back in the Bonanza, and waited at the airport for the rest of the family. A nice way to spend Thanksgiving Day.

I reached several conclusions from the experience. One was that the Bonanza is a lot more rugged than most people give it credit for being. Another is that, in spite of my stupidity, the Good Lord was very kind to us that day. I also learned to treat snow showers with respect. For a long time afterward, whenever the weather office reported snow showers, I would get a heavy feeling in the pit of my stomach—and decide that it was a good day to stay on the ground.

●

A precautionary landing in the face of an impossible weather situation is still good advice; just make sure you land near some civilization, if you can, so that you can avoid having to take off again the way that pilot did. That means confessing your predicament early. Sure, missing Thanksgiving dinner is no fun, but cooked turkey keeps very well.

Just as an illustration of how nicely things can turn out when a pilot does confess to himself that he is in a bind—while there is still time to do something about it—comes this incident from a wise Canadian.

●

My job as a helicopter traffic reporter for a major radio and television station combined the best of two worlds—broadcasting and flying. Fifteen hours a week in the passenger seat of a Hughes 500 helicopter jetting across the Montreal skies generated enough pay for a few weekend hours in the left seat of a rented Cessna 172.

Just before noon on a crisp December day, our newsroom received a report of a spectacular train wreck near the city of La Tuque, 137 miles northeast of Montreal; the television news director wanted film for the evening news. Speed was of the essence, so the obvious solution would be to hop in the helicopter. But La Tuque Airport had no JP-4 fuel. Without refueling, the return trip would have been possible but marginal, and our helicopter pilot did not like marginal flights. The alternative was to charter a fixed-wing aircraft.

"Rent the plane and I'll fly it," I offered. "You'll save the cost of a pilot, and I can cover the story." I arranged for another announcer to cover the afternoon traffic shift, then headed for suburban St. Hubert Airport with a cameraman and another television reporter.

The previous night, a cold front had moved through the area, dumping a mixture of freezing rain and snow on the city. When we arrived at the airport, the linemen were still struggling to remove the ice from a half-dozen Cessnas while an impatient group of pilots waited to take off. We were fourth in line for an airplane, and the 172 assigned to us was still parked on the ramp, covered with ice.

We found a deiced airplane and made a deal with its pilot, whose need to fly was somewhat less pressing than ours. We took his thawed-out Cessna and promised to pay for his flight time.

The flight north was uneventful, and we arrived over the wreck just as the daylight was beginning to fade. I flew low passes up the valley where the train had derailed until the cameraman signaled that he had sufficient footage.

After landing at La Tuque Airport, we separated. I would call the station and report on what we had seen, then ready the airplane for the return flight. The reporter and cameraman went to the wreck site by taxi to shoot some more film from the ground. It would be impossible to get back to Montreal in time for the six o'clock news, but there was plenty of time to make it for the late news at eleven.

Although the airport's only structure, a ramshackle shed, was locked, a helpful sign indicated the airport manager's home. In the bitter, below-zero cold, I debated whether I should take him away from his warm living room to replace the third of a tank I'd used on the flight north. I had enough fuel to get back to Montreal, with a 45-minute reserve, but when I was a student pilot, I had come to believe that an airplane wouldn't take off without full tanks. I phoned the airport manager, and he left his dinner table to unlock the pump and fill the tanks.

Another phone call, to the nearest weather office, in Quebec City, yielded a forecast of scattered snow showers in the La Tuque area, but VFR conditions were anticipated. Montreal was reported clear and was expected to stay that way; winds were out of the west. I figured, then, that the flight should take about one plus 20, and there appeared to be nothing in it that a 200-hour VFR pilot with a night endorsement (a requirement in Canada) could not handle.

It was 7:30 before my companions returned. If three and a half hours of stamping my feet in an effort to defeat the numbing cold had been unpleasant, their experiences were enough to make a man swear off the glamorous news business for good. The cab driver had gotten lost, and they had walked three miles along a railroad track in waist-deep snow. They had hitched a ride on a snowmobile and then commandeered a farmer's truck. But they had gotten the film. At 7:55 we got rolling.

On climb-out, we were solid IFR in a snow shower at 800 feet. I put my head down and climbed another thousand feet, breaking out on top of the scattered cloud to review the situation. Behind, the runway lights were visible, twinkling against the blackness of the surrounding hills. To turn back would entail the risk of encountering IFR conditions again on an unfamiliar approach with few ground-reference points. Ahead, the lights of farms and villages beckoned, and beyond, a solid horizon was visible.

We continued climbing to 4,000 feet, well above minimum en-route altitude and just at the tops of the murky cumulus clouds. The air was still, and the velvet sky, speckled with stars, stretched to eternity. In Canada, VFR on top is illegal, a thought that crossed my mind as the cloud deck closed up solid beneath us. Better illegal up here, I thought, than dead against a mountainside down there in the darkness. An hour ahead of us, the clear skies of Montreal would permit an easy descent.

We passed the town of Mattawan, 35 miles along our track, on time and on course. The next 40 miles would be without ground-reference points, for it is rugged land, lacking farms, towns or roads. Ahead and to the left, the lights of towns along the St. Lawrence River Valley provided a comforting horizon. It was just a matter of maintaining course and climbing now and then to stay above the tentacles of clouds.

Thirty-five minutes into our flight, I called St. Hubert Tower, estimating our arrival at 9:15, as filed by telephone prior to departure. The familiar ATC response was further reassurance that all was well. To back up my visual navigation, I dialed up the St. Jean Vortac, 17 miles due south of our destination. The lazy swing of the needle to the distant beacon would lead us directly home. I corrected slightly to the left and climbed to 6,000 feet as we neared the end of the blacked-out land beneath us and the clouds edged higher. Through the undercast, the hazy lights of villages could be seen.

At 8:50, two things became obvious: The omni signal was not getting stronger, and the continuing blackness below was now solid cloud. Where was the expected clearing in the St. Lawrence Valley? I steered farther eastward in the hope of clarifying my position and seeing some signs of life in the CDI. A check of another omni, northwest of Montreal, yielded no needle life. Radio reception continued to deteriorate until further attempts were useless. Was the radio fading, or was I moving farther away? There followed several minutes of garbled conversation with other aircraft and Montreal International Center. I requested a fix on my position, but that proved fruitless.

The situation at 9:15 (our original ETA) was discouraging. VFR on top of a solid overcast without navigation or useful radio. At least I had fuel enough for two and a half hours of flight. If anybody could find me and offer vectors, I was confident that I could make an easy letdown through the clouds with lots of room underneath.

On the emergency frequency, I called Montreal Tower and received a reassuringly strong response as I explained the problem. In the right seat beside me was the reporter, a 2,500-hour Air Force veteran, who was following my predicament with interest. Dozing in one of the back seats was the cameraman, on his second lightplane flight.

He awoke with a start when the tower asked: "Cessna ZWT, do you wish to declare an emergency?"

I thought for a moment. Lots of fuel and lost on top. Sitting comfortably with no panic. But that gas was not going to last all night. At this rate, I'd have to declare an emergency sometime, and I'd rather do it without the cold sweat pouring down my brow.

"Roger, Montreal. ZWT declares an emergency."

There followed several minutes of discussion about my possible position. During the past half hour, I had maintained a generally easterly heading in the hope of reaching the end of the cloud bank and locating a familiar landmark, so I was likely well north of my St. Hubert destination and flying at cross angles to a track leading to it.

There was in the sky that evening a DHC-6 from a regional airline deadheading back from the Far North. He broke off his approach to Montreal and picked up communication with us. At his suggestion, I attempted to get a VOR reading on several frequencies and relayed them to him, but they were found to be contradictory, so triangulation was not going to be a solution. The strongest indication came from a VOR near Sherbrooke, about 50 miles east of St. Hubert. In the rich baritone all airline pilots seem to have, the Quebecair captain suggested a turn to 240. As I completed the turn, lights suddenly appeared, sparkling brightly beneath us. There was a city and, marvel of marvels, an airport. It looked familiar, and it was: Sherbrooke Airport. To the right, I could see St. Hubert, and beyond, the lights of Montreal as we descended around the edge of the cloud deck.

"Quebecair Five-Four-Zero, Cessna ZWT. We're VFR over Sherbrooke with VFR conditions from here to St. Hubert. You can go home to bed now."

"ZWT, we're halfway down to meet you. We'll continue."

The little Cessna and the Twin Otter made rendezvous in the night sky about 40 miles from St. Hubert. A hundred yards off my right wingtip, the airliner throttled back and, with flaps hanging, kept pace. We chatted.

"Five-Four-Zero, ZWT. We're in good shape, I've got Hubert in sight."

"We'll stay around, ZWT. We weren't going anywhere tonight anyway."

We flew in silence for a few moments, creeping along beneath the overcast.

"ZWT, Five-Four-Zero."

"Yup."

"How do you feel?"

"Good."

"You sounded very cool back there."

"I had lots of gas. I still have almost two hours. Thanks for your help. And say thanks to Montreal when you get home. Nice to know there are so many people around to help when you get in trouble."

"That's what flying's all about."

"Rog. I'm changing to St. Hubert Tower, Five-Four-Zero. Thanks. And goodnight."

At St. Hubert, I made one of the super landings of my life. Our film was too late for the news at eleven, but we were home, and I had learned a little more about flying.

●

He made it sound as if the emergency were no emergency at all but almost business as usual.

What about pilots who are rated to fly in instrument conditions? Does their IFR rating make them weatherproof? Here is an account from one experienced instrument-rated pilot who got his first lesson in what ice can do to performance on what might otherwise have been a ho-hum flight from New Mexico to California. It is the classic tale of icing, and in the relating of the pilot's emotional reaction to the situation, recalls Evelyn Burleson's feelings from some three decades previous, when she found out what the inside of a cloud was like.

●

There are some things you can learn all you need to know about in ground school; others have to come to you in the cockpit. I had read as much about ice as the next person and could recite the catechism of cliches about it: that it raises stalling speed, lowers cruising speed and increases the drag and weight of the airplane; that once you have it, it's hard to get rid of; and that it's very bad stuff. On the other hand, I had read many references to routine operations in icing conditions, or with a load of ice, so I felt that ice, like hypoxia, could be lethal but rarely was. It was inevitable that with such a patchy knowledge of the subject, I would eventually find myself in the midst of the real thing, and that the outcome might depend more on luck than knowledge. So it was. I had my baptism on a winter flight from Albuquerque to Needles, California, in a Beech Sierra.

I had gone with a friend to Albuquerque for the weekend. She had to be back in Los Angeles for work by midday Monday, and I got the Sunday afternoon weather outlook on which to base a decision about when to leave—that afternoon or early Monday morning. There was a front near Prescott, Arizona, right astride Victor 12, which was the logical choice of an airway home. The wind was out of the west at 40 to 50 knots at 9,000 and 12,000. The icing level was on the surface to somewhere near Prescott, and the MEAs were mostly 10,000 and over. A course deviating to the south via Phoenix seemed to avoid the front, or at least delay problems until the line of high mountains that rings the Los Angeles Basin to the east; but it was somewhat longer than the direct route along Victor 12.

I mulled over the alternatives, getting additional weather briefings at intervals, and noticing that while the same facts appeared in all the briefings—strong headwinds, icing possible in clouds, heavy weather in Prescott—some of them were decidedly more cheerful in tone than others. Since I knew that Rocky Mountain frontal weather can be quite spotty, and since one report gave the Prescott front as moving eastward at 45 knots, which would put it over the low, flat Painted Desert area by the time we got there, I decided finally to file IFR and see what happened. There was comfort in the fact that not a single case of icing in cloud had been reported—other than light rime ice—by other aircraft. Monday morning, furthermore, would be no better, and possibly worse.

We took off with sufficient fuel for six hours of flight at about 3:15 in the afternoon, climbed to 10,000 and settled down on the autopilot. Our DME groundspeed was about 90 knots. After an hour, we entered what I thought might be the front in question, though it was rather far east—well east of Zuni, in fact. We remained in cloud for an hour or so, picking up very light rime ice, but the going was smooth, and we emerged from the clouds about 40 miles east of Winslow in a transparently beautiful post-rainstorm aura of limitless, crystalline visibility, slanting light and rich color. More cloud buildups were in sight west of Winslow in the vicinity of Mormon Lake, but I persisted for a while in the notion that we had passed through the front and that the clouds ahead were merely local terrain effects.

We reentered cloud between Winslow and the mountains. ATC had by now gotten some reports of light to moderate rime icing from a Bellanca that was westbound ahead of us; the Bellanca had requested 14,000 and at that altitude had broken out on top in the clear. Because of the headwinds, I stayed at 10,000 for quite a while, but when the leading edges looked fairly furry and the windshield had a Christmasy frosting, I requested 12 and soon thereafter 14.

Dusk descended, and then gradually darkness. Level at 14,000, which we reached with some difficulty in what I took to be extensive downdrafts, we stayed in cloud for a long time, but the ice did not seem to build any further. Finally, we broke out above an irregular mass of cumulus that slanted downward in the moonlight to the west.

At this point, we were about 10 east of Prescott Vortac. Prescott, which at one point had been reporting obscured sky and one-eighth in snow, was now clear with cu in all quadrants. While we were still struggling for altitude in the clouds, I had intermittently toyed with the idea of landing at Prescott. Now that we were in the clear and the frosting had evaporated from the windshield, if not the leading edge, I felt heartened in spite of groundspeeds of about 70 knots. I had filed for Needles with the thought that even if I could not refuel there at night, we would be west of the weather; with this in mind, I decided to go on.

I now made a singularly poor decision: to descend to 10,000, where the headwind was a little less strong (I hoped). I reasoned that if it put us back into cloud and we began to pick up ice, we could always climb back out and let it sublimate, as we had done before. So far, there had never been more than an eighth of an inch of ice visible on the leading edges of the wings.

After passing Prescott, we were cleared to descend to 10,000 —the MEA—into a deck of clouds with tops just a shade above that altitude. We immediately picked up some windshield rime ice and some sink. We dropped down to 9,400, in spite of my best efforts and those of the engine running at max rpm, full throttle and best-power mixture. I was uncertain of the terrain height west of Prescott, but I knew it was rough country, and wanted to get back up to the MEA. At this point, we had neither radar nor radio contact with ATC, being in one of those blank transition areas between sectors of which the West has many.

Finding myself unable to climb even at an IAS of 75 knots, and certainly making no headway over the ground, I decided to deviate slightly to the north, where the clouds were lower. Twenty miles or so to the south was a busy thunderstorm. I was beginning to get quite nervous about the inability to climb, which seemed puzzling in view of the fact that there still was only a slim coating of ice at the very nose of the wing.

We shortly broke out of cloud on a northerly heading, to our great relief; my friend, who had slept through the earlier pseudo-front, was in fine form for appreciating this one, and was keeping pace with my apprehension.

At this point, something happened that I still cannot explain: The engine quit. It did so only momentarily, for two or three seconds, but it was the kind of gulp that could not possibly be mistaken for automatic rough.

It was as though someone had suddenly pulled the mixture to idle. My immediate response, apart from jumping out of my skin, was to push the mixture to full rich; as if in response, the engine roared back to life—but only coincidentally, I'm sure. I scanned the instruments for some hint of explanation, but none appeared.

Thoroughly shaken by now, I waffled around for another couple of minutes and then decided to turn back to Prescott. We were still below 10,000 but clear of cloud. I gave ATC a call on the last frequency, and when they did not answer I tried Prescott on 122.2. When there was no answer there either, I called Prescott on 121.5 and got an immediate and very clear response—not surprisingly, since we were only 18 DME past Prescott, a distance it had taken us nearly half an hour to cover. Prescott got an approach clearance from ATC, and for the first time on the flight, I put on an oxygen mask to get myself primed for the approach. The oxygen made no apparent difference in my vision or anxiety, but I felt pleased to be doing the sensible thing.

The VOR approach at Prescott was a disaster. Prescott was still under a big hole, but I felt for some reason that I ought to do the approach since I didn't know exactly where the airport was. Surface winds were gusting to 50, and the upper winds were worse. After crossing the VOR and turning left to intercept the outbound course, I could not connect with the radial even with an intercept angle of 90 degrees! Finally, I glimpsed the rotating beacon, abandoned the approach and landed visually without much difficulty, though the winds were fierce and I was constantly having the unusual experience of hitting the aileron stops in my control movements.

Throughout the approach, I kept hearing odd cracking and splitting sounds that I couldn't quite place. When we landed and parked, I learned the cause: Although only a thin crust of ice was visible on the leading edge, there was a plate of the stuff perhaps a foot wide and half to three-quarters inch thick *underneath* the leading edge, where I couldn't see it. There were proportionate buildups on the fuselage and horizontal tail. Much of the ice had fallen away during the approach, and there were chunks of it tracing our path across the ramp. I suppose I pulled 15 or 20 pounds of it off the wings—an elated celebration of being back on the ground in icy winds so strong they blew the chocks away from the tires.

The FSS man, whose shift was just ending, very cordially drove us to town; sleety rain began to pour down, and our host cheerfully offered that if we had continued, we would certainly have gone down.

Reflecting on the experience, I realized that he was probably right—if only because at the rate we were going, we might never have reached Needles; by the time we landed at Prescott, we had already been airborne for four and a half hours.

Reflecting further, I tried to see where I had made the blunder that would have been reported by bland accident-reporters as the "pilot error" that undid us. I saw several blunders, starting with the whole attempt and going on to such particulars as descending again into the icing once I had managed to get out of it; but given the state of my knowledge at the time, I can't say that any of my decisions was absolutely contrary to reason. The pivotal problem was that I did not realize the amount of ice we had picked up, and the reason for that was that I did not know—I have never read, never been told—that it can collect entirely on the underside of the wing, out of sight of the pilot. You might think that I could have deduced from the deteriorating performance of the plane that we had a load of ice somewhere; but if you look out the window and see virtually no ice, such "obvious" deductions are not so obvious.

Another instant criticism of my actions is that I did not use oxygen although I was at 14,000 feet for some time. Again, perhaps because I am young and do not smoke, my own experience had been that oxygen did not make much difference at altitudes up to the Sierra's rather modest ceiling, at least in such subjectively testable areas as night vision. Some people say that a hit of oxygen at night is like turning on the lights; for me, it isn't. At any rate, the question is whether I did something that night that I would not have done with a normal amount of oxygen; and I cannot say that I did. In view of what I thought about ice in general and our ice in particular, I would probably have gone back down into the clouds, oxygen or no.

Furthermore, I did not really start feeling helpless and thick-brained until the Prescott approach, when I was well stewed on oxygen but badly shaken by the engine stoppage. In the bewildering position of being unable to intercept an omni radial two miles from the station with a 90-degree cut, I was beginning to succumb to that awful state of mental viscosity in which the instruments cease to provide information and seem to crumble into a useless hodgepodge of meaningless arrows and numbers.

Though grim, it was a worthwhile experience—because the meaning of icing has become three-dimensional for me, and I have the beginning of a handle on its real-life, rather than storybook, implications. I realize now that you need lots of engine power to handle it—a 200-hp four-seater, even half empty, isn't enough. I realize that it is one thing to pick up ice at 10,000 if the terrain is at 1,000; it is another to pick it up at 10,000 if that's the MEA and down means out. I realize, intimately, what an ice-logged airplane feels like, and what a helpless, struggling beast it becomes. I realize that looking down at the leading edge doesn't tell much about icing, at least if you're mushing along at high altitude to begin with. I realize that as the situation begins to deteriorate, the tension tells on the pilot and he himself deteriorates, becoming less and less competent to deal with more and more demanding developments.

I also received one more lesson in what must be the fundamental tenet of every pilot's creed: that there's no Monday work for which it's worth dying on Sunday.

●

Unless the airplane is equipped with deicing gear—rubber boots that expand to break ice off wings and empennage, or heated panels on leading edges and propellers—ice is still something to be feared. Airplanes, from light twins up, usually are capable of carrying deicing gear; even some single-engine lightplanes have it now. Still, ice is not something the wise pilot goes looking for.

Thunderstorms are a threat to all airplanes, no matter what size or how well equipped. One curious Army Air Corps instructor actually went looking for a thunderstorm. He wanted his student to experience the storm's effects, but the instructor himself ended up getting the lesson.

●

The heart of Old Man Thunderstorm has always held my careful respect, but it took a special occurrence to teach me equal respect for his whiskers.

I was instructing in B-24s, flying out of what was then Tarrant Field at Fort Worth. We were off airways and my student-officer was flying partial panel instruments with artificial horizon and DG covered—doing a pretty good job of it, too, in smooth air.

Off in the west, a front was moving in, with a very definite line squall lurking near the horizon. Thinking to give my student a little rough-air experience, I handed him a heading that would approach the storm. I had no intention of flying into it. Just a brush along the edge to pick up some turbulence would be enough for my purpose.

Nosing along on the heading I had given him, the student picked up turbulence as scheduled. A boost on one wing; the student recovered. A drop of the nose; again he recovered. Suddenly we were in rain—not a gentle drizzle, but an honest-to-goodness downpour—and there was no need for an instrument hood.

Good experience, I thought, glancing at the student. We'd skirt along the storm a little more, then head for home.

Then it came—BANG! An explosion. It seemed to come from the interior of the airplane. As we stiffened to alertness, there was another bang, followed by a series of explosive noises. I turned my head to shout a question to the crew chief standing beside me. That action probably saved my eyesight, for the next instant the heavy windshield on my side came crashing in upon me, cutting my neck and face. There was no need to question the crew chief. We knew the answer—hail. It sounded as if someone were hitting the fuselage with baseball bats.

Tearing off the covers hiding the artificial horizon and DG, I yelled out a heading that would take us away from the storm area. In a minute we were out of it. The crew chief handed me a souvenir—a chip, an inch and a half in diameter, from the hailstone that had broken my windshield. A terrific blast of air whistled in through the hole where the windshield should have been, and my face was numb. We limped back to the base.

An inspection after landing showed that the rugged old aircraft had come out second best in the encounter. All the glass in the plane except the left front windshield and the side windows was broken or cracked. The bombardier's nose and the top turret were wrecked. Engine cowlings were badly battered. There was a hole in the horizontal stabilizer big enough to plunge a fist through.

One reads a great deal about how to fly through a thunderstorm and about the weather squadrons who fly through anything. With all proper respect for those who fly through thunderstorms, I give them a wide berth.

At no time did we fly into the storm. We never got beyond the edge of it, but we learned that the edge of one storm can be as rugged as the center of another. I have sometimes seen hail show up as a green haze on the edge of a storm, but there was no green haze that day, so the absence of this phenomenon does not necessarily mean the absence of hail.

That experience taught me a lesson I've never forgotten. It's not only the middle of a thunderstorm that's to be avoided; the edge may be just as bad.

●

So you see that it's not just airframe ice that is to be feared; ice also comes in the hard pack.

Oddly enough, the phenomenon of thunderstorms that ground-bound people fear most—lightning—has the least effect on airplanes. Lightning strikes on airplanes may affect electronic components, but the bolt usually passes through an all-metal airframe with only minor damage at its points of entry and exit. Hail is the bludgeon that strikes hardest, with violent winds running a close second. There is one horror almost too terrible to imagine that would simply overwhelm any airplane unlucky enough to stumble into it: a tornado. The tornado is first cousin to a thunderstorm, both weather conditions spawning in acutely unstable air. One pilot who nearly flew through a tornado—at least he guesses that's what it was—told how it looked to have a front-row seat as a tornado was born one day in Nebraska.

●

We had been tooling around the country, generally heading west, following our inclination, with no particular destination, and letting our interest determine how long we stayed. We had rented a Skyhawk in New York, stopped off to visit with friends and gas up along the way at Broken Bow, Nebraska.

We were eager to head west and had decided to stop at Denver next, but we were locked in at Broken Bow by weather. By "locked in" I don't mean that it was no-go, but for two days running, Denver had reported severe thunderstorms, and central and eastern Nebraska was socked in by 800-foot ceilings.

By the third day of inactivity, salted with several trips to the airport to read the ticker and look at the sky and discuss conditions, and after three calls to North Platte FSS, I decided to move. From Broken Bow southwest to Imperial it was overcast with 800- to 1000-foot ceilings. But Akron, in Colorado, was reporting scattered and 10, and Denver was reporting scattered thunderstorms with possible light hail, which our forecast said "should be easily circumnavigated."

I filed by phone with North Platte FSS and we got off the ground at 3:55 P.M. Nebraska time. I contacted Denver Center and confirmed my clearance. In 15 minutes we were on top at 8,000, the sun shining, beautiful billowy clouds beneath us.

By Holyoke Intersection we had breaks in the overcast, and

over Akron the cloud layer was replaced by broken clouds and towering cumulus, all quadrants. I had been instructed to call Denver Center on 124.1; if unable, Akron FSS. I was, and we did. Akron FSS acknowledged my call, gave me a new clearance and told me to try Denver Center on 124.1 again on the hour. Again it was no-go, and back to Akron FSS for further instructions.

Meanwhile, however, the cu that was so pretty and white and billowy 20 minutes earlier had been replaced by darker stuff, and it was clear that we were running into cumulonimbus. We could see jagged streaks of lightning in the distance at ten o'clock and at two. Lucky, I thought, that I can get between 'em and maintain my flight path as called for in the clearance. Now, however, the two-o'clock cell was getting close, and I sneaked a degree or two to the left of my course.

I still had no luck in raising Denver Center on 124.1, and flight service suggested I try approach control on 119.3. That was also negative. I learned later that they read me loud and clear, but I could get no reception.

Now, however, our situation had changed a bit. We were under about 70 to 80 percent black sky cover, and we had been experiencing a mild and variable chop for some time. The large cell on my right was now at three o'clock and no longer a factor, although still close. Our ten o'clock storm was still at ten but now closer, and here at one o'clock was a new cell perhaps 10 miles away. This one did not seem nearly as severe as its predecessor on our right, as its sheet of rain was lighter. However, snaking out from the canopy of black overhead at approximately twelve o'clock, *outside* of the main rain area, perhaps five miles ahead was a tornado. I recognized it intuitively although I had never seen one before.

There was still a clear area ahead, however, and with a further deviation from course to the left (taken on my own initiative since I was still unable to raise either Denver Center or Denver Approach, although I did apprise Akron FSS both of my course deviation and of the funnel), it appeared that I could still get by both the severe cell at ten o'clock, now perhaps 10 miles away, and also the funnel at twelve.

At this time I noticed another curious phenomenon on the ground just ahead and slightly to the left of my course. The air over the ground seemed clear under the black canopy of cloud, but on the ground was a cloud of dust, perhaps a mile in diameter, roiled, several hundred feet high and moving seemingly slowly. As we came abreast of it and perhaps no more than a half mile from it at our nine-o'clock position, the turbulence suddenly increased enormously. Now we were buffeted with solid thumps which we felt alternately against our seats and our seat belts, and we gained and lost 200 feet at a time. I throttled back and changed course slightly toward the funnel at twelve o'clock. Just then my wife hollered what I feel may have been true—that what we had seen on our left and nearly flown through (I say "flown" euphemistically) may have been the formation of another funnel.

Although we did not know it then and although we still had to skirt several more cells, the worst was over. The funnel on our right simply dissipated as we watched, leaving a little trail of dust on the ground, and we were past the disturbance on our left. Now Denver Approach Control was responding and we reported our course deviation, flew direct to Denver Vortac and took vectors from there to Stapleton.

I guess countless thousands have skirted thunderstorm areas and have done it easily—no sweat. But it is now clear to me that the storm you dodge is not especially, or necessarily, the one that is dangerous to you. Thunderstorms can spring up *anywhere* when there is unstable air. Although you can dodge the one ahead to get to a clear area at 90 degrees to your original flight path, the clear area can be replaced by a new cell—or much worse. The same conditions that produce thunderstorms also produce tornadoes and, when the conditions are right, you can get funnel formation and perhaps not be able to see it clearly because it has not yet hit the ground and raised dust and debris to color it.

Naturally, we read the papers avidly the next day. Although cloudbursts and wind had lashed parts of Colorado and done some damage, the funnel reported east of Bennett ripped through crops but caused no injuries or property damage. I was grateful that our names weren't in the paper.

●

Of course, it doesn't necessarily take a visible storm to wreak havoc upon an airplane. Clear-air turbulence is as vicious as the fury inside the thunderhead. An Air Force B-26 crew found out just how bad it can be—and in a setting conspicuously serene. Imagine what went through the minds of these unsuspecting airmen as they were ambushed by invisible violence.

●

It was one of those drowsy mornings, murky outside, with a slight drizzle coming down—a perfect morning for sacking in. The time was November 1954, and I was serving with the 11th Tactical Reconnaissance Squadron, formerly of K-14 Korea but recently moved to Itami Air Base, Japan.

That morning I was scheduled for a routine flight to Tachikawa Air Base, near Tokyo, to pick up some parts. We checked the weather at operations and found that the 1,000-foot overcast we had was just a temporary local condition, and our route and destination were clear. I filed an IFR clearance, then checked my plane and crew, a weather B-26 with navigator, weather observer and radio operator. I taxied out, receiving IFR clearance and pulled up the gear at 0900. The flight to Tachikawa normally took about two hours. Climbing through the overcast, we broke out in the clear at 4,000, continued to climb to 9,000 and leveled off. It was beautiful up there, in contrast to the murky weather down below, and I believe without exception every member of the crew was trying to think of a legitimate excuse to spend the day and night in Tokyo. It had been quite a while since we had had a milk run like this.

As we approached Tokyo, Mount Fujiyama loomed up in its majestic splendor, a sight that makes you thrill to nature's magnificent handiwork. It was the first time any of us had seen Mount Fuji naked, so to speak, without a cloud in sight. Since we were well equipped with cameras, we decided to fly over to photograph Japan's highest peak. I called and checked the weather at our destination, canceled our IFR clearance and informed Tokyo Radar we were deviating from our flight plan to take pictures.

Mount Fujiyama is more than 12,600 feet high, so to be safe, I climbed to 14,000. We circled the top once, grinding away with movie cameras and snapping pictures like tourists, circled a couple more times, looking over the shrine within the crater, then headed for Tokyo. Just as we left the ridge of Fuji, all hell broke loose. The plane rocked crazily, and the altimeter was winding and unwinding. We dropped 2,000 feet, hit bottom with a jolt and just as quickly climbed 3,000 feet. The airspeed fluctuated from zero to 400 mph. I yelled over the intercom to tighten the belts, but it was too late for that; all I could do was try to keep the plane level and ride it out. I looked out and the wings were flapping like a hound dog's ears. At that moment I could have sworn it was impossible for them to stay on. To this day I'll swear that the wingtips touched, both above and below the fuselage. The VHF transmitter tore loose, bouncing around the cockpit along with the Very pistol, and dirt and maps from the floor. My navigator was leaning over with his hands on his head to keep from hitting the Plexiglas canopy. Along with attempting to keep the plane level, I also was trying to buckle the chest strap of my chute. (I always flew with it unbuckled for comfort.) All of this was over in a matter of seconds, but it seemed like an eternity, and just as quickly as it had started, we were in smooth air again.

A glance told me that everything except the tumbled gyros appeared to function normally. A check with the crew found the radio operator bleeding from a cut on his head, the weather observer okay, and my navigator shaken up but okay. After talking, we decided that since Tachikawa was closest, we would head there as planned. By this time oil was trickling from the cowling of our right engine, which appeared to be hanging slightly. I trimmed it up for a 100-fpm rate of descent and headed for Tachi. I couldn't contact anyone, but I caught a weather report that Tachi was clear and had five miles' visibility. Now our only worry was whether it would hold together for another hour.

We made it to Tachi and touched down as gently as possible. After answering a maze of questions, I headed to Weather to ask a few questions myself. What caused all the turbulence? Why was it so rough, while the sky was clear? The only explanation I could get was that we had hit some upslope turbulence, which is common in mountainous regions, and is unusually severe around isolated peaks.

A later report from Maintenance, after they had torn into the plane, disclosed two cracked stress panels in the wings, some 30-odd popped rivets, buckled skin in several places, and sprung engine mounts on the right engine, causing it to hang downward. It had been no ordinary turbulence.

Turbulence is something pilots will always have to contend with from time to time. However, if every pilot understands what turbulence can do, and where heavy turbulence may be encountered, he will be forewarned. I thank my lucky stars I was flying a plane that could take it.

●

Being slammed around so hard that your airplane nearly breaks in perfectly clear skies is the kind of thing that can make a pilot ask, "Why me?" When they are unexpected, the forces at work in the air can seem doubly brutal.

One area where an airman expects to find bad weather is in the Canadian bush—IFR practically guaranteed, along with all the worst that the weather can dish out. Sit in with this experienced pilot, then, as he allows a grudge to bend his judgment and take him into the wildest conditions any airplane has ever found itself in.

●

When I had returned a week overdue from a mercy flight to Lethbridge, the boss had been none too happy with the delay and reminded me that the charter business does not flourish without aircraft. In his opinion, our Cessna had lingered unreasonably long.

There were things I wanted to tell him about the high winds and turbulence I had encountered, about my two unsuccessful attempts to get home, but another rush charter was waiting. I was to fly a Seabee through the Rockies to Edmonton to photograph a train wreck.

Accompanied by a news photographer and our base engineer, we took off hurriedly. The flight to Edmonton was uneventful, and the next morning I figured we would shoot our pictures, return home, and I would defy the boss to criticize me.

So it was that we were up before the sun and wasted little time with such things as weather maps. We knew that there would be fairly strong headwinds, however, so we planned to refuel at Calgary, then follow the rugged but shorter Canadian Pacific Railway route through the mountains. We reached Calgary somewhat later than I had planned. The headwind was so strong that even heavy trucks on the highway below reached the city before we did. What with the wind and the late hour, we would have shown good sense to hold until the following morning, but I was still doing that slow burn from the previous trip, so I fueled to the hilt and headed toward the rock pile.

The going to Banff, though rough, was much faster because we now had a crosswind. We were cruising about 1,000 feet above the tracks to get maximum shelter from the mountains and still maintain sufficient altitude to turn around. Although we braced ourselves for a beating when entering the Kicking Horse Pass, after a few violent bouncings, the weather relented. The Seabee whined toward Golden into the teeth of a strong westerly which funneled down the valley.

Even at this point it would have been good sense to turn back, as our groundspeed was cut badly and it was well on into the afternoon. But the sun was shining and we were going in the right direction. With luck, we would be in Kamloops by dark.

At Golden the wind dropped and ice fog started to sneak up on us. A few feet at a time, almost without notice, our 1,000 feet dwindled until, at the entrance to Roger's Pass, where the railway turns west again into a narrow valley, we were a scant hundred feet over the trees and following the right of way with difficulty. It took three circuits to find the valley entrance, and I belatedly considered turning back, but there was not enough daylight left to reach Calgary. We had to keep on the west of Revelstoke or find some emergency landing spot.

It started to snow. Visibility dropped to near-zero. We made three attempts to land in the Columbia River, but drifting ice floes made it impossible. The airport at Revelstoke was our only hope and it was up the now totally obscured valley.

At telegraph-pole height, the white double-track right of way was just visible among the dark trees. The engineer was desperately reading the chart, calling off the flag-stop stations as they passed beneath, and warning of turns ahead. Deeper into the storm, the temperature rose and the snow began to stick. The Seabee's nose became coated. Soon the only visibility was out the side and through the tiny space I managed to keep open by reaching out the storm window and scraping the freezing snow off with my fingernails.

It was suicidal to push farther. If the valley would only straighten, I would go in, wheels up, between the tracks. We banked around another corner and suddenly faced a black wall. We had come to a tunnel!

By banking violently I was able to do a 180, but there was no place to land. We had to put the Seabee through the tunnel or over the top of the crag.

A desperate check of the map showed a pass to the right of the railway which looked like 4,500 feet would clear. The moment we climbed, the railway disappeared in a white shroud of snow. We were on instruments doing a climbing turn in a narrow valley.

By maintaining a constant-rate turn and a very sharp watch out the side, we were able to keep out of the trees on the mountainside. The valley became wider as we ascended, and it looked like we were going to make it, when the rate of climb started to drop off rapidly.

The engine had long since been wide open and was trying gamely, but the load of ice was too much for it. Before we had time to assess our new predicament, the airspeed went out completely. The pitot head had frozen solid.

Then Chuck, the engineer, thought he could see the pass. We headed in the direction he was indicating, held our breath for an eternity, then suddenly broke into the clear.

There was a train far below stuck in a snow-slide. The knowledge that there were people below, even if we couldn't contact them, seemed to break the tension and we shouted our joy at being alive.

Our rejoicing was premature, for the break lasted just long enough to allow us to get back down to treetop height, when the snow closed in again. We reached Revelstoke shortly afterward, but by now it was dark and snowing so heavily that it was impossible to find the airport, although I was getting close to home territory and knew the country well. The only hope was to press on to Three Valleys' Lake some 12 miles out of town, where there was a chance of being able to land.

The temperature was dropping again, but at least we were not picking up any more ice. The wind had risen, though, and turbulence, especially at track level, made flying difficult. Darkness had now forced us so low that there was no hope of turning in the narrow valley. It was either reach Three Valleys' Lake or make a forced landing on the tracks.

At Three Valleys' Lake the weather suddenly became CAVU, and in the last light of evening we could see that the lake was a churning mass of whitecaps. A landing there was impossible. We could only push on and hope to find some shelter on the Shuswap Lakes at Sicamous.

The weather was not through punishing me. A few miles from Sicamous, it again began to snow, robbing us of what little light was left. When the lights of the town finally showed up, it was too dark to see the water or to determine the wind direction or force. We had to land. We could go no farther.

Fate saved our good fortune for the last. As we circled the town, a passenger train pulled into the station and stopped. The tracks at this point are right along the water's edge. The lights from the coaches shone out upon the water, forming a welcome flare path.

I dumped the Seabee in downwind. It hit hard but stayed on. The hull took a mighty pounding as we ploughed through the waves, but it held gamely, fell off the step into a wallowing trough, and we were safe.

Veteran railroaders say that our day in the high Rockies was one of the worst days in their experience. We learned that, during those anxious hours, the telegraph operators were charting our progress, passing the word along from station to station so that they could keep tab of the plane's well-being (or absence thereof!). Twice during this period we were unreported. Two trappers at Beavermouth heard the plane zooming low over their isolated cabin and watched it trying to find a path through the towering mountains. They were so certain that we had

crashed they had dressed and tramped through the storm toward where they thought we had come down.

It was an experience that I have never forgotten. I learned
that a childish "I'll show you" attitude can lead to real trouble.
The photographer got no pictures on that harrowing day, but
I at least profited by the realization that there is nothing to be
gained by being petulant—not in flying.

●

It's a good thing the train was on time that night, or the story
might never have been written. That's one flight that almost
anyone would be glad to say he missed.

Who catches the blame for misadventures with the weather?
Pilots talk out of both sides of their mouths on that one. When
the weatherman, with a grisly forecast, advises them against
going, they resent it; when he says things will be fine and the
weather turns out rotten, he catches hell again. Weathermen
can't win.

In the real day-to-day professional situation, pilots and
meteorologists actually work together, the pilot dependent upon
the data only the weatherman can supply and the meteorologist
dependent on the pilot's eyes to confirm or deny the educated
guess. The relationship has evolved into a curious symbiosis, each
one needing the other—and griping about it all the way. The
friendly banter between pilots and weathermen is part of the
folklore of aviation, something that was captured perfectly by an
Army helicopter pilot who found some time to meditate—while
he was stuck, fogbound, on top of a mountain.

●

All weathermen lie, and after all these years I should have
known better than to believe this one. As I sat stranded on that
mountaintop, I reflected sadly upon how I had been had again.
Not that I can blame them, you understand. If you had to mess
around all day with those dumb dew points and musty milli-

bars, you'd try to inject a little humor and excitement into your life, too. The first thing they do when they come on shift is study the charts for possible ways to screw you up, and this day had been the perfect opportunity. Tropical storm Delia, a frustrated hurricane, had counterclockwised clouds all the way up to the Sacramento Mountains of New Mexico, and I could see them peeking slyly at me as I drove to work.

The weatherman who stood facing me was wearing Air Force blue (it doesn't matter whether they come in scarlet or chartreuse; all must swear that secret oath to create confusion), and his smile was disarming. He bowed his head, probably to hide a malevolent smirk. "Ferrying a helicopter from Holloman Air Force Base to Corpus Christi, Texas. What an interesting flight! Wish I could go with you." (Oh, as I sat later on that New Mexico mountaintop—clouds to the right of me, clouds to the left of me—I remembered what an oily voice that was.) "Well, you ought to have a nice flight. Minimum ceiling should be 2,000 feet, visibility five miles, winds less than 10. A few clouds over the mountains. We don't have any reporting stations there, but you should be able to go under." (Did you get that about not having any reporting station? That's his out, see, when you whip that hazard report on him. Oh, devilishly clever. And smooth.) "Have a nice flight," he says, smiling. He probably fell over his crystal ball laughing when I left. May his weather balloons have holes in them.

We cranked up, two olive-drab Hueys. These two were camouflaged for the jungle and were to get a new coat of paint at the Army overhaul facility at the Corpus Christi Naval Air Station. My partner on this safari was a big, cheerful fellow, hands like hams, graying at the temples, an excellent pilot and maintenance man; he was good to have along, but he ruined everything by being a compulsive talker. When he arose each morning, the day was a blank canvas waiting to be covered with words, and he never failed. You have to admire such an artist. You'd think I'd have been safe in my own helicopter, but he had that all figured out in advance. "After we get airborne, go to frequency 126.95 so we can stay in touch in case of emergency." With him, an emergency is not having a listener. This wasn't my first trip with him, though, and I've developed a system that keeps us both happy. About every 10 minutes, I switch to his frequency, wait for a pause in the running commentary on the way his machine vibrates, the growth of antennas, the landscape or whatever, give him a "Roger that" or "That's affirmative" and cut him off again. Most big talkers don't listen to you anyway.

He could hardly wait to switch from Holloman Control to the en-route frequency because he was fairly bursting with exciting things to say. Click, he was gone, and I could contemplate the brown, barren desert falling away below as we began our climb eastward. We were at 6,500 feet in our ascent above the rocky western slopes of the Sacramentos, once the stronghold of the Apache. At those higher elevations with more abundant rainfall, the rocks give way to tall pines that would swallow a downed airplane.

My attention was diverted from the mountainside by a fine mist falling on the Plexiglas bubble, and I could see there was trouble ahead. The ceiling was lowering as we passed Pinon VOR, and I could see the tops of the towering cumulus soaring thousands of feet above. Click, "Rough in that stuff," "Roger that," Click. Piston engine goes boing, boing, boing, but Huey goes wopwopwopwop.

We headed south, where it looked brighter, and probed for a way through. The clouds were down on top of the hills, and so were we. We slowed our forward speed, and I started one of the smartest maneuvers in flying, the 180-degree turn, when suddenly we were in the stuff. We broke out, and I glimpsed a flat spot ahead. My partner was with me as we hovered and set down in the clearing.

It would have been dangerous to switch to his channel just yet, so I sat, silently cursing all weathermen and the day I decided to get into this profession. Why didn't I listen to my mother and become a garbage man? ("Out in the fresh air and all you can eat," she used to say.) If we couldn't get out of there soon, we would have the AF, FAA, CAP and a few other letters looking for us. Our commanding officer would be mad, and something cold had just told me that the canopy leaked.

I could barely make out the next ridge a hundred yards away. My partner walked over, mouth flapping, spreading noise pollution all over the mountain. It didn't matter that I couldn't hear him. I held the door so he couldn't get in, but he's bigger than I am. "—and I just found some elk tracks," he said. I lost my cool. "Here we are stuck on this God-forsaken mountain, running out of flight-plan time, and you're looking for elk tracks!" I shouldn't scream like that. It always hurts my throat. Might as well be nice. "Come on in and have some coffee. Nobody will be looking for us for a while."

So we sat, drinking coffee, and me listening to his war stories as I watched the clock and worried about our flight plan. I tried a few calls on the emergency frequency, but nobody was listening. Then the wind began to pick up—a good sign. At least it began to move the clouds around. My friends the birds were having trouble hanging onto the rotor blades. "Hey, I can see that ridge over there," my partner said, breaking a 15-second silence. "Let's try it." We started up and cautiously hovered over to the next hill. It might have been our rotor wash, but never mind, the clouds were moving—not much, but enough. After 10 trying minutes at treetop level, the eastern slope of the mountains began to fall away and the ceiling to improve. I got Carlsbad Radio and advised them that we were en route. The visibility wasn't anything to be proud of, but we slipped into Carlsbad Municipal.

I tuned my partner out as we sloshed across the ramp and into the terminal building. The weatherman was rubbing his hands eagerly and smiling disarmingly as we entered. I thought to myself, I have lived this before. With head bowed, he oiled,

"Carlsbad to Corpus Christi. What an interesting flight! Wish I could go with you. Well, you ought to have a nice flight from here on. The worst weather is behind you. It should be mostly clear flying from here. Oh, a little low stuff here and there, but you should be able to go under."

3/LOST AND FOUND

Flight gave man the final dimension with which to measure his wanderlust. Surface transport—the ship, the oxcart, the Ferrari—was the captive of plane geometry, yet it was with a plane that man was finally able to travel UP. (And, inevitably, DOWN.) So relentless was this upward urge that a flying machine went *up* to the moon eventually, and then it was no longer a plane but a spacecraft.

That an airplane was capable of a third dimension was incidental to its value, for aircraft were not for going up and down like an elevator, but for moving from one point to another. That moved aviators back into plane geometry; pity, for if they'd had only to move vertically, pilots would never have learned how to get lost.

This peculiar talent for going the wrong way is not limited to people named Corrigan. Almost all pilots, from the beginning of the science of air navigation, have connived to arc off toward distant horizons with none of the blessings God gave such lowly creatures as pigeons, which manage to find their way with little fuss. Humans have a rotten sense of direction. Given the advantage of height conferred by air travel, one might have expected us to do at least a little better than our meager biological inheritance allows. But no. Put a human in the air and that piece of ground he treads daily will look as foreign as Lilliput. Charts and compass only obscure the issue further, using symbology and abstraction to clarify confusion, which hardly ever works.

Getting lost is grim stuff if one uses up all the fuel before finding a place to land. Every pilot who has gotten lost has known that weird constricting in the gut which accompanies the growing realization that he hasn't the foggiest notion of where he is. All the tools that science has provided him—beacons, airways, omnirange, various instruments—are but trinkets if he loses reference to a known point. Granted, time and technology have greatly improved the well-trained airman's chances of finding himself; a vast web of electromagnetic signals now laces increasing portions of the globe with the equivalent of highways that one merely follows or uses for reference.

Students of flight spend as much time acquiring the skills needed to keep track of where they are as they do learning the behavior of aircraft. Because air travel is rapid, it takes only a moment's lapse to lose the track. Err only a few degrees off course and after an hour you are lost by miles. It is easy to get lost, which may account for its popularity.

Getting lost is a tense time for everyone, but worst for the lost one. To the spectator viewing the stupefied pilot through the lens of the stories that follow, there is a certain poignant humor in each situation, perhaps because the poor pilot's fix reflects something of the human condition. Being just a little bit wrong is so very different from being exactly right. The following accounts were written by pilots who found out they had gone wrong at some point in a flight—in one case, after the landing!

Devon Francis, aviation editor for the Associated Press and one of the founders of the Aerospace Writers' Association, was an experienced hand in the cockpit and past the point of being awed by a few low clouds; but he wasn't beyond allowing the weather to confuse his pilotage.

●

The weather was not good, but it was not bad. The clouds were in two layers, both broken. For an hour, drizzles had come intermittently from the scud below. My route was Lock Haven, Pennsylvania, to Flushing Airport, just east of La Guardia Field. I had flown solo over the eastern Pennsylvania "hills"—

some of the ridges rise to 2,000 feet—before, and had a mind's-eye picture of the terrain and route.

It seemed to be clearing as I fastened my belt. An occasional shaft of sunlight came through. The Cub Cruiser with its 75-hp engine had felt fine on a check flight, and I had been surprised at its pleasant landing characteristics. Because the tail rides high when the ship is at rest, the amount of backward stick travel at the moment of full stall is negligible.

At the end of the runway I braked the ship to crosswind position, ran up the engine, tested the mags, wheeled upwind and took off. That was mistake number one.

I took my time climbing, scanning the clouds as I gained altitude. It did not look bad at all. Coming back downwind, I had 2,500 feet, so I set off across the first ridge enclosing the winding river. Ahead of me, almost at right angles to my course, the river made a turn. Almost immediately, the scud began bothering me, and I turned toward a lighter spot. I was not more than three miles south of my course when the river appeared. I spotted a checkpoint, headed slightly south of east and checked both the deviation and variation of the compass. So far, so good.

Here the terrain played out, affording me plenty of places to get down in case of engine trouble. I was about to lean back with a sigh of satisfaction and light a cigarette, when scud began whipping by. Rain spattered against the windscreen. I throttled back and nosed down, an eye on the altimeter and the tops of the hills. Should I turn back? The return to the airport would be easy, I knew that. But from 2,000 feet, light spots appeared ahead and it was hard to give up the quest. I decided to go on.

That was mistake number two.

Now it was nip-and-tuck with the scud. I couldn't get over a 2,000-foot ridge without pulling up into the stuff, and I was no instrument flyer. I reasoned that I could go through a notch in the range at the right, keeping a valley of a branch of the Susquehanna in sight for 15 or 20 minutes for safety. In that valley within easy range were three airports, at Riverside, Berwick and Wilkes-Barre.

The clouds kept pressing down. I found myself at 1,500 feet anxiously peering ahead at the ridges in my path. They ran from 1,500 to 2,000. Ten minutes elapsed. I cut through a notch in another ridge. Now, for the first time, I was not quite sure of my position. I studied the map anxiously as turbulent air occupied my stick hand. Landmarks were at a premium. I still had time to cut north to the river and follow its valley to the haven of an airport. But if I did that, I might be stuck there all night.

I elected to abandon all thought of the river and to rely on my compass. If I held to a course slightly south of east, I reasoned, I must, with a following wind, come reasonably close to my objective. If unconsciously I veered south, I had to pick up Staten Island or, at worst, the South Jersey summer resort shore. If I veered north, I was bound to cross the Hudson River.

I hadn't remembered so many hills on the course. And here was a lake I could not place on the map. Still, just south of east had to get me there—unless the compass had been calibrated wrong. I drove on, getting a little mad. I was sure I would cross and recognize the ridge split by the Delaware Water Gap. It was raining now and then, and the windscreen was getting dirty.

I couldn't turn back if I wanted to. I didn't know where to turn. Ducking up valleys had destroyed my sense of direction, and as for the map, it had gone completely cockeyed. I certainly would tell the Civil Aeronautics Administration about that! I scotched my worry with a singsong reassurance that just south of east *must* bring me out at some recognizable place. But the ship was pitching and, more often than not, I was not sure just where south of east was. Lightplane compasses swing like a blues singer.

I went on. The choice was not mine. Happily, the hills were lower. I measured them by rule of thumb and the altimeter as the ship went over them.

The tanks held four and a half hours of fuel; no worry on that score. The rain had stopped, but the visibility was getting worse by the minute. For the twenty-fifth time I glanced at my chronograph. I had been out two and a half hours.

Suddenly, ahead of me loomed a shoreline. It was a straight shoreline, what I could see of it, and for all I knew, the water stretched eastward for 3,000 miles to Europe. The fact was that I could not see 500 feet ahead of the ship's nose.

Well! I wasn't so dumb after all. I knew now. This was South Jersey. I drew a sigh of relief, leaned back and lighted up. Now I would fly just east of north, crossing the New York Lower Bay and Brooklyn to Flushing. That might take me 20 minutes, maybe 30. Through the haze I saw the shoreline bear left sharply. The map corroborated that. But I couldn't see the sand spit stretching north from the Atlantic Highlands. Well, the visibility was miserable anyway and I was right on an airspace reservation, so it was best to follow the shoreline. With something below me I might recognize with a little study, I failed to check my map. That was mistake number three.

The terrain failed to gel. What should have been Raritan Bay turned out to be a little inlet. Now, instead of returning to the shoreline, I struck inland. I don't know why. I was bewildered and, for the first time, definitely uneasy. Where was I? I could not be north of my course. I would have crossed the Hudson. Obviously what I had seen back there was not the Jersey shore. I began wandering northeast, afraid to go back under miserable visibility conditions and find the ocean.

A shoreline sticks out like a sore thumb. That was mistake number four, according to my count. More accomplished fliers probably have added up a dozen by now.

Now if I *were* north of my course, I argued, and *had* crossed the Hudson, a course due south would bring me to Long Island Sound. I turned south, flying five minutes to the second. I gave up. Too soon, as it turned out. I was more than three hours out. I had something more than an hour and a quarter of fuel left.

I had best pick a field and get down. My ability to reason had been swallowed up by fright and embarrassment. I was thoroughly scared under the existing visibility conditions and I did not want to hurt the airplane in a forced landing.

I looked around, spotted a field, dragged it and pulled up for an approach. The area was a little hilly. What wind there was appeared to be west-southwest. It had two 250-foot fields, one plowed, one sown in clover, without a fence between. I would have to land slightly crosswind, coming in over the plowed field —which was badly furrowed—and touching on the lip of the other one. The ship squatted nicely and braked to a stop. The landing was the first sensible move I had made since leaving Lock Haven.

No one came out of the house at the end of the first field.

"This is going to cost me," I ruminated.

A hired hand outside grinned. "Lost?"

"Yes, where am I?"

"Redding."

That was in Connecticut. I felt my face getting red. Then I *had* been north of my course and I *had* crossed the Hudson— but how I had done it without seeing it, I could not figure out. The track I had made began crystallizing now. I had been blown ever so slightly northeast. In 175 miles of flying, the better part of it by compass alone, I had emerged over the shore of Long Island Sound at a point where the shoreline ran in almost a north-south direction. That had confused me. At that moment I had been less than seven miles off course.

The farmer, surprisingly enough, was pleasant. If the ship was equipped with a tailwheel instead of a skid, he said, I hadn't done much damage. He, his wife and the hired man walked out to see me take off. The ship staggered aloft. Now I would fly slightly west of south, strike the Sound and follow the shoreline. That was mistake number five. I should have flown directly to Stratford and checked the weather. But Flushing Airport could not be more than 20 minutes away.

The visibility kept getting worse. I dropped from 2,000 feet to 1,500 and finally to 1,000. The Sound popped up out of nowhere. I cut southwest, flying just offshore. The shore was hard to see, so I edged closer. Then, as I strained my eyes to keep the shoreline in view, a squall struck.

The ship was tossed around like a leaf in a gale. I had to keep an eye on the horizon or run the risk of stalling and spinning in. I dropped to 100 feet. The line between the Sound and land was dim. If I stayed over land, I ran the added risk of colliding with something. By dint of pulling and hauling, I managed to get the airplane headed out over the Sound. Now I dropped down to within 10 feet of the water. I had to. The rain was coming down in sheets.

I was riding on a miniature gale, lashed by rain, straight east over the choppy waters of the Sound. Updrafts and downdrafts rocked the ship. For the first time in the eight months since I had received my ticket, the idea entered my head that I was going to join that select company of pilots who had not been able to walk away from an airplane.

This was my last ride. In the next three or four minutes the conviction that my number was up became so fixed that, even while fighting the ship, I found myself wondering when and how they would find the wreckage.

Then, to the south, I saw a lighter spot in the sky. I could not turn but I could crab, foot by foot. Presently the rain began to lessen. From my meager 10 feet of altitude I climbed for a space to breathe. I was soaked through, but whether from rain that streamed into the cabin or from sweat, I did not know or care. As I turned, picking up the Long Island shoreline, I could see the squall still raging over the water.

The visibility was not too good and rain still pelted the ship, but the way to Flushing Airport was clear. Afterward I measured the distance from the point where I encountered the squall to the point where I came out. In an 85-mph plane I had been blown 12 miles in five minutes.

As I climbed out, shaken and weak, in front of Speed's Flying Service, the imperturbable "Speed" Hanzlik, who has been taking his airplanes in stride for more years than he cares to remember, was lolling in the doorway of his office.

"Just get in?" he asked, glancing incredulously at the whipping windsock.

"Yes, I got lost, badly lost."

"Lots of guys get lost," observed Speed.

"But not like I got lost, or as scared as I got," I objected, reaching for a chair for support.

"Lots of guys get scared, plenty scared. How's about a cup of coffee?"

I felt better, somehow.

●

It would have been difficult to come up with anything that could top what Speed Hanzlik had already lived through. Experience shows; which man was sitting comfortably in his office drinking coffee while the other was out flying to Flushing by way of Connecticut?

If an American can miss the Hudson River in the rain, a Briton can miss an airport at night, as this RAF trainee demonstrated conclusively.

●

In 1936 I was serving with a Royal Air Force fighter squadron based near Cambridge, about 50 miles from London. The squadron was equipped with the Gloster Gauntlet, one of the last of the biplane fighters and a really wonderful airplane to fly, having no vices at all, which is one reason why I am able to write this story.

In those carefree prewar days, most of our time was spent training and preparing for the big scrap to come. Part of this training called for night cross-country flights, which consisted chiefly of beacon crawling from one fighter airfield to another, with perhaps one daring leg purely on dead reckoning. The overall distance covered in these flights seldom exceeded 150 miles. It was on such a flight in December 1936 that I learned a very sharp lesson.

I was scheduled to fly south from my base, Duxford, to another fighter airfield just outside London, then across the north of the city to a civilian airfield, and thence due north, on the dead-reckoning leg, to a third airfield, and finally a short leg, due east, to my home base. I took off, climbed to 12,000 feet and set off toward the glare of London. Everything went well, and I soon saw the neon beacon flashing the identification of the airfield. On arriving over the top of the turning point, I found that London, lit up in all its prewar glory, looked so attractive that I decided to have a really good look at it.

In order to take in as much as possible, I made a wide circle over the south of London, then went on to the civilian airfield instead of going directly to it across the north of the city. I arrived over this next point very little behind ETA, which should have warned me that something was wrong—but it didn't! Had I taken the course originally planned, I would have noticed a very rapidly increasing drift.

Taking careful note of my time over the civilian airfield, I set off for my third turning point. Sure enough, it appeared right on time and dead ahead. There was no positive means of identifying this airfield, as it did not have a beacon; but the flare path was lighted and it appeared where it should have. I was quite convinced that everything was going according to plan, and consequently, I turned east and headed for home, calling the base on the radio.

The radio in those days was high-frequency, and if you were very lucky, you could sometimes carry on a two-way conversation with your base over a distance of 30 miles—always providing, of course, that you had sufficient height. It was because of this poor radio reception that I had not bothered to call the base before this. Now that I was well within range, I did not expect any difficulty. It came as rather a surprise when I received no reply to my calls. Eventually I heard the ground station calling me, but it was very faint and although I replied several times it soon became evident that it was not receiving me.

About this time I noticed that there were not as many lights on the ground as there should have been in that part of the country. Those that I could see had an orange tinge to them that denoted ground mist and I began to suspect that something was radically wrong. Suddenly I saw the beacon—I was home! One dash, two dots and another dash, a very welcome letter "X." I throttled back and started to descend. As I approached the base, however, I noticed that there was no flare path laid out, so I looked at the beacon again and found that it was flashing one dash and three dots, a most unwelcome letter "B." This really puzzled me as I knew of no airfield with this identification, nor could I find one on my map.

After circling this strange airfield a few times, I decided to fly south again, find London, reorient myself and return to base by beacon crawling. With this in mind I turned south and climbed back to 12,000 feet.

I had been flying for approximately 10 minutes on this new course when, with a splutter, the motor died. I glanced down, saw that I was out of fuel and quickly turned on the reserve supply, praying that there would be sufficient in this to enable me to get down somewhere. I turned back toward the no-longer-unwelcome beacon and found, to my surprise, that it was still quite close. Throttling back to conserve my fuel, I glided back toward it.

When I got down to circuit height over the airfield, I found it impossible, there being no flare path laid out, to tell where the actual landing area was. I picked out what appeared to be an open space, owing to the lack of lights, and, turning into the direction I estimated the wind to be from, came in to land, setting off a magnesium wingtip flare as I did so. This was a mistake, as it glared very badly against the ground mist, and for a moment I could not be certain what attitude the airplane was in. Fortunately I was very low, and before I lost control of the aircraft I saw below me a plowed field, which enabled me to keep the airplane in a level attitude. Almost immediately I saw a row of trees directly in my path. There was nothing that I could do except shield my face with my left arm, ease back on the stick and stall into the trees. This I endeavored to do, but I had a little too much speed and, instead of going into the trees, I ballooned over them and came to rest unharmed, and the aircraft undamaged, in a field just beyond.

I sat very still trying to make myself believe that I really had made it, when a man came running over to me waving a flashlight. When he reached the airplane, he looked at me in amazement for a moment, then said, "Where in hell have you come from?" Before I could reply he went on, "This isn't the airfield, you know; it's my back garden and for your information you have landed in between a stone quarry and a concrete gun emplacement! The airfield is on the other side of the road."

●

And as if that wasn't bad enough, the gentleman turned out to be the base commander. He also turned out to be a good sport about his garden being thrashed, though, and found the maladroit young fellow in the airplane a bunk at the officers' club and a noggin of whiskey to sleep on.

Blunders like that one could never happen today, right? Wrong. Here's the promised comedy of errors in which everybody got into the act—pilot, controllers and a strong wind—to find the wrong airport.

●

"Five-Four Fox, radar vectors for ILS approach Runway 18, descend and maintain 3,500."

As Kansas City Approach Control talked, a little bell in my head started to ring—but not loud enough to get through a limited-experience brain that had been battered by over two hours of instruments, which was punctuated continually by turbulence, rain and vectors away from the heavy stuff. As that Kansas City approach controller offered his radar hand leading to the localizer, new confidence and relaxation took over.

My wife and I and another couple had planned an early Sunday departure from DuPage, outside of Chicago, to put us in Colorado Springs for a four-day business convention a little after noon—hopefully in time for a quick nine holes before dark.

As our brand-new Cessna 210 lifted four people and a Pullman-size load of luggage into the clear skies of northern Illinois, it was hard to visualize anything but a "severe-clear" or a little "violent-scattered" flight to Kansas City. Our route was V9 St. Louis, V4 to Kansas City's Mid Continent Airport, which had just opened and was still unspoiled by the congestion of commercial traffic.

Those blue skies were soon punctuated by strong, building cumulus to 20,000 or better, slightly south of the Joliet Vortac. Instrument flight in a new airplane was becoming a reality, and this airplane had all one could ask for in electronic equipment.

Turbulence through the next two hours was a constant problem, despite the fact that repeated checks with Chicago and Kansas City Centers assured us there was nothing but rain in our vicinity. Finally, a handoff from Kansas City Center to Kansas City Approach brought that welcome approach clearance. The Mid Continent 18 back-course approach plate was already on the lapboard, as the ATIS had given the wind clue for such an approach. I briefly wondered if the FAA had thoroughly checked out the backside approach to this new kerosene Mecca.

Approach Control had us on a 270-degree heading and we were still solidly in the soup when the query came: "Do you have the 727 in sight?" A negative reply brought a new heading of 320 degrees and the comment that radar thought we just might follow the 727. The controller continued and told a Braniff to report the outer marker.

Somewhere in my head, that bell rang.

Moments later, we flashed downward through layers, and in those two or three seconds a 727 was indeed seen heading south between layers three or four miles from our position. The bell got louder, but not loud enough. Approach Control started our turn to the left and 180 degrees, but still no center needle. On the same frequency came Braniff's report of the outer marker. Back down into another layer, the mind started to spin. We're doing a back-course approach on which radar says the localizer should show center, but we still have a left-pinned needle. We have had a flash visual sighting of a 727 and the only other airplane on this frequency is Braniff; they fly 727s, but this Braniff is obviously doing a front-course approach on which they are reporting an outer marker. Yet Approach Control has suggested we follow a 727. Something was wrong. I knew I'd better put it together quick. We were on the *wrong* side of the omni to make the intersection. Now I *had* to hear the bell: The term "ILS" doesn't apply in controller's language to a back-course approach; this can't be Mid Continent!

"Hey, Approach, we're going to *Mid Continent.*" The controller came back quickly: "How did I miss it? It's right here in the corner of the tape—Mid Continent. We've got you coming into Kansas City Municipal. Turn left 090 degrees." We started to turn to 090, and the outer marker lit up. As the blue light faded, Approach came back with a special weather on Mid Continent of 200 and a half. We advised that wasn't for us even if it were legal, and what was Kansas City Municipal?

"Four hundred and one."

"Okay, we'll buy it."

Approach Control came back: "Continue your turn and roll out on 180 degrees." Things were now coming fast as I found the new approach plate, hit 180 and the outer marker all at the same time. I was quickly running out of hands as well as brains.

Back on the power and follow that nice new glide slope, a heavy right correction for strong west winds, and our heading went beyond 200 degrees to maintain the localizer.

Now, watch altitude—minimums not too far away. The cloud lighting was giving clues that the bottom was close at hand; however, I stuck with the needles. Just as we broke, my fledgling friend in the right seat hollered, "There it is!" Leaving instruments at 400 or 500 showed the Missouri River in a break through the clouds, followed by a runway straight ahead. What a sense of accomplishment, landing in heavy rain after a full-ILS approach in a brand-new airplane . . .

"Kansas City Ground Control. Five-Four Fox off the active." "Five-Four Fox, suggest you contact Fairfax Ground Control." For those of you who haven't landed at one airport while talking to another, a check of a Kansas City Sectional will tell you that we were not only at the wrong airport, but in the wrong state. While doing an ILS to near-minimums, no less. The end of Fairfax (Kansas) Runway 22 is only a mile and a half from the end of Kansas City (Missouri) Municipal Runway 18 and is only about 2,500 feet to the right of the localizer for Kansas City Municipal. With a low ceiling where you break out close to the end of Runway 22, and a strong west wind that can put your nose on 200 degrees or more, you can begin to get the picture.

After 15 minutes on the ground at Fairfax, we realized we would still have to go to Kansas City Municipal in order to eat. Sweeping up the pieces of my pulverized pride, I finally got the courage to push the mike button and ask the tower how I could get an instrument clearance to go the mile or so to Kansas City Municipal. The tower replied, "Funny thing . . . you don't need one. We just went VFR."

●

Even surrounded with all that electronics, our man up front can often manage to trip over the threshold. Any second-guessers be

*warned: That story is not the first, last or only instance of a good
pilot landing at the wrong airport. It happens frequently enough
so that pilots unfamiliar with an area would be wise to pause
before canceling IFR, especially at night in a big city with several
airports close together. All beacons look alike, and so do runway
lights. Follow the approach procedure to minimums even if you
are contact and you'll minimize your opportunity to repeat the
mistake our hero made.*

*Maybe that proliferation of navaids is too confusing. Maybe if
a pilot had just one simple task—a single instrument to monitor
—he'd be better off. Flying a simple heading shouldn't be too
tough, should it? Don't bet on it.*

●

When you were taking your early flight training, did it ever
seem to you that your instructor was going overboard by insist-
ing you perform flight procedures by the book each time you
flew? Mine raked me over the coals once for failing to call out
"Clear prop!" when I started the engine after landing on a
vacant field. He also insisted I do a complete preflight check on
an aircraft that had just taxied up to the gas pit in perfect
condition. He would go into orbit when, after setting my directional gyro, I would forget to spin the adjustment knob to make
sure the gyro was uncaged. These and hundreds of other rules
were drummed into my ears by a voice that, after years of
practice, could easily outroar a lightplane engine running at full
power.

I thought I could never forget those rules, but five years later
and hundreds of miles south of the Mexican border, the truth
came home.

My two companions and I were returning in my Cessna 182
from a week of fun in the warm November sun of Baja California. Our last stop had been at the luxurious new resort at Punta
Chivato, located on a point just north of Mulege on the Gulf
of California. The night before, we had picked up a weather

broadcast that told of a large winter storm moving into southern California, so we were anxious to cross the border as soon as possible.

After a late breakfast and a wait for some box lunches, we hopped into the Punta Chivato truck and jolted out to the airstrip. After a week of sharing the loading and check-out tasks, we now made short work of them. Soon we were airborne and climbing out beneath a high, thin overcast.

The air was unbelievably smooth, so we decided to fly the geologists' route up the rugged backbone of the peninsula rather than the customary and safer Gulf route. When we reached cruise altitude, the Gulf was already disappearing off our right wing. I turned to a heading of 312 degrees, set my directional gyro and settled back to enjoy the conversation and the rugged beauty of central Baja as it slipped beneath us.

For almost an hour, we cruised northwest with the Gulf out of sight. I was eyeballing the mountains ahead, with only an occasional glance at my directional gyro, which indicated each time that I was right on course—312 degrees. Then, off my right wingtip, the Gulf reappeared. I decided to fly closer to it to check my position against some recognizable landmarks. According to my chart, we should have been coming up on Bahia de los Angeles, with giant Angel de la Guarda Island offshore; no bays or islands were in sight, though. Perhaps beyond the next bend . . .

About this time, we realized that someone had left the box lunches in the truck at Punta Chivato. But as we flew on and no island appeared, the vague sense that something was wrong made the problem of no lunch fade completely. I began studying the coastline for anything that would be identifiable on the map. Suddenly, my attention was riveted to a detail that had escaped me before. Instead of the gentle waves of the Gulf, what I was looking at appeared to be breakers—the Pacific! How could that be? The Pacific would be off my left wingtip, and this was off my right. I shot a glance at my directional gyro: 312

degrees—on course. I checked my magnetic compass: 169 degrees! Impossible! How could we be flying southeast when we had been flying steadily northwest and had made no turns? I reached up and tried to give my DG adjustment knob a turn. It was stuck in the locked position and needed a pull of another quarter inch before it would spin free. No wonder I had been holding that heading so well!

With the weather deteriorating to the north, I had to make up the time I lost flying west and south, so I decided to head due north, a heading that would bring us eventually to the Gulf and minimize our flight time to Mexicali.

As we approached the Gulf again, we were able to identify Angel de la Guarda Island to the southeast and thereby fix our position. Our concern over whether we would have enough gas to make the border was ended. All the way home, there was a lot of good-natured ribbing about my navigating ability. I finally had time to marvel at how an airplane could turn, and even reverse its direction, so slowly that three pilots, who were all awake and alert, could not sense it.

It wouldn't have happened if I hadn't decided to fly the Baja backbone instead of the Gulf, nor if I had remembered the rule my instructor had tried so hard to implant in me: "When you set the DG, pull out the knob and give it a spin to be sure it's free. It only takes a little twist."

●

All things considered, that closetful of navaids is a pretty good deal. When it comes to navigating, simplicity doesn't seem to work. The trouble with magnetic compasses is that they are passive instruments. They are also fickle. Like impressionable children, compasses will follow whatever happens to be the most persuasive force at the moment. Acceleration and deceleration can throw them off. So can a simple turn. Directional gyros are a help, but they require power, either electricity or vacuum; they also precess—drift slowly off their settings. Larger airplanes have slaved compasses that eliminate most errors; but all compasses, after all, are the "slave" of magnetic lines of force that terminate at a place called the magnetic pole. Is the magnetic pole the North Pole? No, the magnetic pole turns out to be somewhere in Canada. And if that isn't enough to shake one's faith in the whole arrangement, there is a variation in the difference between magnetic north and true north (which is associated with the real North Pole) depending upon where one happens to be flying. It is hardly something upon which to pin one's hopes.

So someone devised airways. First there were lighted beacons along the route. They were no help when the weather obscured them, which is exactly when they were needed. Next up were the radio ranges, which broadcast Morse code for the letters "A" or "N" if you were off course, humming nicely with a steady tone when you were on the airway—better, but not good enough.

●

I was a half hour overdue at Jackson, Mississippi, after a long hop from Spartansburg, North Carolina. Early twilight lowered the already-poor visibility. I was lost and running out of gas. I tried to pick a clear landing spot in the mist-shrouded forest below. There was none.

After 900 hours in the air I was still careless. The more than 10,000 miles and almost 100 hours of cross-country time I had flown in the preceding two months increased that carelessness. I believed I knew the route well—I'd flown it half a dozen times in the past few weeks. How wrong I was!

My last hour's supply of fuel was going fast. The gas gauge crept nearer and nearer empty—with about 40 minutes' flying left. Something about lost-plane procedure and bisector headings kept coming into my mind.

Jackson Radio was tuned in on my range receiver. I turned the volume up and a stream of di-dahs came into my headset. I was almost on the A bi-sector heading, according to my charts. I crossed my fingers and hoped I would soon find the station.

Instead of flying the airway on the 350-mile hop, I had flown direct. At least I thought I had. I used general audio checks on the radio ranges instead of the visual checks I should have made. But neither my audio nor my visual checks had been precise.

My second big mistake came in crossing what I supposed to be the east leg of the Jackson Range. The trees and rivers and the general look of the terrain were familiar. I turned west, blissfully presuming the town was just ahead. I never checked the leg. Soon a twilight N, dah-dits, began coming in. A little south of the east leg, I figured. I banked the plane over a bit to the right. The N was more distinct. Steadily my corrections became larger and larger; yet with each correction the dah-dits became clearer in my headset. Still, I didn't feel too uneasy about it.

When I reached 30 degrees off the inbound heading, I began to wonder. I knew the general direction of the lowering sun was westerly. My compass wasn't too much in error. It read correctly when I picked up the plane at Norfolk, anyway. Suddenly my mouth felt strangely dry. A light sweat broke out on my forehead. I checked the range layout of my sectional chart. My heading was more than 60 degrees to the right of the inbound course! I called the radio range and told them I was lost in an unknown N quadrant.

"Roger," they acknowledged clearly, "continue your orientation. Report when you have determined a fix."

It was my ball again. At last I remembered to check for a build or a fade on the range signal. I tuned the receiver down until only a faint signal came through. Slowly it became less and less audible, then it was gone. It was a sure fade. My heading was taking me away from the station. Wasting no time, I kicked rudder and laid the plane over in a 180-degree turn.

Then an eerie thought struck me. The gas would last only a half hour more at best. I turned up the radio receiver again. The twilight signal soon came through. It became a steady "on course."

I turned to what I thought was the beam heading. Thinking I had joined the west leg, I headed east. Again I failed to check. Soon I saw a town ahead that I felt must be Jackson. The map showed the east-west leg crossing directly over it. However, the clear on-course buzz changed abruptly to a twilight A signal!

The field must be almost dead ahead, I thought. The di-dah of an A definitely replaced the beam signal, though. I couldn't see any field, either. Perplexed, I called the tower again.

"Jackson Tower, this is Six-Seven-Three over unidentified town. Do you have me in sight?"

"Negative, Six-Seven-Three. Could you describe any landmarks?"

I skimmed along the housetops. A lumber mill, a main street, railroad tracks and a schoolyard made up the small town. However, I could see no clues to its name. Then I spotted something that might help.

"Jackson Tower, this is Six-Seven-Three. There's a lumber yard with a water tower near it. The name Woodford is painted on the tower."

The tower rogered my transmission, adding, "Will check. Wait. Out."

I couldn't wait long in the air. I tried a reorientation on the range while the tower checked on my information. I turned to the A bisector heading. The fuel gauge showed me this was my last try. I was at a scant 700 feet, afraid to climb for fear of wasting gas. If I didn't find the field this time, I'd make that crash landing soon.

I pulled the canopy open. A rush of air brought in the smell of the trees. None of the tiny clearings looked big enough to hit without killing myself if the engine quit. And it would quit any minute, I knew. I decided to wait until the last moment, though.

I would pick as clear a spot as possible and hope. I leaned forward against my shoulder harness, giving the straps an extra tug.

"Six-Seven-Three, this is Jackson Radio. An officer at Jackson field knows this area fairly well."

I wanted to cut them off and concentrate on as good a landing as possible.

But they went on: "He says the Woodford lumber mill is just northeast of here. I'll let him talk to you."

For a split second I had hope. But only about 10 minutes' fuel remained.

"Steer 220," the officer told me. "That lumber mill is just about 20 miles from here."

Maybe there was a chance. The bisector heading I had been on for the past few minutes was 215 degrees. The town should be just ahead. I scanned the forest eagerly. Through the slight ground fog I could see only the trees and a long farmhouse. If only I had five more minutes' gas. Suddenly, I saw the range station just ahead. A half mile farther should be the field. A few minutes more, and I'd make it. I was almost over the red-and-white radio towers. The engine was still going. I saw the runways. The engine still ran smoothly. What a relief! I lowered my wheels for landing and started my glide.

"Six-Seven-Three for straight-in approach," I requested. "Am very low on fuel."

"Cleared for Runway 29," they responded. I wondered if they were as relieved as I was.

●

Another device that was supposed to enhance the pilots' dismal record at navigation was the automatic direction finder.

●

"The ADF is a relatively simple device. Its needle points to any station it is tuned to. You can fly a front bearing or a back bearing with equal facility and quickly determine your drift. Most pilots like to fly toward something, but this is purely a matter of personal preference. The ADF with its needle at 180 degrees is no less reliable than the ADF with its needle at zero degrees."

Wrong. I repeat—wrong.

In late April 1966, my wife and I left our home base at Van Nuys, California, and flew our Comanche 400 to Europe. We had installed a little wedge-shaped 20-gallon auxiliary tank between the rear seat and the baggage compartment, increasing our supply of fuel to a healthy 150 gallons, had built in an oxygen system, dug up an ancient HF radio that just fit the glove compartment, rigged a trailing-wire antenna, added a beat frequency oscillator switch (to get a tone from ADFs overseas) to our ADF, collected papers and gear, and grabbed some sky. The trip presented no great problems, and it was not until the recrossing of the Atlantic, indeed the very last water jump, that we learned our lesson about the ADF.

We took off from Narssarssuaq for Goose Bay, which was more than 600 nm in front of our nose. Applying the huge variation of 40 degrees west, we took up a compass course of 268 degrees; the deviation was negligible. This we would hold until about halfway across, whereupon we would steer 262 degrees, then 258 degrees from a compulsory reporting point (Capelin) 40-odd miles off the coast of Labrador. No amount of wind shifts or silly mistakes could make us miss all of North America.

We reset our DG and flipped on the autopilot.

We had a back bearing on Simiutak that was virtually nailed to 180 degrees, so there was no drift component. At our assigned altitude of 8,000 feet there was nothing to do but switch tanks, wait for 50 degrees west longitude to show up, and report via HF to the center.

Every now and then my wife would tune away from Simiutak to try for a Consolan fix, using Nantucket (off Cape Cod),

Stavanger (Norway) and Bushmills (Ireland). We had used this system of counting dots and dashes on the eastward crossing with some success, but now all three stations seemed to have gone on vacation. Ocean Station Bravo also was silent.

I called blind on 126.7 and a BOAC jet came right back from somewhere at 40,000 feet.

"British Overseas, could you relay a message to the Bravo boat from Comanche 8483 Papa? We'd like them to turn on their beacon."

"Right."

While we waited, my wife tried to tune Bravo, using the BFO switch and a headset. Silence. Then:

"Comanche Eight-Three Papa, this is British Overseas. Bravo has its beacon on, and requests your position and how long you wish the beacon."

We guesstimated a position, and said that we wanted the beacon kept on until we landed in Goose, checked into the hotel, had a shower and a drink.

"I quite understand. Every pilot feels the same way about that beacon. Are you receiving it now?"

"Negative. But thanks for everything."

And we were alone again.

My wife retuned Simiutak and the needle snapped back to 180 degrees reassuringly. But when she tried Cartwright and Hopedale, both on the Labrador coast, the needle wandered aimlessly.

"I think we're way north of course," my wife muttered.

"What makes you think so?"

"Well, we can't get Bravo, for one thing, and Cartwright and Hopedale both seem to be quite a bit to our left."

"Those bearings are useless. Forget them. We've got a fantastic back bearing from Simiutak and, as far as I'm concerned, we're threading the needle into Goose."

I don't know when I began to grow uneasy. It may have been when we entered snow clouds and light icing (with Goose Bay reporting an 80-degree temperature!), or it may have been when it gradually dawned on me that we were receiving Simiutak from three times the distance we had been able to receive it on the eastward crossing. Either way, the combination of the two was deadly: solid instruments without track guidance. I told my wife to try anything and everything ahead. This time I really paid attention to her bearings on Cartwright and Hopedale. The needle wandered on both, but always to the left.

"See if you can pick up Goose VOR on the Mark XII." She tried it, but no luck.

"How about the low-freq radio range?"

"Can't get it."

"Tune the whole dial slowly on all three bands and try to identify the loudest signal. I'll see if I can contact the center."

I called Goose and Gander on 5626.5 kc. No response. I tried them with 8888 kc, then went to emergency on 2182 kc. I was obviously talking to myself. We were in great shape: IFR, in ice, lost and without communications.

She had completed her sweep of all the bands. Now only Hopedale was identifiable. The needle wobbled horribly, but *always* to the left.

"Retune Simiutak."

My wife groaned but complied. It was still coming in, though faintly, and the needle swung to 180 degrees. I pressed the little red test button, then released it. The bearing was correct, but now, despite the evidence, I distrusted it; and if this bearing from Simiutak was wrong, we were already in serious trouble. Almost five hours at 175 knots true airspeed meant one hell of a distance—and in an unknown direction!

"Tune Hopedale and leave it."

The thought of chasing a wandering needle was not my idea of fun, but there didn't seem to be an alternative. Going back to Greenland was out of the question. We were well beyond our point of no return.

I called blind on 126.7, but this time no friendly airliner

replied. I scored the same on 121.5. That settled one item anyway. If contact was to be made, it would have to be on HF. I set up 5626.5 kc again and called Goose Center.

But precisely at this moment a small hole opened below us. We were crossing the Labrador coast! We both saw it in that split second—a desolate snow-covered shore—and then it was gone. I put the Comanche into a needle-width turn, for this at least was half a fix, and I had no intention of wandering away from it until I gave the matter a little thought.

We circled. What to do? And while I figuratively chewed my nails, trying to make a decision I wouldn't regret later, I cursed every piece of printed material I'd ever seen on ADF, for there was one trifling thing the experts never mentioned. You can home on a front bearing and be sure of reaching the station— but a back bearing *is only as good as your magnetic compass!* Without drift on a given heading, any given heading, the ADF will read 180 degrees. So if you want to fly outbound from a radio beacon on a compass course of 268 degrees, you'd better be damned sure when you're flying 268 degrees you're not flying 290 or 255 degrees.

I say again: On a front bearing your old magnetic compass can go as crazy as it wants to. But on a back bearing, friends, you are at your compass's mercy. It can lure you 1,000 miles off course. So, until somebody discovers how to check deviation during flight, back bearings are to be regarded with a certain amount of skepticism.

"Comanche Eight-Three Papa, do you hear Goose Center?"

The HF was working again!

"Eight-Three Papa, roger. We're over the Labrador coastline, doing 360s, probably north of course. Can you give us a radar steer?"

They could and did. But we were quite late getting into Goose. We had been over 200 miles north of course.

Two days later, over Oklahoma, I discovered what had happened, because neither of us was satisfied with the Labrador pilots' explanations, which dealt with distant storms and meteorological phenomena. I reached out and turned on the HF radio, watching the magnetic compass as I did so. It swung away 20 degrees! A short causing an electrical field? Undoubtedly, because we had swung our compass with the HF radio on before our departure.

In any event, since things like that can happen at any time in any cockpit, I will never *completely* trust a back bearing again.

●

Since there are still many parts of the world which have only nondirectional radio beacons as navaids, ADF is all a pilot has, so that couple's experience carries an important lesson.

Here's another tale of a fellow who flew the ADF without any trouble but got stranded in the sky right over the airport. He was so near—and still so terribly far from—a safe landing.

●

We had picked up our brand-new Turbo Aztec one sunny June morning at Los Angeles International Airport. Our trip, which had been planned in every detail, would take us some 1,000 miles, crisscrossing Mexico and the Central American coffee republics down to Panama. We left L.A. International two hours late because a leak in a fuel drain valve had to be fixed. Our first stop was at Tijuana, Mexico, to clear customs and immigration.

After a brief snack, we filed a flight plan for Los Mochis, Mexico, our destination for that day. We also dutifully made a note of sunset, which we were told was to be at 8:17 P.M. We asked if there was a time difference between Tijuana and Los Mochis, and the official told us that there was none. To double-check, we compared watches.

The flight itself was to last about three hours and 20 minutes. We crossed the rugged and lonely countryside of the Baja California peninsula and the Gulf of California in beautiful weather. We were still over the Gulf and had another 45 minutes to fly when the sun began to set. In spite of all our double-checking, Tijuana had given us the sunset time incorrectly. But that was no cause for alarm, since 6037Y was IFR-equipped and I was instrument-rated. Furthermore, the Jeppesen chart for Los Mochis showed a lighted runway, and Los Mochis was informed of our arrival because we had properly filed the mandatory flight plan.

About 40 miles from our destination, we tried to raise Los Mochis Tower by radio. We received no reply. During the next 15 minutes, we tried again and again. Each time, the result was the same: no reply. We consoled ourselves with the possibility that we were the only expected traffic and that the controller would return to the tower only shortly before our ETA. We began to get the definite sensation that something had gone wrong, however, when we crossed the Los Mochis NDB— located on the airport—and saw nothing but total darkness beneath us. We saw no tower lights, no planes, no runway lights.

To make matters worse, the chart indicated that the airport had to be approached with considerable caution. On one side of the runway, a powerline ran across the airport; on the other side, too close for comfort, was a 550-foot hill. Unfortunately, we could locate neither powerline nor hill. Los Mochis Tower stayed dark.

I began to fly ADF approaches, pulling up when crossing the beacon each time. After several attempts, we were still unable to locate the runway in spite of our powerful landing and taxi lights. Our fuel reserve had decreased to 45 minutes. This precluded any possibility of proceeding to another airport, especially since we were separated from the only possible alternative by some 120 miles of the Gulf of California.

We didn't have much time to spare for risky experiments. I decided that our only hope was to make people in Los Mochis aware of our presence and problems. This I tried to accomplish by flying over the town at low altitude with all lights burning and landing gear extended, constantly changing the manifold pressure, to obtain maximum attention. During each successive fly-by, I attempted to approach the NDB at a little lower altitude, while maintaining exactly the prescribed radial. Once over the beacon, I would dip the nose momentarily to see if the lights hit anything resembling a runway.

Finally, I took a third step and, for the first time in my career, radioed mayday. I broadcast my call on 121.5 and on 118.1, Mexico's tower frequency, hoping to raise a higher-flying plane that could alert Los Mochis authorities through Mexico Control. In nonemergency situations, the latter procedure had worked surprisingly well for me over some very lonely Atlantic and Persian-desert spots. But this time, no one, either in the air or on the ground, heard my call.

During one of these increasingly desperate approaches, I suddenly saw in the beam of automobile headlights a plane beneath us on the ground, and seconds later a series of kerosene lamps being put up as runway lights. Five minutes later, I landed on a rather bumpy strip. Hordes of people had come to the airport, expecting some sort of sensation. One little thing had not arrived at Los Mochis, however: our flight plan from Tijuana.

From an aviator's viewpoint, I had done everything possible to make the flight and the landing safe. Nevertheless, I learned two things from the experience: (1) When flying abroad, I will never again head for an airport unless I am certain to reach it before sunset, with the exception of large, well-known international airports where the tower is certain to be occupied 24 hours a day. (2) When in doubt over hours of operation, runway lighting or conditions of a particular airport, I will call the tower of that airport long distance and get the answer, no matter how much it costs. You may save more than money in the long run.

●

That's a case where a pilot was "found" in the navigational sense of the word but "lost" without a ground reference. There is no sound lonelier than that of a lost pilot transmitting a message for help, and when no answer comes back . . .

When there is *an answer to the call, nothing can express the relief the pilot feels. Put yourself in this man's place: his family packed into a Cessna 170 on a flight from San Jose, California, to Disneyland—then everything fell apart.*

●

We were lost. Our fuel supply was dwindling to the worry level. We were flying VFR above a solid overcast with boiling tops threatening to engulf us. Neither the airplane nor its pilot was equipped for instrument flying. We were forced to climb ever upward to stay clear of the towering cumulus clouds. At 11,000 feet we were still climbing. Our VHF radio—our only radio—was unreliable and intermittent. Below us, beneath a blanketing layer of clouds were 6,000-foot mountain peaks. To consider a needle-ball-and-airspeed descent through that turbulent blanket of gray was no more than gruesome speculation.

Earlier in the morning, we had climbed outbound from the Agnew VOR and cleared the Santa Cruz Mountains with ease. We picked out the outline of Monterey Bay on the Pacific Coast through open patches in the early-morning fog that blanketed the coast. We soon reported over Salinas on schedule and estimated our flight time for the direct flight to Paso Robles at 46 minutes. Highway 101, which paralleled our flight path, provided us with a ready reference. Near Mesa Del Rey, Paso Robles Radio came in clearly with the latest weather.

Paso Robles had 1,000 feet scattered and 5,000 broken, so we could land and refuel at Santa Barbara, stretch our legs, then press on to Fullerton Airport near Disneyland. The three girls were already asking, "How much longer, Daddy?" Thinking I had it made, I decided to climb on top; we were starting to get quite low, and it would be turbulent in the mountains below this scattered layer.

"I thought you told me that flying on top was pushing your luck," said my wife. She remembered this and some of the other sensible precautions I had explained to her on previous occasions. She reminded me of my flight instructors. I admitted to myself that she was right and I should listen to her, but Santa Barbara was so close and everything else was going according to plan.

We passed over Paso Robles at 9,500 feet and estimated Santa Barbara a short 51 minutes away. The steady, reassuring engine soon lulled the children to sleep. They had accepted the early-morning takeoff without complaint. Now they were catching up on lost sleep.

I turned the course selector to the 133-degree radial and centered the needle. The to-from indicator verified the outbound flight direction. The magnetic compass settled down to a proper heading. Relaxed, I glanced down through the fuzzy holes in the overcast. I turned to my wife and smiled.

"I thought we might see the peaks of the San Rafael Mountains or Big Pine Mountain. They're both more than 6,000 feet high. I guess the overcast is covering them up."

As I glanced over the instrument panel, hesitating on each instrument in turn, something attracted my attention. The magnetic compass had changed several degrees from its previous position. I glanced at the omni needle. It was still centered. I verified we were still flying outbound on the proper radial.

It was possible something had affected the compass, but what? I had swung the compass last week on the compass rose at San Jose, checked it carefully, both with the radio on and with the engine running. Of course, compasses are prone to errors and changes.

I called Paso Robles for a radio check. Everything seemed to be all right; their latest weather report indicated the airports in the San Joaquin Valley to our east were socked in. Paso Robles had a solid overcast and a lowering ceiling. There was no point in thinking about returning there. However, it was good to hear that Santa Barbara was still clear.

Santa Barbara Radio still was out of range, though. I returned Paso Robles and waited. Glancing at the magnetic compass, I noticed that it had changed several more degrees. As I turned to my wife with a look of disbelief on my face, she asked, "What's wrong? You look worried."

"I *am* worried. I'm not sure where we are. The radio indicates we're flying in one direction, the compass says another. They disagree by nearly 90 degrees. We should have reached Santa Barbara by now, or at least picked them up on the radio. I'm afraid we're lost."

Suddenly the sun disappeared. I looked up just in time to see the top fringes of a boiling cumulus as we headed into it. I applied full power and began to climb, determined to remain in the clear. In what seemed hours, but in reality was only a few seconds, we climbed into brilliant sunlight. At 11,000 feet now, I could see cloud tops bulging and building up ahead of me. I knew we couldn't continue climbing indefinitely.

I reasoned to myself: Santa Barbara was clear, but the fog had blanketed the coast from Monterey south. If we were to the right of course and had missed Santa Barbara, we could easily be flying over the Pacific Ocean. If we had flown far left of course, we could have flown over the Coast Range. If we had, we would be over the San Joaquin Valley. The San Joaquin, we knew, was socked in.

I glanced at my watch. It was still early in the morning. At this time of day, the sun is still in the eastern sky. We must have flown left of course. The compass, if it was accurate, would verify that. At this point I was quite sure the compass was okay. At least it agreed with the sun. Our destination must have been somewhere to our right. Anyway, the San Joaquin was socked in, so we couldn't land there. Paso Robles was below minimums, so that was out. Our best bet was still Santa Barbara. It had to be somewhere to our right. That cloud buildup must be over the mountain peaks. The mountains must have blanketed Santa Barbara Radio, and that's the reason we never received them.

The sun was dead ahead now, and at this hour it seemed a foolproof indication of direction. Thinking back to our last known position, I now made my decision. I made a 90-degree right turn. It would keep me out of the overcast and would start us in the direction I was sure we needed to fly. The compass settled down to the new heading. By now it was obvious the radio was unreliable. I glanced at the fuel gauge and rapidly calculated the remaining flying time. One hour for sure, perhaps as much as two. With the sloshing because of the turbulence, it was hard to determine.

In desperation, I cranked the handle on the radio. I turned the dial from one end to the other. Suddenly I heard another airplane talking to a station. It was in the San Joaquin Valley. I called, and waited. Almost immediately, he returned my call. He listened patiently to my problem, then advised me to take bearings on three stations he identified by call sign and frequency. I began immediately. In rapid succession, I tuned in each station, identified it, jotted down the bearing and checked the to-from indication.

Trying to maintain a heading (and not fly in circles or fly aimlessly), and at the same time draw a straight line on an undulating map spread out over knobby knees in moderately turbulent air, seemed impossible. I called the station, relayed the readings I had jotted down and was told to stand by. Perspiration was dripping off my nose.

"Cessna Five-Seven Pop," snapped my headset after what seemed an interminable interval, "check your third reading." Quickly, I tuned in the station, jotted down the reading and transmitted the new figures. Again that frustrating delay. Moments later, the headset sizzled to life. "Take a heading of . . ." I noted with satisfaction that the heading given nearly coincided with the heading I had taken in desperation.

Now a new development entered the picture. Suddenly, out of the corner of my eye, I caught sight of another airplane as it crossed below and just ahead of me. I relayed its identification to the ground station. Minutes later, just before we feared it would disappear from sight, the twin Cessna in military garb changed direction and circled into formation with us. The ground station had contacted it on another channel. Although we couldn't communicate directly, the ground station relayed our transmissions. The pilot of the twin Cessna volunteered to remain with us until we got into the clear.

The Cessna had difficulty slowing down to remain with us. At first, it flew around us in circles like a mother hen tending her brood. It was a comforting feeling to be able to waggle a wing in recognition.

Minutes passed. We were advised to switch over to Santa Barbara Radio. I held my breath as I tuned the radio. Santa Barbara answered at once.

The overcast had broken now, and ahead it was obviously scattered. Below were the Santa Ynez Mountains. We had flown far left of course, and as a result, had overflown our destination. We were descending now in the clear, and as the range of mountains dropped off to the Santa Barbara Channel of the Pacific, our Air Force guardian buzzed by and waggled its wings as it departed. We waggled our wings in a return salute. Before the Cessna was out of sight, Santa Barbara Radio had relayed to the crew our message of thanks and appreciation.

●

Here's a riddle: When is terrain as useless for navigating as an undercast of cloud? The answer: when the terrain is called Alaska.

If that Disneyland-bound pilot had been able to see through

the cloud, he might have been in better shape. But having contact
with the ground is no help when one hill looks just like the other.
Bear in mind the admonition about the uselessness of compasses
in the north country as this woeful pilot recalls his darkest day.

●

On the wall of the CAA office at Weeks Field in Fairbanks is
a map of Alaska covered with colored thumbtacks. They are
scattered from the fogbound Aleutians to Point Barrow; from
Kotzebue on the Arctic coast to Ketchikan, first Alaskan city
on the mountainous Pacific coastline. Each tack marks the
wreckage of a plane down somewhere in the mountains or
tundra. I learned about flying in the hardest possible way: by
contributing another tack to the map.

The great majority of lessons of this sort did the pupils no
good; they were either found dead or not found at all, the
only trace being a note fastened to the instrument panel:
"Am walking southwest down the creek, have rifle and
three days' food . . ."

Sudden spring came to Alaska, and I decided it was time to
get some more cross-country time. I bought a 1946 Aeronca
Chief. It had no radio and only a basic instrument group, but
it had good range and was in good condition. I could hardly
wait to undertake a breakfast flight to Circle Hot Springs.

Circle Hot Springs is a resort hotel about 120 miles northeast
of Fairbanks and about 7 miles south of the Steese Highway,
a gravel road about 150 miles long from Fairbanks to Circle,
Alaska, on the Yukon. Most of the way, it runs along the south
shoulder of a line of ridges averaging 4,000 feet in height. The
highway is only about a quarter of the way up the ridges from
the floor of the Chatanika River and is virtually invisible from
the air when approached from the north.

With the assurance that all I had to do was follow the highway, I took off, and an hour and a half later was gliding into
a landing at the Circle Hot Springs strip. Here I encountered

a short field 1,000 feet above sea level. I overshot but managed to avert an accident by ground-looping, an embarrassing performance with my instructor and fellow student pilots looking on.

I made my second mistake by not fueling up before taking off. I had dumped the auxiliary tank in the Chief, which holds eight gallons, just before landing, and the main tank holding fifteen gallons was full. So what if gas was 60 cents a gallon? In about two hours I would happily have paid $6.00 a gallon.

I took off and flew to nearby Central Airstrip, shot a couple of landings for practice on short fields and then headed back along the highway. I had just passed Miller House, a mining camp along the road, when I ran into a thunderstorm.

A student pilot's first encounter with a thunderstorm is not easily described—something like being tumbled about in a concrete mixer. As I bounced around in the ship, my stomach got queasy. Leaning as far out the side window as my safety belt permitted, I let the cold air wash over me.

Refreshed somewhat by the slipstream, I turned back to the job of flying the airplane. I looked down, saw—or rather didn't see—something which made me break out again in a cold sweat. The Steese Highway was not in sight. I was lost somewhere over interior Alaska with only two hours' gas.

First, I tried to orient myself by the compass. A lightplane compass is a fractious thing at best, but with a variation of 30 degrees and a dip angle of 77 degrees the northerly turning error makes one virtually useless up there. Then I did some figuring. If I were north of the highway and on a northerly heading, I would come out over the Yukon River Flats in very desolate country. My chances of being found there would be small. If I headed southwest, I would come out on the Tanana Valley, fairly well populated for Alaska, or possibly the Alcan Highway. Accordingly, I took a course roughly southwest by the sun.

At first, I was optimistic. A succession of green ridges passed under the wings, each one looking like its neighbor. I strained to catch a glimpse of the level green plains of the Tanana Valley. An hour and a half went by. The gas gauge was showing near-empty and bouncing around, and I knew a decision would have to be made in the next half hour.

I passed several saddles and ridge tops that were free of trees and looked fairly level. I could probably have made a safe landing on one of them, but I kept putting it off. After all, the Tanana Plain was certain to be beyond this next ridgeline. I was just crossing a deep valley between the ridges when the engine coughed and quit for good.

It was Dr. Samuel Johnson who said, "Count on it; if a man knows he is to be hanged in a month it concentrates his mind wonderfully." Similarly, if a man knows that in a minute he is apt to be rolled into a heap on an Alaskan hillside, miles from any other human being, it likewise stimulates him.

I recall only an icy calm as I cut the switch and trimmed the ship for the normal glide. I decided that my best chance was to pancake the ship into the creek bed. Accordingly, I headed for a place where the creek seemed widest, meanwhile avoiding fir trees whipping past the wingtips. The creek bed came up fast as I brought the nose up into a three-point attitude. There were cracking and crunching sounds as the ship plowed through the willows and brush along the creek bank, a splash as it hit—then silence except for the gurgling of the water.

Unpacking my emergency equipment, I made camp on the creek bank. I was on a flight plan and had reasonable hope of being found. Yet I had heard of many planes disappearing in the north without a trace.

About 8:30 that evening the USAF 10th Rescue Squadron came over, and a more cheering sight I have never seen. I discharged an emergency flare, and although they gave no sign of having seen it, they continued to circle. I concluded that I had been spotted. Exhausted, I dropped off to sleep and awoke about one in the morning to see a helicopter hovering over me in the continuous twilight of the Arctic summer night. Tenth Rescue had come through for me!

I got in the 'copter and was deposited 45 minutes later at Ladd Field, very glad to be alive. It turned out I had been 12 miles south of the Steese, about 40 miles west of Miller House. I must have been unaware of recrossing the highway, since it lay on the south slope of the ridge.

●

The Aeronca couldn't be recovered, and the hapless pilot sold it where it lay. One moment he knew where he was, then that diversion to settle his stomach stole his attention and he was lost.

4/WHAT IF IT BREAKS?

Four forces affect an airplane in flight: *thrust, lift, drag* and *weight.* The last of these forces should really be labeled *gravity,* since that is what attracts the mass of the machine toward the earth. Of those four forces, three are mutable. Thrust is limited only by the power we can extract from engines. Lift varies with airfoils and airspeed, not to mention air density. Drag is related to lift and to the resistance of the air to the bulk of the airplane passing through it. Only gravity is constant.

High-performance airplanes now have so much thrust available to them that they are able to accelerate vertically. It is the aviator's way of thumbing his nose at gravity. Because gravity's engine consumes no energy, it runs perpetually; it has a timeless, inexorable quality and infinite patience. That flyspeck of a pilot and his airplane must come down eventually.

Gravity is a great equalizer. An airman feels like the king of all he surveys, so long as his source of power never runs out; if it should fail him, the results are quite humbling, and King Airman is tumbled from his lofty throne. Perhaps that is what makes a mechanical failure such an emotional experience. The very act of flight involves a lot of pride; flying may well be man's proudest accomplishment. The pride is faintly colored with defiance, though, giving it a quality the Greeks called *hubris.* Early fliers were thought to be acting contrary to the Divine Will. ("If man had been meant to fly . . .")

This business of leaving the ground, then, is a commerce that relies on overweening optimism. When pilots take off, they also take leave of their more conservative senses. If they could witness close at hand the tortured iron that sustains them up there, they might realize how slender is the mechanical thread that sews aviation together. The pistons, valves, struts, longerons—and lately, transistors, capacitors and resistors—usually perform anonymously, which is just fine with the captain. Like workers on an assembly line, the individual parts of an airplane never attract any attention until they refuse to work.

The suggestion that there is a degree of frailty to this mechanized circus is difficult to face. It batters at the airman's carefully shored-up faith that the flight he is about to make is a predestined success. The foundations of that faith are the statistics, which overwhelmingly support the pilot's expectations. Failure is a long shot. Turn those same statistics upside down, though, and they become a chilling guarantee that once in a great while something will break. The true stories in this chapter all describe that eventuality, in one form or another.

One of the four forces that govern flying is definitely not *fame*. Airplanes pay absolutely no heed whatsoever to the notoriety of the pilot. Roscoe Turner was famous as an air racer and a colorful, heroic personality, but when his engine failed, he had no advantages over anyone else in the same fix.

Turner was hoofing it across the mountains of Arizona—at 250 mph—in his Wedell-Williams racer, Number 25, and looking forward to more competitive successes. This was 1932, before the Pratt & Whitney "Hornet" in the nose had any provision for carburetor heat.

●

The ship and engine were in perfect shape. I'd made certain modifications in streamlining, which had speeded it up. I'd had it painted a shining, shimmering gold. And as I cruised about a hundred miles southeast of Holbrook, Arizona, I was sure that it would break my transcontinental record, established when I won the Bendix race in 1933, and probably win the Thompson Trophy.

Then the engine sneezed a couple of times. When one of those streamlined kites starts acting up—with a thousand horses in the nose and just a couple of paddles for wings—you worry and look at the terrain beneath. The mountains didn't look reassuring.

"If she quits," I told myself, "I'll bail."

But I got to thinking it over. The ship belonged to me. No sense in tossing it away like that. I shoved the throttle forward. The engine picked up. I felt easier, and flew at top for a while. Then, wanting to save the engine, I eased back into the "loafing" range again. I decided that the sneezing was caused by the engine's cooling off a little. The fact that it was icing didn't occur to me. This was a phenomenon that few of us knew much about. It seemed warm. My outside air temperature gauge showed 65°.

Then it started dropping rpm again. As long as I planned to stay with it, I swallowed hard, braced myself and headed north. My chart indicated flat country and some population in that direction. If I hurt myself, I didn't want to be isolated in the off-trail wilderness below me. And about this time I did some more thinking and started getting sore. I was sure that somebody had failed to connect a device I'd thought up—a throttle spring that opened the engine wide automatically in case of throttle or throttle-connection failure. By this time I was kicking her open again and again and getting no response, and I was sure the throttle had gone haywire and the spring hadn't been attached.

I started losing altitude as my rpm fell off more and more, and I knew trouble was with me for sure. I spotted what later turned out to be an Indian reservation. There was a small green field that looked long enough to take my landing speed, even with 60 gallons of fuel and at high altitude. I didn't have a choice, anyway. There wasn't anything else, so I circled.

I have only a hashed-up memory of what happened from that time on. I recall straightening out, coming in over a fence. I hit once and bounced, which was nothing out of the ordinary, since

Number 25 has no shock absorbers. I struck again in something soft. The next thing I recall—just a flash—was seeing the ground in front of me and I felt the tail lift. The next thing I remember, I was looking at blue sky. My ribs hurt and my neck hurt. My safety belt was digging into my middle.

I looked behind me, which was *up,* to see what damage I had done to the tail surfaces. I was surprised to find there weren't any. In fact, there was nothing much to speak of aft of the cockpit. The leading edges were okay. The trailing edge of the left wing was shot and the right aileron was damaged.

The first thing I did was pull myself out of the cockpit, getting untangled from a can of tomato juice and the crank. I managed to get the cowling off, still sure that the automatic throttle control hadn't been connected. But it was. I saw fluid dripping from the carburetor. I felt it, smelled it. It was water. For the first time, I began thinking maybe ice had caused the trouble. However, the ground temperature at this point was 90°. How could it be?

However, whatever it was, the plane was stacked; it was 18 miles to the nearest telephone and 35 miles from there to the railroad station. I was washed out of both the Bendix and Thompson and thousands of dollars. A three-year run of bad luck began.

That night I visualized the marks my ship had made on the field again and again. I finally figured out what I had done. I had hit the ground a second time, nosed over, slammed down on the tail; the tail had dug in and sheared off, and I had gone over once more to right side up. I'd ended with the ship—what was left of it—standing on the wheels and nose.

But I still couldn't figure out the reason for the engine's quitting. While still in the hospital in Los Angeles—where I spent a week after the doctor who attended me showed me X-rays of my vertebrae and told me the fact my neck wasn't broken was a miracle—I started checking with airline pilots. I found that they, too, had had engine trouble in that vicinity on that day and at that time—and that they blamed carburetor ice.

It shocked me to realize that for all those years Jimmy Wedell, and I and all other speed fliers had been hopping around the country without carburetor heaters. The only thing that had saved us was that we'd been running at full throttle, thus blowing out the treacherous ice as fast as it formed.

I knew, now, that ice could strike at any time and under any conditions. When Number 25 was rebuilt, I ordered a heater on the carburetor even though it meant abandoning short stacks. When my new Turner-Laird was built, the first thing I insisted on was a heater. And I would no more think of making any kind of a hop today without one than I'd think of flying without wings.

My lesson was expensive. I tell the inside story of that flight and its disastrous end for the first time in the hope that young pilots will learn about this particular phase of flying at less cost, both physical and financial. The time may soon come when all engines are delivered with heaters as standard equipment. But such unequipped engines now in service may cause anything from a dead-stick onto the airport to a stack-up in mountainous country. Kicking the throttle wide open is a very poor and uncertain remedy, as my experience points out.

●

Turner felt an obligation to write about his experience despite the sting of his loss; carb ice was something other pilots should be warned about. It could fail an engine as fast as a broken rod or a swallowed valve. Turner's advice carried a lot of weight, but it didn't carry far enough. Another pilot, this one in a modern Skylane with ample carburetor heat, failed to get the word.

●

My route took me over the northern edge of Columbus, Ohio. The clear skies over the western plains had yielded to a scattering of cumulus riding atop a thick haze layer at 9,000 feet, and now a few of them were building up. I had been cruising at 9,500 and now climbed to 11,500 for smoother and cooler air. Ground temperature at Quincy had been 93° F. Even at altitude, the air was heavy, wet and sticky, and the OAT gauge read almost 70°.

The loss of power must have been very gradual at first. When it registered that the manifold pressure was quivering at 16 inches instead of a normal 18 or 19, it made me aware that I had been unconsciously holding back-pressure to maintain altitude. The airspeed indicator read between 125 and 130—a bit low for the Skylane even at 11,500 feet.

With full power and a slightly enriched mixture, I watched in disbelieving fascination as the MP needle gradually sank to the bottom of the green arc. I was thinking something like: If that overhauled engine quits, I'm going to carry it to Colorado —on my back, if necessary—and get a refund! But the humor somehow escaped me at the moment.

I also remember asking myself what Ohio's provisions were for landing gliders, and hearing again the voice of my instructor saying something about "Good pilots know where they are at all times . . ."

Good pilot or not, I had to be a few miles north and west of Zanesville. The next few seconds consisted of finding the Zanesville frequency, tuning 111.4, verifying that the VOR was on the field (close by might not be good enough), centering the needle, making a shallow turn to the right to keep it centered, and sweating a lot.

Full power was not enough to maintain altitude. I had 48X headed toward a strong but invisible Zanesville VOR, and as the altimeter began to unwind, I struggled to get my mind to think about why the engine was quitting. The only thing that would come to me was that the mechanics had left me with an overhauled lemon, and there was nothing I could do about it in the murky air over Ohio.

I passed through 6,000 feet before reaching Zanesville Radio and informing them of my situation. At the same time, I spotted what might be a town through the haze just to the right of my course and a few miles ahead, and what might be an airport nearly dead ahead and just to the east of what might be a town. I recall feeling just a bit miffed at the calm, well-adjusted voice from FSS, providing me with a routine airport advisory.

In seconds, the intersecting runways east of Zanesville gave me a positive visual identification of the airport, and things sort of added up to the fact that I was too high for a straight-in approach to the active. The engine was not producing enough power to inspire confidence for a normal pattern entry, so I advised FSS I was making a right base entry for 22. Again that calm voice repeated the advisory and added that there was no other report of traffic. Doesn't anything upset those guys?

Over the fence I was a bit high, but 48X was slipping well into the light crosswind from the left, and there was plenty of runway left after roll-out. The engine was running but very rough. As I applied power, from habit, to turn the airplane onto the taxi strip, a surge of power startled me. A pilot watching from a hangar as I taxied to the ramp told me later that the engine was putting out some black smoke, as if it were running very rich.

Next morning, the Cessna service mechanic pulled the top plugs and checked compression. All six cylinders checked out okay. We ran it up on the ground and again it checked out okay.

"Next time," the A&P said gently, "you may want to try carburetor heat."

Even overnight it had not come to me. On a hot day in July, flying clear of visible moisture with the throttle nearly wide open, I just had not been able to make myself *think* carburetor ice. I had accumulated 1,400 hours in a variety of non-fuel-injected aircraft and had never encountered a perceptible instance of carburetor icing. With that newly majored engine, it just had to be something basically wrong—mechanically, I thought.

Everybody knows about the intense and rapid cooling of the air that can take place in the carburetor throat. Everybody knows it; but everybody doesn't necessarily remember it when the OAT reads about 70 while flying clear of visible moisture at cruising power. It's too easy to forget how much water the air can hold, and how quickly that water can freeze inside a carburetor.

●

Ice is one thing, but what about the kind of engine failure that involves parting of metal? One always imagines that an actual failure of a part is followed immediately by a silence so final and irrefutable that further decision-making is abruptly simplified. Such is not always the case, as the following two histories point out.

Alma Heflin was on vacation in Alaska when a valve broke on her aircraft's four-cylinder powerplant.

●

Engines don't always conk completely, and you can do a heck of a lot of traveling on two cylinders if you have enough altitude to glide.

A friend and I had flown from New York to Seattle, shipped to Juneau and then flown on to Fairbanks, Alaska, over country that could have been conceived only by God and the Devil working in amicable partnership.

We had purred along at a happy 1,000 feet, even dropping sometimes to a bare 50 to check direction of a river current to confirm our navigation. Having arrived safely at Fairbanks and completed some side-trips, we felt our summer plans were practically fulfilled. Someone told me of a herd of buffalo at the ferry on the Tanana River. When a friend found himself stranded that same afternoon with no charter plane available in time to make his boat-sailing at 8 P.M. in Valdez, we decided I could get some good pictures and deliver him to the dock at the same time.

We started from Fairbanks with a quartering tailwind, and although rainsqualls were reported by trading posts ahead, we had a 3,000-foot ceiling even over Isabel Pass. Blue cumulus clouds massed over the mountains should be blowing away steadily. We turned southward, found the buffalo missing at the ferry, then started climbing before reaching the mountains. Rainsqualls were bad in the pass, masking the windshield with sudden deluges, with the wing-strut thermometer barely over freezing. We had 6,000 feet and were on the lower fringes of rain clouds over the field at Rapids. Later, I checked the field there and found it merely a cleared spot that no one would especially seek— but it was to look good later.

Shining Summit Lake was ahead when the engine coughed, stuttered, paused. We were chattering about something but choked to sudden silence. I pumped the throttle and the engine started. We looked at each other in frozen shock. It was running rough and nothing is worse than not knowing how much danger you face. A shorted plug, wet by the rainsqualls? But I was sure the engine was too well cowled and, anyhow, the miss should be more constant if it was plug trouble. Water or dirt in the gas? If that, then complete failure might come any minute. I climbed for more margin.

Then the engine banged, stopped again, started as I leveled out of our climb, stopped . . . and then snarled back into an ear-racking pounding like a boiler shop at top production. I grabbed the chart frantically. To turn back into Isabel Pass might be suicide. A forced landing on the peaks if we did not reach Rapids 30 miles back would be no simple matter of sheared-off wings. The road, strung along the edge of the mountains, was too winding to set down on. It was either the road below us, narrow and shelving as it was, or the next field 75 miles beyond at Gakona with rolling hills, stunted trees and tundra between us and safety.

Tundra is the sparse covering of much of the sub-Arctic. Frozen ground, melted a scant few feet in the summer, is covered with moss and weeds. It is buckled into domes by the freeze-up, and the thaw leaves nearly hollow caps of knotted vegetation that almost invariably nose over a plane forced down on them. If we went down in a wooded area, the plane would be washed out, although we would probably not be hurt; the plane would be landing slowly, and the roots of the slender trees are massed in a funny shallow little pancake hardly more than a yard across and not a foot under the surface.

To one side wound the highway, though, and perhaps we could get down there. I wheeled the plane over, leveled over the narrow, snaky road, and lifted the nose skyward for an exploratory moment. The air-speed dropped alarmingly, so we leveled again.

We still had 1,800 of our normal 2,350-rpm cruise, oil pressure was up, temperature was normal. Wing temperature was up now to 45°, so at least we didn't have to worry about icing. Vibration threatened to tear the whole engine from the mount, though, and airspeed was down to 60 mph. But we had 6,200 feet, and if the engine didn't conk completely—and if it stayed on the plane—we should make Gakona in about 50 minutes.

"Here's the situation," I told my passenger. "We have a fair chance. If we land on the road, we probably lose wings and landing gear, but we probably won't be hurt. If we go on, we'll possibly get to Gakona even though we're settling. But we may lose the engine, and I doubt if I can fly it if the engine tears loose. It's your life, too. Shall we land or gamble on the ship's hanging together?"

I should have known better. It was his first cross-country, his second airplane flight—but he races outboards, and his eyes were shining.

"Go on!" he said. "Gosh, this is swell! I wouldn't trade this thrill for a thousand dollars!" I felt a sudden irritated urge to tell him to save his thousand dollars, he might need it for a funeral, then I laughed. Good guy. I turned to nursing the plane along.

My throat was swollen shut with plain fright, but the ship was under good control even though the stick was making my hands tingle and shoulders ache and the rudder pedals were spanking my feet. The engine was turning an even 1,800, but we were settling. In 15 minutes we were down to 5,000 feet. A quick check of the map showed Gakona still all of 50 miles away. A private field belonging to a mine was about 30 miles to one side of our course, another about the same or a little closer on the other side. But below us was the Valdez Trail, where we might land if worse came to worst. Between us and those other two fields were only tundra and trees. We clung to the path above the road and clattered on.

About 35 miles farther, there was a clank in the engine that stopped time as the propeller stood still across our horrified vision for a third time—and for the third time it started again. Now the noise was worse, we lost another 150 rpm and vibration increased. Now we were settling at an even 100 feet per minute. The Poplar Grove, an Alaskan Road Commission camp, came below. Men ran out of their tents, staring up at us as we limped along. The road widened here. Perhaps we could land. But Gakona was only 10 miles beyond now. We staggered on.

Gakona is five miles off the road, a trading post built in the days when freight came up the Copper River. On the farther side of the Cooper River Canyon, at right angles across our course, is Gulkana, with a fair field, but I could never have raised the nose to climb the slope on that side. We wheeled eastward and sighted Gakona.

Alongside the field, like a tired horse that drops at the end of the race, our engine stopped dead. No false alarm this time, no shamming; it was dead. I cut the switch and set the stabilizer with shaking fingers. We glided around the field into the wind, slipped to lose the last thousand feet of precious altitude and dropped onto the grassy runway. We climbed out, waved at the approaching Indians with quivering nonchalance and called it good. Fifty-five minutes of mortal fright, and safety!

Two cylinders were cold. A valve stem had broken between the guides, and for the first 15 minutes it had run with only an occasional miss; it had been riding up and down, just hanging there. Then the head had been broken off and driven into the piston. That cylinder had then cut out immediately. The other cylinder had eventually cut out with plugs fouled by backed-up gases. I shivered again as I noticed that the paint had been flaked off the mount by the shuddering of the tortured motor.

●

Lest anyone think that occurrence, which Heflin wrote about in 1941, was some kind of fluke, pay heed to this air-taxi pilot's experience in 1973. He was more worried about his job than about terrain, but the effect was the same—he had to keep a sick engine running.

●

A good rule of thumb for an air-taxi pilot is never to turn back if he can make it to the next airport on his schedule. I turned back once in a Piper Aztec because I didn't like the way the engines sounded. I was climbing after takeoff, with a full load of passengers, when I decided to return to the field and land. Even though a postflight run-up yielded mag drops of 25 rpm on one engine and 125 rpm on the other, my boss said my action was unjustified, because three passengers had been badly frightened and the other two annoyed by the delay.

The company policy, I was told, was that any mag drop of less than 200 rpm was insufficient reason for not continuing, at least back to home base. I could have flown all day with the engine running rough, and had the plugs cleaned the next morning if they hadn't cleaned themselves in the meantime, he said. The boss demonstrated his faith in that policy by flying the airplane home, switching magnetos off and on and jockeying the mixture levers until the roughness disappeared.

At least I kept my job, which paid all the flying time I could stand plus $89 a week. Twice afterward, I turned back after takeoff because of engine roughness, but never again with passengers. A rule was forming in my head: Change airplanes if you have a spare; cancel a flight if necessary; but once you load up with passengers, don't bring them back to the departure airport with both engines running.

Meanwhile, the company was doing well. The safety record was perfect, the customers were happy, business was good and the owner was making money. The policy of never turning back seemed to be working. Major problems failed to appear, having been exorcised, one hoped, by preventive maintenance and the owner's keen sense of what was really necessary to keep an airplane flying.

I was called on a day off to fly a rescue mission for another pilot, who was stranded away from home with a flat tire and a load of passengers. A spare Aztec was parked on the home ramp, supposedly fueled and preflighted, and all I had to do was fly it. I struggled through afternoon traffic on the way to the airport and then took time to make another preflight. It was getting late.

The inboard fuel tanks were unusually low, but we always kept 15 gallons in the outboards to keep the rubber in the tanks from drying out. I could burn some fuel to make up the difference. The right fuel strainer made a puddle of water on the ramp six inches across before any gas came out of the drain. Rather than take time to find the sampling apparatus, I soaked my hands by running all six drains until nothing but clean gas was coming out. The engine checked out okay, and the half-hour deadhead was uneventful.

When I arrived, we put four overweight passengers and one infant in the back seats and 300 pounds of baggage and freight in the baggage compartments; it was just as well we were light on fuel. I offered the left seat to the other pilot, but he said, "It's your flight." He sat in the copilot's seat, which is normally a passenger seat, and I cranked up and taxied out.

I noticed that with both tachometers reading the same, the manifold pressure needles were split slightly. I tried to remember if they had been that way the last time I flew that airplane. Our company didn't do engine run-ups with passengers aboard, so I taxied onto the runway and started the takeoff roll.

The owner's policy was to use 25 inches of manifold pressure instead of full throttle, to save the engines and to synchronize the propellers on the ground for a smooth takeoff. I set the throttles and started to synchronize the engines by sound. The left engine ran faster in that airplane, and it usually took a half-lever-width reduction of the prop control to bring it in sync with the other one. I gradually pulled the left lever back until the wow-wow-wow became a wooww-wooww and then checked the tachometers to see why they hadn't synced. The right engine had 2,450 rpm, about a hundred low, until just before we lifted off the ground. When it came on speed, it surged past the left one, which by then was back to 2,500. I pushed the left engine back up, raised the gear and set climb power—24"/2,400 rpm. The right governor must be acting up, I figured, not giving us full rpm on takeoff. I pointed to the right tachometer, and my companion shrugged. I headed home toward a pink sunset.

The next 20 minutes were normal except that we seemed to be flying 10 miles per hour slower than we should have been. That one of my engines had lost a cylinder, and that parts of that cylinder might soon grind layers of metal off the rest of the moving parts, was the farthest thing from my mind. That, in fact, was now happening—I was losing an engine.

I emerged from beneath a layer of broken clouds and added power to climb 500 feet; both engines responded normally. Five minutes later, I was making a base-leg entry to the traffic pattern and lowering the gear for landing.

On final approach, I synchronized the engines with the throttles—at low power, the props operate in fixed pitch—but I had to keep the right throttle way ahead of the left one, and the right manifold pressure stayed up around 20 inches. I pointed out the gauges to my copilot, and he shrugged again. There was no reason why both engines shouldn't have been behaving the same, but if we hadn't been so accustomed to abnormal conditions like this one, we might have concluded that something was wrong. Still, everything sounded and felt fine. It was not until we were taxiing back to the chocks that we both realized that we had just missed having to feather one prop at low altitude and at near-maximum gross weight. The left manifold pressure was 12 inches and the right was 20; both engines were idling smoothly at 800 rpm. There was obviously a hole in the intake-manifold system on the right engine, probably a bad valve or a hole in one piston. The clues all fell into place, starting with the manifold-pressure split before takeoff. The rpm hadn't come up for takeoff because the leaky manifold had produced an artificially high pressure reading that was not an accurate measure of the fuel-air mixture going to the cylinders. In addition, there was probably a dead cylinder. With the 25-inch throttle setting, the right propeller had not come out of low pitch until increasing airspeed had taken part of the load off the right engine and allowed it to wind up to speed. The low rpm was thus a warning that an internal component of the engine had failed. It was my one chance to abort a takeoff for good reason, and I had blown it.

An autopsy showed that the exhaust-valve seat for the middle cylinder on the right side of the right engine (where I would be least likely to hear it) had come out of the jug and was dangling around the valve stem like a loose bracelet, chipping away parts of the cylinder head and leaving its mark in the shape of a crescent on top of the piston. The exhaust valve could never fully close, and exhaust gases from the good cylinders were being sucked through the bad cylinder whenever its intake valve was open. That must have leaned out the mixture some-what in the intake manifold, but not enough to affect perform-ance noticeably. The real problem was in the lubricating sys-tem, where the metal chips were slowly destroying the engine. If the flight had lasted long enough, the engine would have seized or come apart.

I was assured that I couldn't have flown on one engine with the load I had, it being an article of faith in general aviation that single-engine performance claims for light twins are exag-gerated. I couldn't speak with authority on that subject, having been lucky, but I was comforted to find that a sick engine can take off, cruise for half an hour and land without quitting in the air.

Nevertheless, I had obviously made the wrong decision when I continued a flight in an airplane that wouldn't develop full rpm on takeoff. I was going too fast to stop when I noticed the problem, but I could have returned and grounded the airplane.

Several questions remain: What would have happened in another hour or two of flight? When the engine finally died, what would have gone first—power or oil pressure or what? How would I know it was time to feather it, to give up nursing it along and to commit myself to single-engine operation for the rest of the flight? I've picked up a lot of different advice on that subject, but I probably won't be able to answer those questions until the next time I fail to heed the signs of impending engine failure and keep on going. The fact that minor problems were my daily bread made a serious problem hard to detect. If one pilot won't fly it, the boss can find another one who will. That makes the go/no-go decision difficult.

●

Perhaps the lesson in that is to avoid tired, run-out airplanes and stick to new equipment. That's what Tex Rankin thought, too, but he found out differently on a flight in the Northwest in a factory-fresh trainer. He had picked up the new Great Lakes in Cleveland and was on his way back to Portland, Oregon.

●

I was accompanied by Ray Bartley, my chief mechanic. The first day I started at dawn and flew as far as Cheyenne, Wyoming, landing at dusk and remaining overnight. I took off from Cheyenne the next morning just before dawn and flew to Pocatello, Idaho, and from there to Walla Walla, Washington, arriving at about 3:30 P.M. Upon landing, I was exhausted, having flown more than 20 hours in two days. Before I took off, a trimotor Ford en route from Portland to Spokane landed. I asked its pilot about weather at Portland and he reported a ceiling of 1,000 feet. He added that at the time he left, fog was right down to the water in the Columbia River gorge through the Cascade Mountains. From Walla Walla to The Dalles, Oregon, the east entrance to the gorge, he reported CAVU. He advised me not to attempt to go into Portland.

We didn't have beam or station facilities of any kind at that time. I had discovered several years previously that if I flew in a direct line with Mount St. Helens and Mount Rainier I would pass directly over the center of Portland's East Side district. Then, by a simple matter of triangulation, when Mount Hood was at full right, I knew that I would be over the Columbia River at a point four miles east of my airport. Following this, I would let down in a northwest direction and come out beneath the overcast over the lowlands near the confluence of the Willamette and Columbia Rivers.

Of course, I had always obtained information regarding the ceiling by telephone from Portland previous to this and never had attempted a letdown of this type with a ceiling of less than

1,000 feet. Such procedure was anything but wise because the ceiling could drop from 1,000 feet to zero within a short time and a letdown with ceiling zero in all probability would have proved fatal.

If I had used the type of judgment I have since learned to use, I would have put the ship in a hangar at Walla Walla and would have spent the night in that city, particularly in view of the fact that Bartley and I had flown almost 10 hours since daylight. However, being anxious to get home and having tremendous confidence in this brand-new ship with a proved cruising range of four hours at 90 mph, I decided to fly to Portland, only about two hours away.

We went over The Dalles at five o'clock at an altitude of 10,000 feet. Shortly thereafter we encountered solid banks of clouds that forced me up to 12,000 feet in order to remain above them. I continued westward until six in the afternoon when, theoretically, I should have been over the city of Portland. However, when I looked for Mount Rainier, Mount St. Helens and Mount Hood, I discovered that these snowcapped peaks were covered with clouds. It would be impossible to work out a letdown problem with any degree of accuracy because the hills along the west side of the Willamette River within the city of Portland are at least 1,000 feet high. A slight mistake in my bearing easily might cause me to strike the hills instead of emerging over the lowlands.

I decided to turn back and land at The Dalles, where the weather should still be CAVU. The Dalles was only an hour away, and I had gas for two more hours. The little Cirrus engine was barking merrily along, and I was not in the least bit worried, although everything below me was a sea of clouds. The ship and engine were brand-new, weren't they?

About 15 minutes after I had turned back toward the east, Bartley called my attention to the fact that the gas gauge registered empty. Smilingly I waved assurance that there was no cause for worry. I had flown many Great Lakes trainers whose gas gauges had read empty when the tanks were full. I honestly believed that there was enough gasoline in the tank to carry us all the way back to Walla Walla if we cared to go that far. Fifteen minutes later the engine suddenly spluttered and died. I realized then that the gas gauge had not been wrong. Here we were more than 12,000 feet high with a solid bank of clouds just a few hundred feet below us, a dead engine, no parachutes, and we were directly over the Cascade Mountains' backbone.

In just a few seconds, we plunged into the clouds and my heart sank almost as fast as the airplane. I had flown forest patrol over these mountains during the two previous years, and I knew that they furnished some of the roughest country in the United States, all of it covered with a dense growth of Douglas fir trees, most of them about 200 feet high and so thick you could not drop a rock between them without striking a branch.

I told Bartley to watch ahead and when he saw any dark object to pull back on the stick in the front cockpit. I watched my instruments, kept the ship level and glided down as slowly as I could. Down we went—11,000—10,000—9,000. Everything was just a dark, gray soup. I knew that Bartley must be thinking of his wife and children at home, and I cursed myself for ever having gotten him into this jam. I knew that we were close to Mount Hood, the icy slopes of which are more than 11,000 feet high.

Down we kept going—8,000—7,000. Each time the altimeter needle slipped back a hundred feet, I knew we were coming closer to the inevitable crash. Then, as we neared 6,000 feet, Bartley, who had been straining his eyes forward waiting for some dark form of disaster to emerge in front of us, shook the stick and yelled, "There it is!"

I jerked up my head just in time to see the top of a mountain directly in front of us, perhaps 50 yards away. I started to pull back on the stick. Just before we struck the mountainside, I had it full back to make a pancake landing. The ship crashed amid a growth of young fir trees and remnants of burned-over logs.

It turned upside down. Bartley and I scrambled out without a scratch. We were both mighty happy to be on the ground and able to walk away from the ship.

Fortunately we had landed on the only spot in miles that was not covered by a dense growth of timber. This particular spot had been burned by a forest fire many years before, and the saplings which now grew on it helped to check our impact and probably saved us from serious injury. We were doubly fortunate in cracking up only a few yards from a forest ranger's lookout station. The ranger heard the crash and came to the ship. When he found that we were unhurt, he showed us how to get down the mountain and gave us a lantern and a map. We found that we had landed on the top of Mount Hillockburn, 6,200 feet high and about 10 miles southwest of Mount Hood.

Later we were able to salvage about 50 percent of the $4,000 airplane by taking it apart and hauling it down the trail in sections. Upon careful examination, we found that the gas tank had cracked along the bottom for about four inches, probably due to vibration. After the accident, the makers of the airplane changed the tank material from aluminum to steel.

No one should have implicit faith in an airplane engine or aircraft, whether it be new or old. An airplane engine is dependent upon the uninterrupted functioning of many different mechanisms and things.

During the break-in period, extra vigilance must be used. Adjustments should be made and there should be frequent inspections. Certainly there is no excuse for *less* care at the beginning. Most forced landings of new ships are due to some trouble which in almost every case proves to be minor—mine was an exception—and easily remedied *ahead* of trouble.

●

Apparently no one is immune, then, from the caprice of the machine, which seems to delight in jumping the pilot at the very moment when he would be least likely to wish disaster upon himself. If one fears such eventualities, perhaps it is wiser to put a bold face on, to almost wish for it. What else might have prompted the instructor in this story to advise his student with these words?

•

"You're not a pilot until you've made a forced landing." My basic flight instructor always heralded another simulated emergency with that adage. I had some reservations about the statement at the time, but after my moment of truth I realized what the words meant.

I'd had enough terrestrial and scholastic expenses to limit my flight time to three or four hours a month—just enough to maintain a fair degree of proficiency. When the start of spring vacation gave me a week of freedom, I decided to fly down to Taos, New Mexico, for a day of skiing, spend the night and then head west for Palm Springs, California. My flight down to Taos was scenic and uneventful, and after a marvelous day of skiing I made a quick call to get the weather forecast from Santa Fe before turning in.

While running up the engine the next morning, I was surprised to note a drop of about 300 on the right mag, but as the engine warmed up, this discrepancy disappeared, and after getting several normal readings, I took off and headed southwest, planning to check it again over Santa Fe, where I knew I could find a mechanic if the problem reappeared. Although the Cessna was a 1958 model, it had just undergone its 100-hour inspection, and two inflight checks of the magneto put my mind at rest.

Just southwest of Mormon Lake, my state of bliss was suddenly shattered by a highly unpleasant roughness of engine, accompanied by a series of most unpromising coughs and sputters. A few quick glances at my airspeed and altimeter revealed that the majority of my horses had stopped powering. A sweep of the gauges gave no hint of the problem, and although my fuel gauges had proved inaccurate on the previous day, I knew that I was only three hours into a five-and-a-half-hour supply. Switching tanks failed to improve the situation, and increased throttle with reduced pitch was equally ineffective. Although atmospheric conditions precluded icing, I hopefully eased in some carburetor heat; it only made the problem worse.

These frantic activities had taken about a minute, during which I was also negotiating a gliding 180-degree turn away from the now-forbidding higher elevations and toward the road-studded plains of Winslow. As I recrossed Mormon Lake, I rapidly analyzed the situation. Oil pressure, engine temperature and generator were normal, and I still had plenty of fuel.

I was fairly certain that my problem was an electrical one, and I remembered my momentary trouble with the right mag that morning. I still had some power and reasoned that my best chance lay in trying to limp back to Winslow, which, although some 40 miles away, at least was downhill and in flat country. With such a rough engine, I surmised that one magneto was gone completely, and not wanting to risk losing what little power I had, I resisted the impulse to try switching mags (a decision that proved to be wise).

Unfortunately the situation soon took a turn for the worse, as the engine began a series of stops and starts that naturally steepened my descent to an alarming degree, in view of the marshy terrain beneath. As soon as my problem had become a true emergency, I called Prescott on the omni frequency (not having enough time to dial in 121.5). I knew that the mountains would soon cut off radio contact, but I figured that I should at least report an ETI (estimated time of impact) so someone could locate the pieces.

Looking westward across the lake, I noticed a meadow that obviously was my only chance for landing intact. I coaxed the plane toward that alluring spot. As I drew closer, I noticed that the field was bisected by what faintly resembled a dirt strip. A look at the chart confirmed this vision, but it looked more like a mud flat than a runway.

I was now fairly certain that I could make it to the field, but a close inspection of the strip revealed several problems that would require skill and accuracy. The near third of the strip was still a prop-bending quagmire, and the middle looked a bit mushy. The not-so-far end seemed dry enough but ended abruptly at a barbed-wire fence with big, fat posts.

I glided in over the wet end at about 80 mph and 100 feet, aiming for a spot about halfway down the strip. Bit hot, bit high, I thought and gently pulled in one, then two notches of flaps. I flared out, let it settle, then quickly dumped flaps to hasten a permanent contact with the ground. For a few seconds I was worried about that fence looming up ahead because the dirt was still too wet for hard braking, but I dropped full flaps, and these aided the mud in slowing me down.

Terra firma never felt better as, weak-kneed and dry-mouthed, I made my way across the field to phone the Prescott FAA, just as three state patrol cars screamed up the dirt road and slid to a dusty halt. The officers showed happy surprise at the news that I had come in without a scratch, and they radioed to Flagstaff for an aircraft mechanic.

When the mechanic arrived, we tore down the magnetos, and my suspicions were confirmed. Apparently overheated from lack of oil in the felt liner, the plastic rotor casing had cracked and burned through, creating a short in the right magneto. The left mag, unequal to the continued strain, showed evidence of shorting out inside several of the plug wire holes on the outer cap. I think that later-model mags have a better rotor lubrication system, but I suggest that a proper magneto inspection include more than just pulling the outer caps and replacing condensers.

By late afternoon I was airborne again, sporting two brand-new mags and consoled by the thought that the sizable hole in my wallet was far less painful than other holes I could have received.

I had met with a real emergency and found that I could handle it without panic. A subtle sense of confidence had been born in me, but recollection of the sudden seriousness of my adventure would always warn me against any overconfidence. "You're not a pilot until you've made a forced landing." At last I really understood these words.

●

A common thread begins to emerge. The pilot who is prepared for the eventuality of a failure in any of the aircraft systems is merely inconvenienced in most cases, and seldom harmed.

There is more to our airplanes these days than just the engines. Avionics and instruments now share an important part of every pilot's attention. Routine IFR flight depends on their reliability. If something goes wrong, though, it is not the end of the world if the pilot puts his training to use.

●

The malfunctioning artificial horizon had just been overhauled and checked out in my flying club's Cessna 182. The airplane was now working perfectly, just in time for a trip that my nonpilot business associate and I were planning to Las Vegas, Nevada. Even the weather was cooperating: CAVU and expected to remain that way. We arranged to meet early at the airport, and I readied a VFR flight plan from Albuquerque, New Mexico, to Las Vegas by way of the Grand Canyon.

Next morning, the northern route was no longer VFR due to a fast-moving cold front, but a southern route to Prescott and Las Vegas was still reported and forecast CAVU. We filed IFR anyway, and it turned out to be a good decision. By the time we got off, clouds were invisible to the west, and in 20 minutes we were on instruments. Two hours and 12 minutes later, a swing of the needle announced Winslow—56 minutes late.

Doug was not impressed with our speed. By Oak Creek, we were on top in the sunshine with occasional breaks below. However, with these winds our fuel would not stretch to Las Vegas with reasonable IFR reserves, so we landed at Prescott.

A steak dinner put us in good spirits, eager to continue. An in-person check with the weather briefer showed us the weather we had experienced was the front that had been forecast north of our course, but with support from a deep trough at the 500-millibar level. This was new. Our original weather briefings were by telephone, and no one had mentioned the 500-mb upper air chart. We were shortly to find out how much trouble a 500-mb low can cause. The forecast for Las Vegas was 2,000 feet overcast and two miles, but it was better than that now. The local weather had lowered and closed since our arrival, and snow showers were reported en route. No ice was reported, and temperatures aloft were quite cold, so we filed.

We entered thin clouds at 1,500 feet and soon were in a snow shower. The clouds were depositing traces of rime, but nothing significant. My friend was getting the total weather treatment on his first flight—CAVU when we first left, through a moderately strong cold front, to on top in the sun with breaks below, and now snow showers.

We were still climbing when the new artificial horizon did a snap roll and died. The light rime ice, which hadn't bothered me before, now began to get more of my attention. This airplane had no pitot heat, and in any ice at all, we could lose the airspeed indicator. From our experience getting to Prescott, it seemed reasonable to expect things to get better in this direction, not worse. After all, wasn't the front about 200 nm east of us? Besides, even the trace ice had stopped, and we could probably climb on top. We might just as well make an approach at Las Vegas, where we wanted to go, as at Prescott, where we didn't want to go.

We were at 14,000 feet now, but not on top, so I requested 18,000—about all we could expect of our 182. I toyed with the idea of telling ATC about our artificial horizon, but I figured it had no effect on our ability to comply with our clearance, so I didn't. No point in bothering him, I thought. Meanwhile, the temperature outside was − 25° C., and the air vent, which must be left open a bit for the thermometer to be accurate, had frozen. As we climbed the last few thousand feet, it became rather chilly inside the cockpit. I wrapped a ski headband around the vent and checked to see that the heater was on full.

Shortly thereafter, we popped out of the side of the buildup and were on top. It looked less appealing than ever behind us; below us was not bad. There was another buildup ahead.

"Are we going through that?" Doug asked.

"Probably not," I replied. It isn't very far from Prescott to Las Vegas; the Las Vegas weather was reported to be fairly good and our ETA was rapidly approaching.

We left 18 for 13,000. That's strange, I thought, the manifold pressure didn't change. I throttled the engine—15 inches; full throttle, the same. Another instrument was clearly useless. My concern increased, but I had already decided to go on to Las Vegas, and L.A. Center was clearing us out of 13 for 10. While still on top, I slowed to approach speed and carefully trimmed for level flight. We entered the clouds. Five minutes later, L.A. handed us off. From Las Vegas Approach Control came the news, "Expect an ILS Runway 25, vectors to final approach. Weather now 300 and three-quarters in rain." That buildup we had speculated on wasn't in front of or behind Las Vegas; it marked the spot!

The radio antennas began to howl. Sure enough, ice was building slowly on all the leading edges. "No sweat," I told my friend, "we'll be down in a few minutes." He was looking at all the white. This was a new situation for him. It was new to me, too, but I managed to refrain from saying so. I was busy worrying about the icicle on the pitot tube. As the vectors kept coming in, I began to wonder where we were. The radios were set up for the approach, but the needles didn't center. Fifteen minutes later I was *still* expecting the approach to begin any second. Then approach control told me there was some difficulty sequencing my slow aircraft in among all the jet traffic on the one runway available in this weather. Normally I would have volunteered to speed things up, but with no attitude gyro, no power indicator and the threat of no airspeed indicator, I didn't want to begin a diving power approach, so I remained silent. Besides, I was thinking seriously about all that beautiful weather reported in Los Angeles.

Another 15 minutes, in the middle of a holding turn, things began happening all at once. The air-speed indicator quit, the engine began to sputter and approach control called with a change in landing clearance, from an ILS to a VOR approach. I didn't answer. First things first: I was occupied trying to learn all about partial-panel needle-ball-and-altimeter IFR flying with engine-failure complications. Carburetor heat and a quick switch of mags (fuel was already on BOTH, but my hand still checked) showed one mag apparently half gone, the other rough. Still best on BOTH, I thought. Carburetor heat began to take effect and the engine smoothed out.

Approach control was calling again. "Cessna Two-Seven Golf, maintain 7,000 for obstacle clearance. Do you copy?" I was way behind the airplane, but I started the climb anyway. With my eyes on the remaining instruments, I fumbled for that absurdly located microphone, and gave a hurried "Stand by one." I thought about how nice a boom mike would be. My friend helped me find a new approach plate. Since the engine had begun running rough, he hadn't said much. I called approach control and told my grim story. "I've lost my manifold-pressure indicator, artificial horizon, airspeed indicator, apparently one mag, and I'm trying to locate a new approach plate and set up the radios." I didn't mention the fact that I no longer knew for sure where I was. He offered an immediate approach, but just then I didn't need an approach. I needed to get it all together first. Another couple of turns to read the new plate and I was ready.

The localizer minimums at Las Vegas were 255 feet above touchdown-zone elevation (only 149 feet above airport elevation) and one-half mile. In 300 and three-quarters weather, aided by high-intensity runway lights, I felt confident of a successful approach, especially since during my half hour of being vectored, no one else making the approach had missed. Then, approach control switched me to a VOR-Alpha approach, with minimums of 489 feet above airport elevation and one-mile visibility. I was to be the first to shoot the VOR approach since the weather deteriorated. My last known weather would leave me 200 feet in the clouds at minimums. The weather must have improved, I thought. Approach control does not automatically give weather when it is above circling minimums, so I had no idea how much the weather had improved. Where I was, it looked every bit as bad as it ever did.

While being vectored to the approach, I figured out where I was. Somewhere in front of me was a 5,092-foot mountain. No procedure turn. The mountain was not very far on the right. I made sure the needle stayed centered. The possibility of a missed approach really worried me. The lower we got, the more I worried. I was leaving Mack Intersection now for minimums. I should have insisted on an ILS; I was mentally kicking myself. Approach control was leaving me alone. I think he realized I didn't want to switch radio frequencies and spend time getting myself and the tower coordinated.

"I see a house!" my friend said. Sure enough, straight down was someone's roof, and then the airport appeared. Runway in sight, I changed to tower frequency, landed and splashed through the puddles for parking—45 minutes since we began the approach. I was exhausted. My crisp, fresh business suit felt as if I had worn it a week. In the terminal, while Doug was arranging for a car, a VFR pilot approached with the query,

"Think we could sneak out south to L.A.?" I was definitely the wrong person to ask.

I'm no longer so cavalier about bothering ATC with my equipment failures. I respect the significance of a low aloft. Two-Seven Golf now has a heated pitot tube, another rebuilt artificial horizon and a new boom mike on order. My engine problem was a combination of carburetor ice and an open plug wire. The manifold-pressure gauge had frozen condensate in the sensing line. Once warmed, it worked fine.

Of all the lessons I learned on this trip, the most important was the need for practicing partial-panel flying while deleting instruments not usually deleted. In this case, the failures involved power, airspeed and horizon instruments; but at other times, while in less trying circumstances, I have lost other instruments: compass, rate gyro (needle) and rate of climb. Anything mechanical or electrical will fail some day, and no one can guarantee one failure at a time. If you don't practice under the hood, someday you'll practice for real.

●

If you expect it to happen someday, it may not be quite so devastating to your equilibrium if it does. Not a bad philosophy.

It also helps to match that philosophizing with some solid practice. Many instructors simulate failures of various systems so that their students can learn to recognize how the failure manifests itself and can practice remedying it.

This final story has an interesting twist. On a check ride, of all things, the victim recognizes a real failure—and assumes it is just practice.

●

While there had been other milestones in my 12 years of flying —first solo, then private, commercial, airplane instructor, instrument and multiengine flight tests—today's check ride had a special significance.

An instrument-instructor rating, the "double i" as some call it, would represent my arrival as a pilot and as a teacher. With that piece of paper, I would be a more complete flight instructor, allowed to train and recommend other pilots for the instrument rating; even to send others, on my signature, to the FAA for "double i" and airline-transport-pilot check rides.

The 1965-model Cherokee 140 had only one omni. I had flown it the day before for a couple of hours—the first time I'd been in a Cherokee for quite a while. It seemed adequate, so I preflighted it, got in, made sure I had my logbook and the signed recommendation form for the check ride, started and taxied out.

During run-up, the only thing that didn't check out was the ammeter needle, which indicated a discharge. It seemed to me that this was probably just an error in the calibration of the instrument, since it had done the same thing yesterday and the battery had seemed strong during the engine start we had just made.

Haze limited visibility to only five or six miles; because of that, and for practice, I had filed an IFR flight plan. The flight to the GADO went smoothly, and I shot a VOR approach without a hitch.

The secretary at the GADO took me to the desk of the FAA inspector I'd been assigned to. I had not known until that moment whom I'd get, and he turned out to be a man who was rumored to be extra tough. You never know for sure if the rumors about case-hardened inspectors are true or just started by pilots who were unprepared and deserved to bust. The mill had it that this fellow was quite demanding in mastery of subject and precision of explanations. I'd studied hard, though, and most of my answers were letter-perfect.

When there was something I didn't know, I didn't try to bluff; I admitted it at once. He'd hand me a copy of the regs or the *Instrument Flying Handbook* and say, "Show me where to find it. Look it up. Explain the correct answer to me."

After two and a half hours of oral exam and discussion, I still felt good—great, in fact. He glanced at his watch. "Well, let's go fly for a while," he said. After I performed what I thought was a good preflight inspection, he suggested, "Why don't *you* sit in the left seat. I know you can fly from the right side; you're already an instructor. You'll be able to see the attitude indicator better from the left, and I don't want you to have any excuses for failing." A sly Snideley Whiplash grin spread across his face.

On run-up, I told him to ignore the low ammeter reading. "Always does that," I said.

After we got away from the airport traffic area, he put me under the hood and we ran through some unusual-attitude recoveries, partial-panel flying, demo of compass errors, preferred order of control manipulation for starting and ending climbs and descents, determining time-to-station by flying 90 degrees to a radial—whew!—and more.

Then he asked me to hold at the intersection of two omni radials. With only one receiver, I had to keep cranking from one radial to the other and switching frequencies, but I was managing. One glitch: The course-deviation indicator began to respond rather sluggishly, as though we were flying at an altitude too low for good reception.

"All right," he said, "tune in the VOR at the airport and take us back for an approach."

I tried to but couldn't get a signal. I fiddled with the radio awhile, then checked the circuit breakers and fuses because the radio was by then definitely dead. The inspector just sat there blissfully, watching for traffic.

I gave up. "What did you do?"

"What do you mean?" he asked.

"The radio. It's dead. I've checked everything, but I can't find out how you simulated the failure."

"I didn't do anything," he said, coming alive with interest. He too checked over our receiver; then, at the same instant, the realization came to both of us.

"Take the hood off," he said, "and find out where we are." It was not a test question. We had only a rough idea of our position relative to the intersection I had departed several minutes earlier.

"Find some checkpoints on your VFR chart," he said. My heart did a kind of funny thump.

"All I have with me are instrument charts," I said.

He raised an eyebrow, then produced a current sectional chart from a small plastic case he had set on the floor behind us as he'd entered. He started looking for landmarks, while I tried the transceiver to see if we could get a DF steer from the tower. The transceiver was also quite nonfunctional, which I reported to him.

The air had stayed hazy all morning or we'd probably have found our location almost at once. As it was, we were in doubt for only five minutes before we found a town and positively identified it.

"What are you going to do?" he asked.

"Go back to the airport," I said. When we got there, I circled the tower, rocking my wings. Tower gave us a steady green light. We landed, got a flashing green and taxied to the ramp.

"Drat," I muttered under my breath. Then I suggested that I could rent a plane on the field so we could shoot some approaches, but he said that it was already long past noon and he was getting hungry.

He told me that my oral had been excellent and the flying was all right. "But you don't know it all," he said. "You need to get into the *Instrument Flying Handbook* and learn it perfectly. That's the bible. Every word."

We kept walking. We were headed back into the GADO office. He had a grumpy look on his face; then he spoke again.

"I'll sign the forms, and the secretary will type out your temporary certificate."

Upstairs at the secretary's desk he wished me luck, then headed out the door for lunch.

When my friend and I got out to the plane, I did some troubleshooting and found a loose belt—the one that drives the alternator. I indulged in a moment of self-directed profanity, then said, "I'm some instrument pilot. I take off without an adequate source of electricity."

"Yeah," he said, "that ammeter must have been working after all."

All things considered, it was a lucky day. I passed my flight test and even got a free boost to start the Cherokee's engine. I flew home, with a new "double i"—and a lot left to learn.

5/THE PERILS OF IMPATIENCE

That the airplane could lift a person into the sky would appear to have been enough of a gift. To fly like the birds —what could be a greater achievement? For starters, flying *faster* than the birds could. As soon as there were enough flying machines around to make it interesting, one of the first things the newborn aviators did was to stage a race. Naturally, the losers left with a high resolve to turn things around next time.

Airplanes became faster because they bore the promise of speed; however, the promise must not have been so obvious at first. The Wrights approached the military with their machine by describing it as a platform for observation—it could take a man up high. When the military airplane became a fighter, it was first designed to maneuver well and was highly valued if it could do so at very low airspeeds. Later, some shrewd tactician discovered that one would never be shot down if one's opponent couldn't get close enough to shoot. By the time of the strategic nuclear stalemate, the paramount tactic had become straight-line speed and acceleration. The passenger-carrying airlines had to concern themselves first with reliability. The Pan American Airways "Clippers" were flying boats in part because they could always alight on the water on their way across the ocean if trouble developed. After that nagging worry was out of the way, the race to get there fastest began in earnest; that race slowed only recently, when the SST provoked the question of whether the costs of another speed increase might be greater than the traffic would bear.

So the airplane, in addition to liberating man from the grip of the earth, also freed him from the traditional trammels of time upon travel. The time required for a given journey has been reduced exponentially as increasingly sophisticated machines have borne the burden of the passengers within. It must be with considerable chagrin that these same hell-bent passengers look themselves in the eye and admit that the only thing they do with the time they save is to hurry a little more.

Humans act as if they are profoundly uncomfortable with their own mortality. Life is, when reduced to its temporal essence, simply a long countdown; never long enough, though, and time is the single commodity toward which we demonstrate the most greed. The airplane has become a lever with which to pry more time from life so that we may hasten to the next task. If it saves us time, the time is always spent. Find one person who makes a trip in an aircraft, lands, notes the time the trip would have taken by slower means, puts his feet up for the interim and relaxes. Don't keep looking for too long, though. You might waste time.

Although it seems unreasonable for pilots to hurry, a remarkable number do. The illusion of speed is all that really counts, and as airplanes have been improved to perform better, a perceptual paradox has arisen. A turbojet-powered airliner flies three times faster than a DC-3, but it also flies three times higher; the result is that the ground below appears to be passing no faster than it did at the DC-3's pace. That may account for the behavior of the lightplane pilot who, although convinced of the superior speed of his airplane over that of ground-based transport, will peer down frequently for reassurance, estimating speed by the passage of a main gear or leading edge along the line of a highway below. If only we could *be there*. We're already late. Better hurry. Time flies.

Pilots are all taught to be deliberate, but haste very often sneaks up on them, even if just for a fleeting moment. The fruits of impatience may appear when they are most unwelcome, and then hurry turns to worry.

Before Ernest K. Gann became an airline pilot—and a celebrated aviation writer—he was, like all pilots, just another beginner in a lightplane. Airlines fly by schedules, and yet their operations appear unruffled, unhurried and calm. The lightplane pilot is free to come and go when he chooses, yet he is more likely to choose to hurry. Naturally, Gann the Student was far more impatient to get there than Gann the Captain would have been. From the retrospective vantage of the flight deck, Gann wrote this, reflecting on a time when he had been in a frightening rush.

●

The day it happened, I had 152 hours in my logbook. With that amount of time I should have known better, but I didn't. I still didn't have my sky-thinking completely in line and I fell right into the same trap that has caught so many other pilots.

Ever since I had soloed, I had done more cross-country flying than the average student. I was pretty proud of my avigation and had made a number of two- and three-day flights out of little Christie Airport near New York. On the day in question, I wasn't going very far—just a 40-mile hop to an emergency field at Wurtsboro, New York. I owned an old Waco A at the time, equipped with a Jacobs engine. Not many of these were built. They were the usual Waco biplane design, but the fuselage held an open side-by-side cockpit. It was another attempt to get away from the tandem arrangement whereby the pilot had to yell at his passenger or student through a gosport tube or simply into the prop blast. Although it made the ship very blind on the ground and somewhat so in the air, it was a good idea and is still in use.

The other peculiarity about the Waco A was the combination throttle-brake arrangement. Both were operated by the same handle located on either side of the cockpit. To operate the throttle, you simply moved the handle back and forth in the usual manner. To operate the brakes, you pulled *down* on the handle, kicking rudder at the same time. It was a rather tricky setup on first acquaintance—many pilots (including me) got throttle when they wanted brake, and vice versa. You had to be particularly careful not to pull the throttle in its outward arc of motion when landing or the brakes would take hold. The combined duties of this handle made for a complicated joint affair attached to the fuselage. Its exact construction I cannot remember, and it's unimportant—the lesson I learned from it is something else.

I arrived at the field late. That was my first mistake. Never arrive at the airport later than you originally intend—get there well ahead of time if you can. For some reason or other, the tendency is to make your takeoff when you planned, regardless of how little time you've been at the field. A rushed takeoff means hurrying things, and in an airplane that's asking for trouble.

A friend was to meet me at Wurtsboro Airport at eleven that morning. I hadn't seen him for a long time, and I was anxious to show him that I was now a good enough pilot to arrive right on the dot. I hadn't yet learned that a dash of humility is a sure sign of a really experienced pilot. I grabbed a few maps, took a quick glance at them (after all, it was only 40 miles), then got the ship out of the hangar. There was a ragged overcast at 3,000 feet but that didn't bother me—remember, it was only 40 miles. Such was my haste to make schedule that I didn't even bother to call Newark for a weather forecast. I kept telling myself it was only 30 minutes to Wurtsboro.

As I ran the engine up and tested the mags, I noticed the throttle was slipping back. The control seemed positive but it wouldn't hold in place. Ordinarily it held through friction and the tight ball joint. Everything else worked fine. It was such a little thing (I thought)—if I were starting on a long flight I'd wait and fix it, but 30 minutes . . . well, I'd just hold the darn thing. Nothing to it. Fix it when I got back.

I took off and headed north. At eleven o'clock I was circling the field at Wurtsboro. I could see my friend standing on the ground waiting. I landed and we had a nice talk—too nice. I stayed for three hours. I told him that the throttle was slipping, and we tried to fix it with the only tool available, a chipped screwdriver from his car. It didn't worry me; it was just a nuisance to hang onto it. We thought we had fixed it, but we hadn't.

I shook hands with my friend, took off and headed back to Christie. I climbed to 2,000 feet and slipped along just beneath the overcast. There was a very light rain and some good, dark muck ahead . . . but after all, it was only 40 miles. Fat, dumb and happy, I charged right into as fine a thunderstorm as could be had.

Ten minutes out of Wurtsboro, it really began to rain. I couldn't fly on instruments even if I'd had them, so I let down to 1,500 feet. The hills weren't much below me. Still on course, I flew into what seemed like a solid sheet of water. The turbulence was terrific. It was all I could do to keep the Waco right side up. I was continuously conked on the head with hailstones of various size—and that throttle! Every bump, every twist, would send it scooting back to me. The engine would settle immediately into a nice, quiet idle. The Waco would respond with a rapid descent. What I urgently needed was a third hand. I had one on the stick, very busy, and the other on the throttle to hold it open. This left nothing to hold the map but my tightly pressed knees, which couldn't stay pressed and work the rudder against that turbulence.

I tried sitting on the map, which held it all right, but if I unfolded it enough for a good look, it tried to get out of the cockpit. If you've flown open-cockpit ships in highly turbulent air, you know what I'm talking about. I finally put the map between my chattering teeth and did some thinking: Obviously I couldn't keep this up for long. Even with a good throttle and a steady compass, it would have been a job to stay on course. I decided I wanted to get out of that thunderstorm, and made what I hoped was a 180-degree turn.

The rain got worse, the air became rougher. I was drenched, blue with cold and squirming uncomfortably in a pool of water. I had long before pushed my goggles up because I couldn't see through them—yet with my bare face hanging out, I couldn't see much over the side. The wet map was limp as a rag and kept slipping to the floor. Once it worked back under the seat, and I did a handstand retrieving it. I took my hand from the throttle for a split second. When I raised my head again, the Waco was diving for the treetops. Funny? I didn't think so at the time. I was dressed as an aviator but pulling duty as a deep-sea diver. I gasped for air and got a mouthful of water. I was literally drowning at 1,000 feet above sea level. With the airspeed dropping to 40 mph every few seconds, the water just bucketed into the cockpit.

I called the throttle a number of uncomplimentary things, but I should have turned my scorn inward. Only 40 miles! I had already flown that in circles and was no better off. All I knew was that I was slowly but surely drowning in midair somewhere between Wurtsboro and Christie—but where?

By taking a brutal face lashing, I could just peek over the side. A village slipped past beneath. I circled it for what seemed like an hour trying to identify it on the map. Actually it was closer to five minutes, but I was busier than the proverbial paperhanger. I finally managed to tie the throttle in position with my handkerchief—that was quite a performance too—but not in cruising position. It just wouldn't stay there. It held just enough revs to keep me from stalling in level flight. The slightest climb and off we'd go into the start of a low-power spin. I hated to look at the airspeed.

The map, despite its Government durability, was now a wet mess resembling oatmeal and just about as easy to handle. I finally managed a really good look at it with my stinging eyes and identified the town. I was a good 30 miles off course, and I had two alternatives. There was a little field near the town that didn't look too terrible. It was the first I had seen that was worth considering. I could attempt a landing or set a course for Christie Airport. Now that I'm older and wiser, I would land and fix the throttle. As it was, I elected to carry on to Christie.

By the time I had a new course figured out, I was involuntarily hedge-hopping again—banging through the rain at a near-stall. I was mad and I was scared, and I was kicking myself in the pants—all at the same time.

The only right thing I did was to hold that course once I had set it, through high and low water. I got an occasional bleary glimpse of a lot of strange country. I looked *up* at the top of a few hills as they marched past in clammy procession, but I practically ran into Christie Airport. I landed and poured myself out of the Waco. As my feet squeegeed across the grass to the hangar, they mocked every excuse I could think up.

Forty miles, I thought; maybe only 40 miles, but they grow long or short, as the case may be. An airplane is the fastest method of transport, but give it time before you start. A few minutes saved scurrying around on the ground or refusing to be delayed can turn into embarrassing air hours without half trying.

●

Forty miles proved to be more than enough distance to allow the wages of haste to descend upon the poor fellow in charge of that flying aquarium. The love affair with the sky that permeated all of Gann's books about the world of the airline pilot was only hinted at in that first fumbling effort in the waterlogged Waco.

Gann learned early that the most important part of the flight is the part that happens before the pilot ever gets near the airplane. Given an attitude that yields free rein to impatience, there is very little to intervene on the pilot's behalf once the flight begins. Familiarity with the area may have made the flight seem deceptively easy. In the same way, impatience, combined with a familiarity with the airplane itself, led this cadet to abbreviate the preflight of his Stearman.

•

In the cold, gray dawn of a February morning, the cadets of Squadron A stood at attention in a column of fours on the flight line at the Santa Maria Air Base awaiting the dismissal order from the flight leader. His curt "Squadron dismissed" cracked out above the roar of half a hundred Continental 220-horsepower engines, as the PT-13s were being warmed up before the morning flying period.

We each reported to our respective instructors and were soon being briefed on the maneuvers to be practiced for the day. Minutes later, the Stearman biplanes were taking off one by one en route to their assigned practice areas.

My instructor was a quiet, efficient, earnest man, with many hundreds of hours of civilian and military flying time behind him. One thing he stressed highly was the thorough inspection of the airplane before takeoff. Second to that, he insisted on the use of the checklist—before, during and after flight—no matter how well the student knew his airplane and procedures.

Since I had been fortunate enough to accumulate several hundred flying hours prior to entering the service, my instructor left me pretty much to my own devices except for a periodical check ride. Consequently, I failed to benefit from some of the fine points of his excellent teachings.

One bad habit that carried over from my civilian flying was that I was inclined to skip over my preflight inspection in short order and to inspect only the major parts of the ship. Little did I know then that before the day was over I would be taught a lesson on aircraft inspection.

I was told to proceed to a practice area about 20 miles west of the field and practice right and left spins, chandelles and snap rolls for an hour. By the time I was assigned my airplane, most of the other students were already in the air, so I made a hurried inspection of the plane, checking only the guy wires for tightness and checking the wingtips for evidence of ground loops. I climbed into the cockpit and gave the line mechanic the signal to wind up the inertia starter. At his signal, I engaged the starter and the engine barked into life.

The engine ran very rough, and after a few moments of listening, the line mechanic signaled me to cut the switch. A brief inspection disclosed that the plugs were badly fouled, and the mechanic informed me that a plug change was necessary. Since no other airplane was available, I grew increasingly impatient during the 20 minutes it took to change the plugs. It was necessary to take advantage of every minute of flying time available in order to have the required number of hours completed by graduation time or face the prospect of being held over for the new class.

With the plugs changed and the engine purring like a well-fed kitten, I disregarded everything else and took off, setting a climbing course for the practice area. The air was smooth, the visibility clear, and the Stearman responded to my touch as if it had suddenly become a thing alive.

I was relaxed when I found myself at 5,000 feet over the practice area. I put the Stearman into a smooth 360-degree turn, checked above and below for other planes. Apparently alone in the skies, I lined up on a road, eased the throttle back and brought the nose up a few degrees. At an indicated 75 mph, I fed in right rudder, brought the stick back and flopped over in a spin to the right, One—two—three turns, sharp opposite rudder—rudder to neutral. Stick relaxed in one coordinated motion, back pressure on the stick bringing the nose to the horizon—right on the money. What could be sweeter? A series of chandelle turns soon brought me back to 5,000 feet, where I decided to try a couple of snap rolls.

At 105 mph indicated, I brought the nose about 15 degrees above the horizon, fed in full right rudder, snapped to the right, coming out of it with the nose smack on the horizon. Feeling quite pleased with myself, I repeated the maneuver to the left.

As the plane snapped over, a sudden banging behind my head shattered my pleased feeling with a rude start. I jerked my head around in time to see the baggage compartment cover glance off the horizontal stabilizer and spin crazily off into space. During the moment that my mind was taken from the controls, the Stearman stalled out and I found myself obliged to split-S out.

In trying to regain a normal flight attitude, I found that the rudder didn't respond and the elevators were very sloppy. For a second time, I jerked my head around and saw that the engine cover had seen sucked from the baggage compartment and was draped around the horizontal stabilizer, beating frantically in the slip-stream against the fabric on the elevators.

My first thought was to bail out fast, but as reason began to return, I noted that I had about 4,500 feet of altitude left. My decision was to stay with the plane until I was down to 1,500 feet, and if I couldn't shake the engine cover by then, I would hit the silk.

By gingerly experimenting with the controls, I found that I could maintain a fairly steady and level flight at about 80 mph, still keeping my altitude. After much debate with myself, I decided to attempt to shake the cover by maneuvering the Stearman with as much control as I had left.

I put the plane into a shallow dive. The cover was beating on the elevator fabric until I thought surely the fabric would be ripped to shreds. At 110 mph, I popped the stick back and chopped the throttle in one motion. The elevators took a sluggish hold as I held the stick in the pit of my stomach and the nose came up and over.

At about 45 degrees behind vertical, the ship stalled out and spun off to the left. With one hand on my safety belt release, I neutralized the rudder and popped the stick slightly forward in a normal spin recovery. I half expected nothing to happen, but I heaved a great sigh of relief when I felt the seat of my pants being pressed into the seat as the Stearman recovered from the spin.

A quick look back at the empennage assured me the ship had shed the errant cover. Other than a hollow booming sound the slipstream made in the open baggage compartment, the Stearman seemed in good enough shape to get me back to the air base.

In my nervousness, I landed the plane like a ham-handed novice and managed to taxi it to the ramp without further mishap. I sat there in the cockpit for a couple of long minutes remembering all I had ever been told about preflight inspections. When I climbed out of the ship, I was certain that I would never again fly another airplane without giving it a thorough inspection. I can readily say that in the many hours I have flown since, a thorough inspection has saved me a recurrence of that experience, with possibly more disastrous results.

●

Haste can affect perception. To the pilot who is impatient to take off, a little fluid leak is just "normal." It didn't take this Swift pilot long to change his point of view.

●

Takeoff had been normal, except the landing gear had been slow to retract. This was not unusual, especially on hot days like this, so I simply flipped the circuit breaker off to rest the hydraulic pump and left the gear half retracted while I got a little altitude. Then, as I had often done before, I pulled the nose up, turned the pump back on and pushed the nose down sharply. The slight negative G had always permitted the pump very readily to complete the retraction—but not this time. After two repetitions failed, I decided to extend the gear and try again from scratch.

Down with the gear selector. When the red warning light failed to go out and the green "landing gear safe" light stayed stubbornly dark, I knew I had trouble. I could tell from the visual indicators out on the wing that the left gear was down and locked, while the right gear was almost completely down but not locked.

Well, that's why they put emergency systems on these retractable gears. I broke the safety wire on the emergency crank handle and began grinding away. Soon the crank stiffened and stopped—but no green light. I strained the crank as hard as I dared—still no green.

Then I tried every maneuver I could think of to shake the landing gear down: porpoises, violent yaws, sharp rocking from side to side. Nothing helped. A hard pull-up would be my last resort.

The upper wing skin twanged into a pattern of distinct wrinkles as I horsed the wheel back hard into my lap. The airspeed flickered at about 105 knots, when the Swift shuddered into an accelerated stall. Considering that the normal clean stall speed was about 52 knots, this meant that we were pulling about four Gs. I couldn't risk pulling it any harder. If the landing gear was ever going to lock down, it would have to be now.

As I recovered from the accelerated stall, I was almost afraid to look at the lights. Still red! I had shot my last bolt, and the gear was still unlocked. I might as well land and total up the damage.

Still, there might be one more outside chance of avoiding those loud, expensive noises that go with a belly landing. Maybe a slight sideload would snap the gear into place. It was worth a try. I made my approach a little fast, then leveled off with power and flew down the runway with the wheels just skimming the surface. Very gingerly, I eased down and let the wheels touch, still keeping most of the weight on the wings. As soon as the wheels were firmly—but not too heavily—on the ground, I began a series of slow, gradual swerves from side to side on the runway. As I applied power for a go-around at the end of the runway, I looked at the lights once again—*green!*

lovely, bright, beautiful green. I checked the visual indicators again, and they showed down and locked. The landing was routine.

After the bird was safely parked and tied down, I began checking. I did this somewhat reluctantly, because I had a pretty good idea what I'd find.

First the hydraulic reservoir—*empty.* I had been noticing the telltale oily moisture and occasional droplets dangling from the landing-gear-actuating cylinder. In the Air Corps we used to call this "normal seepage." First chance I got, I figured I'd have new O-rings installed. Meanwhile, I'd just top off the reservoir before each flight to compensate for the fluid lost by "normal seepage." But I was in a hurry to get home and didn't take the time to check the reservoir as part of my preflight. After all, it had never been empty before.

Now, a look at the emergency extension system. Sure enough, one of the cables was off the pulley. The cable had gone slack at some time during an extension of the gear, and had come off the pulley. Why did it go slack? Because part of the take-up mechanism was operating sluggishly from insufficient lubrication.

In each case the guilty party was standing in the same pair of shoes—*mine!* Two postponed maintenance items set up an unsafe condition. In my haste to get on my way, I had hurried through my preflight and forged another link in the chain of circumstances leading from "normal seepage" to an accident. Only a lot of luck prevented the chain from being closed tight around a damaged airplane.

●

The opportunity to learn that kind of lesson rarely knocks twice in one trip—unless you were this poor Tri-Pacer driver on the way from Long Island to Florida with a friend.

●

The visibility was three to five miles with an overcast of 3,000 feet. The first leg of the trip had been uneventful and we landed in Salisbury, Maryland, to refuel. The weather check was okay and we departed south toward Cape Charles, Virginia. We were only 30 minutes out of Salisbury when I encountered my first serious problem.

The cabin of the plane was suddenly filled with burning oil fumes. I broke out in a cold sweat. I looked sharply at the gauges. I didn't want to believe what I saw: The oil pressure registered zero. The cylinder-temperature and oil-temperature gauges were rising. I immediately throttled the engine to idle and began a shallow glide.

My altitude was 1,800 feet. I explained to the fellow with me that we were in serious trouble. "We're going down," I said. "I don't know where, but fasten your seat belt. Secure all loose objects in the plane." He complied, nervously. It was his first trip with me, and he didn't know what to make of it.

My objective was a nearby airport, but the smoke seeping into the cabin changed that plan. I cut the engine for fear of fire and switched the fuel selector to "off." I told my friend to check his side of the plane for an open field while I scanned my side.

We spotted a farm, which gave us some reassurance. I noticed an open cow pasture that seemed most suitable. My altimeter was indicating 900 feet. It meant I had to accomplish a landing in less than two minutes. I estimated the cow pasture to be about 1,500 feet in length. At the far end of the field I saw a herd of cows grazing. A large red barn was behind them. Coming in on final, I realized I was too high. Suddenly, I lowered full flaps and tried to dump the plane straight down. It was too late. My 1,500-foot estimate shrank to virtually nothing and my plane was heading straight for the cows and the large barn.

We didn't know what to expect. Against all rules and risking a stall, I made a 90-degree turn at 100 feet, skimmed over a fence, missed it by three feet and landed in a cornfield. The landing was quick and bumpy. We both held our breaths as the plane cut the cornstalks like a huge scythe and stopped. Luckily, the four-foot-high cornstalks acted as a buffer and then wrapped around our wheels and helped brake our plane to a stop. It cut our landing roll considerably.

We climbed out of the plane relieved and unharmed, though shaken. Nervously we examined the plane for damage. It was negligible, but the right side was covered with oil, from the engine cowl to the tail assembly. Lifting the engine cowl, I noted where the oil hose was broken off and worn at the spot where I had received an okay from the mechanic earlier. The oil stick read "empty."

I contacted a local mechanic who said he had worked on airplanes and assured me he could make the necessary repairs with little trouble. As the damaged oil hose was being replaced, we checked in at a nearby hotel and got some rest. Early the next morning the mechanic called and said the airplane was ready. I checked the hose when we arrived and noted that it was not made of the same material as the original, but the mechanic assured me it was strong material and an able replacement.

Our next move was to get into a position for takeoff. We managed to move the airplane from the cornfield to an adjoining open field that was more suitable for a takeoff. Apparently there was no damage at all to the engine and all mags and pressures were up to par. The new oil hose was holding fine.

It was at this point that we decided to change plans for our trip to Miami. My friend, somewhat worried, said he'd return home by car and meet me in Atlantic City. He rented a car and proceeded back. He took all the luggage with him, as I had to take off from a short field, of about 1,500 feet.

I encountered no problems on takeoff, clearing all obstacles smoothly. I climbed to 2,800 feet, sat back in my seat and relaxed. Everything was humming smoothly and the weather was fine. It lasted just 25 minutes, then everything broke loose.

This time instead of smelling burning oil and fumes, I saw the needle on the oil pressure drop from green to red. *Then* I smelled the burning oil; it was a sickening odor. I cut the engine and fuel-flow valve and radioed mayday to Salisbury Radio, giving my position as approximately 25 miles south of Salisbury. Below there was nothing but woods. Then, to my relief, I noted some cornfields and an open field between them; that would have to be it. This time I had no room for error; the final approach had to be right. The field was enveloped by cornstalks seven feet high on the north and south, with wooded areas east and west.

Again, I estimated the field length as 1,500 feet, and coming in on base I was a little high but managed to lose altitude. I came in at about 65 mph with full flaps. I held my breath, and the wheels suddenly touched ground. The plane jerked, and the ground roll felt solid. Then the plane leaped, bumped, rolled over and stopped. I blacked out. When I came to, I found myself upside down in the airplane but still strapped to my seat. I fumbled with the seat belt, unfastened it and fell to the ceiling of the plane. Quickly, I kicked the left window out and crawled through, sweating in the grime and blood. Once on the ground, I felt every bone in my body quickly. I was breathing like a marathon runner who had just completed 50 miles, but I seemed to be all right except that blood was running down my face from a head injury. Excited and worried, I staggered to a nearby farmhouse. I was exhausted. Someone heard my moans as I made the last step and then collapsed.

An hour later I found myself in a hospital, resting on clean white sheets. The nurse quietly told me there was nothing to worry about. I had no broken bones and I would be released in a few hours.

I returned to the scene of the crash and discovered I had hit a hidden ditch covered with tall weeds and bushes, four feet deep and five feet wide. The plane had nosed over and was demolished beyond repair.

As for my friend, he's never asked to accompany me on a flight again. Did I lose a friend? I wonder.

•

One can only wonder what it was that urged him to take off again from that cornfield with makeshift repairs and plenty of time on his hands. Here's another pilot who got two chances. Having made it through one scrape safely, he took off again and really begged for what he finally got.

•

This story started with a charter flight from Las Vegas, Nevada, to Los Angeles during the summer of 1947, a few days before Bugsy Siegel was slain while sitting near an open window in his girl friend's Los Angeles apartment. It was Siegel who called my office to arrange a charter for his friend Virginia Hill.

It was quite late in the afternoon when Miss Hill arrived at the airport. As I climbed my Cessna 140 out over the south end of Spring Mountain, I realized that if I planned to return to Las Vegas that day I would have to do so after dark. The terrain between Los Angeles and Las Vegas is anything but inviting for single-engine aircraft at night, but there are several lighted fields along the way, and I had flown the route many times. Therefore, even as I departed, I determined to return home as soon as I had delivered my passenger. I had appointments the following morning.

The weather was typical of the desert region over which we set our course; bright and clear with a light southwest wind and the usual afternoon turbulence. Miss Hill was an excellent passenger and apparently accustomed to air travel, for she offered no complaint about the rough air or the monotonous cruise over the desert.

After crossing Cajon Pass, I noted that San Bernardino was completely obscured by a thin overcast of smoke and fog. I told Miss Hill that if the condition didn't improve over Los Angeles,

I would take her to Palmdale and provide her with a bus ticket for the balance of the trip. She objected to this plan and said she had to reach Los Angeles within the hour.

A few minutes later the smog thinned out and we were able to let down over south Los Angeles with a good four-mile visibility. Fog was beginning to roll inland and obscure a portion of Los Angeles Airport, so I landed at Compton, which was agreeable to my passenger. Had we arrived 30 minutes later, I doubt that I could have gotten into the Los Angeles area at all since the fog was moving in fast from the Pacific Ocean.

I made arrangements for a taxi to pick up Miss Hill and returned to the parking ramp. The Cessna hadn't been refueled, and there were several aircraft at the gas pit ahead of me. The sun was sinking fast. The fog was rolling in. There was at least one hour and 40 minutes' fuel remaining in my tanks. I had previously organized a flying club at Silver Lake, about 90 miles southwest of Las Vegas, where I knew the club members kept a barrel of aviation gasoline on hand at all times. If I was going to get out of Los Angeles that night, I knew I would have to take off immediately and refuel the Cessna at Silver Lake.

I taxied out and took off into the waning visibility. During the 20-minute climb to 8,000 feet, the horizon was barely discernible, and by the time I had left the smog behind and picked up the lights of the Big Bear Lake resort off to my right, darkness had fallen. It was one of those desert nights with lots of twinkling stars but no moon, and it was as black as ink in all directions. As soon as I crossed the Sierras, I felt that my troubles were over, and I saw the flashing beacons ahead that would lead me down the airway to Silver Lake. I had a tailwind, charter money in my pocket, and all was well. The air was perfect and the little Cessna trimmed out beautifully. I tossed my charts on the shelf behind the seat and turned the radio to a fine program of band music as I idly observed the beacons move nearer one by one.

For some strange reason, which could probably be explained

only by a psychiatrist, I sat back in this coma for more than an hour before I finally switched bands and tried to tune in Silver Lake. The range signal was so weak that I could barely hear it, and for the first time I began to look around. The compass revealed that my heading was almost due east. I really came to life then, for I should have been flying a northeasterly course. The headlights of vehicles below indicated that even the highway was not where I thought it was. Still following the beacons, I recovered the chart I had tossed in the back and really got down to business. It didn't take long to figure out that I had picked up the wrong airway and was following it to Needles, California. By the time I discovered the error, I was at least 50 miles south of Silver Lake. I tuned in the Needles Range and gave them a call but received no answer. I was too far out to reach that station on the small quantity of remaining fuel. One tank was empty and the other was bobbing on zero. There was but one course of action—to locate a good stretch of highway and get on it before the faithful little Continental sputtered its last. The heavy traffic was a hazard but at least it showed me where the highway was, so I retarded the throttle and started down.

It was not difficult to see by the moving headlights a long stretch of road inclined upward in a westerly direction, into the wind—I hoped. I prayed that I had selected a portion of the highway along which no powerlines had been erected. Spiraling down over the lights of moving vehicles, I leveled off to what I judged to be about 500 feet and got all squared away for a long power approach.

A friendly motorist unknowingly guided me right up to the spot I had selected, but just as I passed over him, another car came speeding down the hill from the opposite direction. I was forced to go around. Likewise, on my second approach an east-bound car cut me out and I had to go through the entire procedure once more. The fuel gauge had ceased to bob as I turned on final and lined up for the third try.

I came up behind a large truck displaying an array of position lights and felt certain the vehicle would slow down upon reaching the incline. Just before passing over the truck, I snapped on the landing lights, which illuminated the pavement before me. The plane was just about ready to settle to the ground, when a small bridge loomed up and I had to use power to get over it. A few seconds later I felt the lurch of rubber tires on the oiled road, and I began to brake the landing roll as much as I dared. I learned to fly on a ranch in Wyoming, and I'm not squeamish about landing on roads or even cow trails, but keeping an airplane straight on a paved highway at night is quite a chore. Perhaps the plane was still rolling a bit when I snapped the ignition switches off and climbed out. I'm not sure. But I saw headlights speeding toward me from both directions as I frantically wheeled the aircraft off the road.

Within moments I had created a traffic jam. Motorists from both directions screeched to a halt to satisfy their curiosity. After getting my breath, I pushed the plane back into the mesquite and turned off the navigation lights so that it could not be seen readily from the highway. An accommodating tourist returned to a small gas station west of the spot where I had landed and brought back some sandwiches and a five-gallon can of automobile gasoline. He told me that I was approximately 40 miles west of Needles. I spent the night on the no-sag spring cushions of a Cessna 140. The desert air was cold and I didn't sleep in comfort, but I was glad to be on the ground.

●

An airplane requires rigorous adherence to the rules, which make it one of the most demanding of machines. No one has yet figured out a way to impart horse sense to an airframe, which leaves the whole thing pretty much up to the pilot.

So most pilots have rules of their own, some based on advice, some based on experience. Faced with the urge to get going, though, a pilot can let even the hardest rule fall to temptation.

That moment of relaxation can make the airplane seem cruelly unforgiving when everything goes sour just because of one lapse.

●

All of us who fly have our own little personal rules for extra safety, but I suspect most pilots feel that the self-imposed strictures really aren't so important as those imposed by FARs. We often bend our personal laws, and when they inconvenience us, we may even ignore them completely. One good scare, however, will prove that a homespun regulation can be just as unforgiving when breached as one devised by the FAA.

Just after I got my instrument ticket and began flying a lot of cross-country, I read an article on night flight in which the author said that unexpected and unforecast weather is so often encountered after dark he had made it a rule always to file IFR on all after-sundown flights. Although I had already flown a lot at night and had never experienced any weather problems, this rule, formulated by a pilot with much more experience than mine, seemed a good one to adopt. For a year thereafter, filing IFR at sunset was something I did automatically, along with turning on the navigation lights.

Nothing exciting happened, and I undoubtedly became complacent. Then, one spring day, my wife and I decided to fly to Cleveland in our Musketeer for the weekend. Weather for the flight was forecast to be 5,000 feet or better with 5 to 10 miles' visibility in light rain; but we would face a 20-knot headwind coming down off Lake Erie, so I knew the forecast might very well go sour shortly after dark. We were airborne from Philadelphia at a quarter to four, though, in plenty of time to complete the 330-nm flight by sundown.

Winds were higher than forecast and the weather lower. About 30 miles east of Youngstown, the rains became heavier, and although the ceiling was holding and visibility to the side was adequate, our apparent visibility over the nose in the fading light became nothing/nothing. Cuyahoga County Airport, our destination, was only 30 minutes past Youngstown, and Burke Lakefront, the reporting point closest to Cuyahoga County, was giving 3,000 and eight. We'd already been airborne in turbulence for three hours, however, so it seemed prudent to land, refuel and have a stretch at Youngstown before plunging into the rapidly approaching darkness.

We parked, ordered fuel and went upstairs to the FSS to check weather. The guy manning the teletypes must have put on rose-colored glasses before coming on duty, for he was full of happy answers and cheery optimism. Without even looking up from tearing the sequences apart and distributing them to the proper clips, he said, "Cuyahoga County? No problem. We're 4,000 and eight, and Lakefront is 2,800 broken, 10,000 overcast and five, and the rain has stopped. Good VFR all the way."

Intuition warned me that he was overdoing the optimism, but he was the expert and I was tired. Rather than pump him further about my destination, I remarked that we had just come from the east and it was marginal VFR in that direction.

"Naw, it's okay that way, too," he answered, as though he hadn't heard what I said. "Phillipsburg and Du Bois and Williamsport are all VFR; it just seems worse at night."

Such glibness from an FSS specialist to a Musketeer pilot on a damp and windy night was so out of character it was spooky —almost sinister. Perhaps that was the reason for my spur-of-the-moment decision not to file. It's only 43 nm from Youngstown to Cleveland straight out on Runway 32 to the Youngstown Vortac, 25 miles to the Chardon Vortac, 14 miles out the 285 radial to Cuyahoga County—over flat and antennaless country, and there are two lighted airports directly on the route. It seemed reasonable to breach my rule this once, and doing so would save waiting a half hour or more for clearance.

We climbed straight out to 2,500 feet, established on the 120-degree radial to Chardon and watched as the town of Bristolville slid by on the left. In the next moment, however, green and red light burst into the cabin as reflections from the navigation lights signaled that we had flown into cloud. We were out again in an instant, but I dropped the nose toward a group of lights in an effort to stay under whatever we were getting into. It was much too dark to see whether it was scattered or broken or got lower up ahead. At 2,000 feet we had good visibility, though, and we were within 10 or 12 minutes of County Airport. I looked up the County Tower frequency, but before I could dial it, we began slicing through the bottom of a cloud and I had to descend another 200 feet to stay contact.

Damn. Down to 1,800 feet in an area where obstructions run to 1,300, with no clearance, mentally unprepared for instrument flying and with my Jepps tossed carelessly into the back. I tried County Tower, hoping to raise a current weather observation from them, but no answer. In the moment of indecision, we smashed headlong into a cloud.

That did it. I pulled back up to 2,000 and began a right 180 directly over the Chardon Vortac. It was very turbulent, and for several minutes I had to concentrate on holding altitude and getting established on the radial back to Youngstown.

Ages later, after we'd already switched to the Youngstown Vortac, we broke out, evidently between layers, for we could see surface lights only occasionally. At the rate they were going by, we must have had a 30-knot wind blowing up our back. That created another problem: If we didn't break out quickly, we were going to be blown right through the Youngstown Control Zone. I called for weather and got 1,600 broken and five miles; but remembering the briefing I'd gotten an hour earlier from Youngstown, I didn't trust this one. It was time to reestablish self-made rules. I switched to the approach frequency and asked for an approach just as the omni needle took off, indicating imminent station passage. But wouldn't you know it! The approach controller was also looking at the weather through rose-colored glasses. In his slowest Ohioan twang, while I began a holding pattern to keep from running through his control zone, he told us that Youngstown was now 1,100 and five and suggested that we continue to the airport VFR.

I can't imagine why he didn't want our IFR business, but there was no time to plead. I called for the VOR approach plate, noted the inbound heading and the circling MDA and switched to tower frequency. Tower cleared us to land, which should have meant they were VFR, but at 1,700 feet, just 40 feet above MDA, we still couldn't see lights on the ground through the cloud below us. I cautiously let down to MDA, looked hard for lights and saw only total darkness. Enough of that. I reached for the throttle to begin a climb, and at that instant we broke out directly over the downwind end of Runway 32. Evidently, the lower layer was just beginning to cover the airport.

I have since counted five FARs that were either badly bent or totally busted on that 40-minute flight—but the most important rule I'd broken, and the one that led to breaking all the others, was the one I had imposed on myself: If you fly at night, file the flight.

●

It takes very little to put an otherwise well-organized pilot right behind the eight ball. Anything out of the ordinary that throws him off routine should be a signal to slow to half speed, to double-check everything. It is the one time to avoid haste with a fervor.

●

Heavily laden with baggage, our Lake amphibian waddled unsteadily down the rough rock surface of the ramp as I aimed its wandering nosewheel for the gin-clear Bahamian water.

The lurching melted into a buoyant glide as the swells took the burden from the wheels. Then one last bump from a submerged conch, the snap of the upgear locks, and we were a boat, our idling propeller and water rudder in contest for directional control with the wind and the tidal current.

The breeze was more than moderate—just right for an exhilarating sail—but stronger than we ordinarily chose for amphibian operation from our exposed location so near the open ocean. I taxied northwest, hiding behind the little island from the searching ocean swells. While my wife checked the VHF and CB transmitters on our field-strength meter (and heard familiar CB chatter on this Out Island party line), I reviewed the gauges and found no hint of trouble.

Despite the comparative complexity of the Lake, with its hydraulic gear, prop, flaps and trim, its electrical system and its water accessories, serious problems had been prevented through four years of tropical salt-water operation by special treatment and careful maintenance. Now she was overdue for a 100-hour inspection, and the plugs had lately seemed prone to foul during long taxis on the water.

Peering through the spray-spangled windshield, I pulled the wheel to my belt and slowly advanced the throttle. The bow rose high and we pushed up our usual wave. The engine struggled in its mounts, and the whole plane shuddered with effort as we strained to climb onto the step. Even with elevator tricks, we could not seem to make it.

Then I saw that although we had our 2,700 rpm, we were not getting the 27 inches that indicated full power.

Left mag—marginal. Both. Right mag—big drop. Both. So that's it. Well, full throttle will blow her clean in a minute. But it didn't. Ice? Possible even in the Bahamas, but carburetor heat gives no effect. Burn out the carbon—slowly back on the mixture till she heats and dies. Now, right mag—marginal, but much better. Back on both—and let's go.

By now, we had passed beyond the protected water and were wallowing in a confused sea, where the following wind waves moved at odd angles to the quartering sea swells. Furthermore, we were steaming like a pot of crawfish in our sun-heated cabin.

Holding full pressure on the left pedal, I turned west across the wind and, reducing drag by centering the huge trim tabs, I tried again.

Now we found the declining face of a long swell, and while the engine strained and I urged with the elevators, the Lake surfed down the slope, and we were up on the step, roller-coasting along on half power like an outboard.

As we swooped and dipped through the waves, the spray drummed on the wings behind, and I gambled a drenching to crack the windshield for a cleansing blast. I retracted the water rudder and the air rudder took over. Now left again, holding the inside wingfloat as high as possible with opposite aileron. As we came up into the wind, I released the crossed controls and added power, and with increased speed the swishing lope quickened to a bash, bash, bash.

Groping through the jolts for the jumping key-switch, I found too much commotion for more than cursory confirmation that the right mag was holding in the area of maximum allowable drop. It was taking full attention to hold the nose within that critically narrow angle with the water that allows best acceleration and avoids porpoising.

Full throttle now as we retraced our wake upwind to the lee of the cay, and that sheltered spot of relatively smooth water where I planned to reach takeoff speed with the least abuse to the hull and ourselves.

We were clipping the crests in a staccato stutter, but something was wrong. Something was holding us back. I glanced down at the airspeed and was not surprised to find the needle fluttering meaninglessly—caused by the usual water in the pitot that would blow out when we got aloft. After 500 hours in the honest little Lake, I no longer needed a speed number for takeoff. I could not divert attention again to the manifold gauge on the far side of the panel.

The seconds, and the precious area of smoother water, were passing without the expected lift. The ride was getting rough again. Although we were gaining speed, we were also rapidly approaching the sand spit that meant the end of all protection.

I became alarmed. Should I abort? It would mean another agonizing effort to make her plane, and our time was limited. Besides, the problem was only a slight loss of power, probably a temporary one caused by dirty plugs, coupled with the drag of our heavy load. And we were gaining, if slowly. Weighing the matter quickly, I resolved to continue.

We nearly made it off that first swell. Almost, but not quite. Bash! I held the nose up. Bash! again, and a high bounce—but again it settled in. After the next ricochet, I horsed it off, and we labored, half stalled, inches above the seas. My heart had bounced to my throat.

Slowly, cautiously, I dropped the nose. The speed increased and we stayed up. Would we make it? We could not yet climb, and the high land at Spencer's Point, rushing toward us, loomed frighteningly close. To pull up too soon meant mushing and certain disaster when we reached the land. Landing now would take us directly into walls of green concrete. I was punished with time for thought, with torturing hindsight.

But now the water was dropping away, slowly, painfully slowly. And as my rigid grip hauled the nose to the edge of a stall, we brushed past the trees on the ridge and saw the land fall away to Cherokee Sound. We were clear.

As the tension knots came loose and my eye swept the panel, I saw—my God—I saw the switch. The switch was on that weak right mag!

●

Had that takeoff been routine, the customary rhythms of pre-takeoff check would have sufficed. But it wasn't routine, and a calm situation turned into a hurried one.

6/BEYOND THE RED LINE

Near the farthest reach of the needle, on the face of the airspeed indicator in most lightplanes, there is a red line. It marks the never-exceed speed, the velocity beyond which the pilot is forbidden to fly; pilots know it as V_{NE}, or the "redline" airspeed. Elsewhere within the aircraft—on gauges, placards, meters, controls—there are lines and markings, all representing limits of one sort or another; they are there to remind the pilot that the airplane is capable of operating safely only within a known performance envelope. Although the term "redline" is most closely associated with the machine's ultimate speed, it is an apt symbol for any boundary which, once crossed, places the aircraft and its pilot in hazard.

Redlines exist in every facet of flight, really, for flight has limits wherever one looks. Some can be measured, computed and tested, and others are intangible. Humans also have limits, so there are redlines beyond which the pilot can't be pushed. Human performance is difficult to compute, however, and most pilots would reserve for themselves the decision about when enough is enough. Regulations and advice that try to force the issue invariably lead to resentment and surreptitious disobedience. No one—especially the airman—likes to be told where or when to stop.

Although pilots in training may not recognize it, much of their learning experience is designed to increase their confidence in both their own ability and that of the airplane. It is dangerous to fly without feeling confident, for the resulting anxiety can affect judgment. Each successful flight has the added benefit of positive reinforcement, enhancing the airman's confidence in the training. Once a rating is achieved, the pilot is on his own, and then confidence can really flower.

The trouble is, there must also be limits to confidence lest a pilot feel that he or she is so good as to be above it all. Overconfidence then affects judgment just as adversely as did anxiety in the beginner. The pilot becomes the airport ace, the show-off, the swaggerer who writes his or her own rules and begins to take short cuts through time-tested procedures.

Once again it seems appropriate to open with a lesson learned while still on the ground—in this case, while starting the airplane. Two instructors who thought they knew it all found out which end of the airplane bites.

●

It was the kind of thing that never should have happened, especially considering our experience. We were both flight instructors for the aero club in addition to being rated military pilots. It occurred while a friend and I were F-105 pilots assigned to an Air Force fighter wing in Germany. Like a great many military pilots, we never lost the love of lightplane flying or the joy of teaching others to fly. With the indulgence of our commander and the help of several dedicated NCOs, airmen and fellow officers, we formed an aero club. And our first airplane? Well, naturally it had to be a J-3 Cub or an Aeronca Champ—in our case, the Champ.

As the only two licensed flight instructors, the two of us had been alternating the students, about 15 each at the start. In time, a couple of other instructors showed up, and business was booming.

One day, my friend, his student in tow, stuck his head in my office. "How about some help getting started?" he asked.

"Meet you on the line in five minutes," I told him.

While they preflighted, I hung around the end that bites, shuffling from foot to foot, trying to recall the details of propping an airplane from my distant J-3 past. Eventually, of course, they climbed aboard. Will peered out from the front seat and called, "Let's get going."

With studied casualness, I faced up to the prop. "Chocks in place and brakes?" He nodded affirmative. As a double check, I gave a light tug near the thick hub of the wooden prop. The brakes were holding, and the wheels were obviously locked.

Now, ordinarily, a guy with any regard for his extremities goes about hand-cranking an aircraft as if each swing of the propeller would bring that snarling, hand-hungry engine to life —this even though he may have properly given the ageless call of "Switch off" before the five or six blades required to get the thing primed and ready.

But not me; at least not on this particular day. This was the old-pro instructor about to demonstrate some smooth, show-biz, hand-over-hand, up-close technique that had suddenly returned from the deep subconscious.

I was 17 once, and it was during that period that propping airplanes day after day had become second nature. Besides, at the little airport in Alabama, we all talked alike, partly because we all had the same flight instructor. As things turned out, it was the words we had learned to say—which were different from the way they say it in some other places—that caused me to be as close to tragedy as I have ever been.

I stood up close, grasped the prop with both hands, then looked at my friend. "Switch offfff," I cried. It's always noisy on a flight line, but he hollered back something that sounded like "Switch offfff." Well, I stood there smiling and began my smooth, hand-over-hand, show-biz propping technique. It lasted about two blades, when——

I did manage to move away from that roaring, feisty engine, but it sure was an impressive lesson. I had not been aware that the engine was already warm and thus would not require the priming strokes of the hand-turned prop. He, of course, assumed that I knew.

If we had not been so experienced, there would probably have been a short prestart briefing to talk over signals and such. When he returned my call of "Switch off," he had actually answered, "Switch on." I was expecting "Contact" for mags on —the way we used to say it back at Auburn.

Last week I gave my 16-year-old son his first flying lesson. As any good instructor/father would do, I gave him a lesson in propping an airplane by hand. I guess it looked pretty silly, a grown man standing there, feet and knees about four feet back, body bent at a 90-degree angle and arms stretched out in front trying to turn that slick metal prop. But as I told him, "There's one thing that's never, ever safe, switch on or switch off, engine hot or engine cold, and that's that machete mounted up front —the prop."

●

Chances are that both those instructors found their complacency shattered after that incident. If pilots are lucky, they have an experience of one kind or another that serves as a warning light to tell them that they have overstepped the line, that they have become overconfident.

Often the decision to press beyond the limits has the best of intentions behind it. That doesn't make it any less hazardous. Here's another instructor who was simply trying to do a better job of teaching, even if it meant bending the rules a little.

●

I was a very eager instructor. In fact, you might say I was too eager. Not content with giving the usual verbal, illustrated instructions at the ready-room blackboard when questioned by my students about what to do in case of an emergency situation, I would follow through whenever possible with a demonstration in the air, simulating the emergency and utilizing my recommended procedure for coping with it. These procedures were not always in the book, but I was determined to give my students the full benefit of my vast knowledge of airmanship.

After spending most of World War II as a basic flying instructor with the Army Air Corps, I found myself a civilian again, doing what I liked best—flying and teaching a class of young vets to fly under the G.I. Bill at Week's Field, in Coeur d'Alene, Idaho. It was a good school. We had Piper J-3s, Cessna 140s and 170s, Stinsons, Fairchild 24s, Waco UPF-7s for aerobatics and twin Cessnas for multiengine. The school offered all the CAA-approved courses. The curriculum was very complete, but I couldn't resist adding to it a little here and there by passing on some tricks of the trade I had picked up.

One day, one of my extracurricular demonstrations persuaded me that the course was complete enough without my little additions. I was always sure to explain to my students that without proper instruments and training it was impossible to maintain control of the aircraft under instrument conditions. But the question was, "What if you become trapped above an overcast in an aircraft like a Piper J-3 with no instruments for IFR flight?" I pointed out that if you knew positively that there was a 1,500- to 2,000-foot ceiling under the cloud deck, one way you could let down without losing control and building up dangerous airspeeds would be to put the aircraft in a true spin and hold it there until you broke out beneath the clouds, make a normal recovery and continue under the overcast.

On my next dual flight in a J-3 with one of my advanced students, I decided to demonstrate this technique. There was a fairly stable cloud deck at about 2,000 feet extending out from the mountains east of the field, with a well-defined edge out about six miles to the west. After takeoff, I directed the student to climb out to the northwest over a little-used practice area to the edge of the cloud deck.

We climbed up to about 3,000 feet and doubled back over the top of the cloud layer. I could see the tops of a familiar group of mountains sticking up through the clouds about five miles to the east, so I knew our position over the ground though it was obscured beneath us. Explaining the "spin through the overcast" technique to Pete, I talked him through a spin entry at about 200 feet above the top of the pillowy cloud layer. The entry was good, and we plunged into the clouds.

Immediately all sense of motion ceased. It's a very strange sensation sitting in a cloud with the stick all the way back and full rudder on, watching the altimeter unwind. I periodically cleared the engine and looked back at Peter to reassure him. We should break out in a few seconds, I thought. The time dragged by and still we sat there, an opaque whiteness all around us. The altimeter was unwinding very slowly, I felt a slight buffeting and fought back an impulse to make a recovery. Finally, after an eternity, we broke out and the ground came into view with a pinwheeling rush. We made our recovery and looked around. We were at about 1,800 feet. I could see the field to the southeast, but the sight that chilled me was that of the mountain range sticking up into the overcast about a mile off our wingtip. These were the peaks that had been five miles away when we entered the overcast. Somehow, we'd been blown about four miles to the east during the time we were spinning in the cloud.

While my student was flying the ship back to the field, I soberly reflected on the folly of my overzealous demonstrations. We could very easily have been carried farther into the mountains, with disastrous results, to say nothing of the fact that I had completely ignored the current regulations regarding proximity to clouds for VFR flight—all this with a student pilot whose training and guidance were my responsibility. I determined then and there to confine my flight demonstrations in the future to those approved in the curriculum, and to limit my instructions for unusual inflight situations to the blackboard.

I realized I had allowed my enthusiasm for realistic training to overrule my judgment, and by setting this poor example of flight safety, I had probably been achieving the opposite of my goal of producing safe pilots.

After parking the ship on the line, I went over the flight with my student. I pointed out the dangers we had been exposed to, some of which he was already aware of. I cautioned him against any repetition of this sort of thing when on his own, and further, that with any degree of foresight, the chances of a pilot ever getting into a situation where such a remedy might be valid were so remote as to be almost nonexistent.

●

Good intentions don't count with mountains. It's probably safe to say that his students were lucky that incident occurred or they might have continued to get that same "lesson" and might have tried the technique one day. Spinning down through cloud is no longer legal for precisely the reason that was illustrated by that little adventure story.

Garland Lincoln did the first in the series of pilot-written true stories collected in this book. He too was nearly the victim of his own good intentions when he pressed beyond the redline limit of weather and pilot skill to rescue a missing Russian crew in Alaska.

●

Maybe you remember. Sigismund Levanevsky, the famous Russian aviator, and a crew of five had been pushing a four-motor Russian job over the hump from Moscow to Los Angeles—smack across the Pole. One flight had been successful, and there was talk of a Moscow-America airline.

The four-motor job was making a survey. It had lifted out of Moscow, streaked across the Pole and was winging it down the 148th meridian when the world last heard. There were planes from all parts of Alaska scheduled to fly into Point Barrow (where Will Rogers and Wiley Post lost their lives) to continue the search.

The report came down from Point Barrow that there was no hope of making an adequate search unless the rescue fliers had gasoline, and there was none at Point Barrow. Harbors were packed with ice, the seas were filled with icebergs and pack ice and it was impossible to get to Point Barrow with vessels. The only answer to the problem was aerial—a cargo airplane must be equipped with tanks and sent north.

The only ship available was a Ford Trimotor at Los Angeles, a 14-passenger job with three Wasps totaling about 1,500 horsepower. I was chosen as pilot; Frank Tomick would be my copilot and Charles Marshall, one of the motion picture industry's best-known flying cameramen, was assigned to go along to film the rescue attempts—and possibly the rescue. I know none of us would have stepped into that ship had we known what lay ahead.

The trip north was financed by the head of an American oil company. Under my supervision, the seats were taken out of the Ford, and gasoline tanks capable of holding 1,800 gallons and oil tanks with 450 gallons' capacity were installed. I lined up a lot of Commander Byrd's equipment, including a rubber boat, sled and ice picks, and stowed it away. We were ready to go.

Bear in mind that the gasoline tanks so filled the rear compartment that the door was no longer usable, and to get in and out of the ship it was necessary to use a steel ladder to climb on top. From that point, we dropped in through the emergency hatch over the cockpit. In case of trouble, we had to go out the same way.

The first leg from Los Angeles to an Indian village was uneventful, save that we encountered a lot of bad weather; but we pushed right through that. We were on a rescue mission and the chief item, to our way of thinking, was elapsed time. I really poured the coal to the old Ford, and we stopped only for refueling, and then not for long. Gasoline and oil were available at Fairbanks, so we were traveling with empty cargo tanks.

When we finally found our way into the Indian village, we were told, "You'd better not go on. Weather's bad. Fog's right down on the ground."

"But we have to go on," I told my informers. "To save the Russians, the searchers must have gasoline."

Ceiling was zero at this point and we stuck around for just a little while hoping for a break. We didn't get it, so Frank, Charlie and I climbed up the steel ladder, dropped into the cockpit and took off into the soup. I climbed for about 45 minutes as there were a lot of mountains around and I didn't want to get messed up in them. At 15,000 we were still in soup; we never came out of it at all.

I had done a little groundwork and was flying by dead reckoning. Luckily, the same weather conditions that brought the fog and clouds had brought no wind. The air was dead, so I merely had the job of figuring my course with three compasses, allowing for variation and deviation. We were on course about two hours, when Marshall said, "The radio's dead."

About this time we were beginning to ice up a little, so I guessed what had happened: The antenna had iced up. But I hadn't guessed all of it. It had iced up and broken off. So we just pretended we hadn't brought along a radio. I watched my instruments plenty carefully.

I'd done a lot of blind flying before, but never had I been so dependent on instruments. We pounded north, and I watched the minutes ticking by, checking my airspeed indicator among other things, and trying to figure what I must be over if I was on course. Then, about 125 miles south of Fairbanks, I got my one and only break. We came out of weather into a comparatively clear section. The ground wasn't visible, but I could see mountains. I recognized them, from previous trips, as a range bordering the Pacific at Sitka.

Then we ran into soup again. I flew for a few minutes over an hour, and then throttled back. I signaled Frank and Charlie to come close.

"We're over Fairbanks," I said, "And we're going down." I began my glide.

"How do you know?" Tomick asked.

"I just feel that way," I said. That was all I was ever able to say about the strange hunch I had. I went down and down and down, until instinct told me that if I didn't level off pretty soon I was going to plow into something. The elevation of Fairbanks and my altimeter just about coincided. But we couldn't see anything.

"Get out of this," Frank said. "If you don't, we'll hit something sure."

"Pull up," Charlie urged. "Maybe this mess'll lift."

"Okay," I agreed. "We've got just about two hours of gas."

So up I went. The minutes dragged by into one hour, and then into two hours. During this time we did a lot of work.

"It looks like a crash," I told my companions. "We might as well make it as safe as possible."

That was just like saying that we had an hour or so to live. But the boys went to work. They disconnected the batteries, they disconnected the radio and they tied everything down. Then Charlie got the portable typewriter and started writing his will—he wrote it nine times. In fact, he was still writing it when we hit. Just as we were getting down to our last gasoline, I told the boys:

"I'm going into a power dive at a safe altitude. I'll open all the motors wide, and then I'll cut the master switch. That'll let anyone know—provided I'm right and we're still in the vicinity of Fairbanks—that we're making a crash landing."

I did just that. As the motors coughed for the last time, Frank cut off the main lines and leads, kicked the safety valves open, and down we came. I leveled off considerably, until we were gliding between 58 and 65 mph.

The first things I saw were three spruce trees, almost directly ahead of me, then a sort of brown grass. I missed the trees, hit what I thought was the grass. It wasn't grass; it was marsh, or tundra—a mucky, messy, watery formation like a bog. The ship skidded across it for about 75 feet, started settling and then rolled over on its back. We were down, all right—and how!

Muck and slime were pouring into the ship and it was settling into the slop. We couldn't get out at the rear because of the empty gasoline tanks, so I smashed the cockpit windows. Ooze and slime poured in. But I poured out. I grabbed at Tomick.

"I'm stuck!" he yelled. "Something's grabbed me!"

He had his left foot stuck in the wheel of one of the cockpits. Charlie came out last. There we were, ship upside down and sinking fast in the muck. We were pondering what to do, when we heard yells. Pretty soon some men came up.

"Where are we?" was my first question.

"About half a mile from the edge of Fairbanks," one fellow said. "We've been listening to you for the last couple of hours."

I don't know and never will know how I did it, but the point of the story is this: I never should have done what I did, even with orders to get through any way possible. Good navigation? Yes. Good piloting, as far as handling the controls was concerned? Yes.

But there, on the tundra, lay the wreck of a good airplane. By the grace of God—and I say that with all due respect—three men who had been in the ship were alive. The plane itself could never perform the service for which it was intended. In fact, with motors gone, I hear it is still bogged down in the ooze of that tundra. We learned later that the Russians had undoubtedly struck an iceberg and had perished. Three deaths might have been added to six.

The lesson I learned? Whether or not lives are at stake, taking chances is silly. A lot of us take chances in airplanes every day with no lives at stake. We get all excited about something that has to be done and we fly madly to do it. Sometimes the results are disastrous.

Today, after that experience, no matter how urgently I may think I have to go someplace, I stay on the ground unless the flight looks reasonably possible to make successfully.

●

Maybe Lincoln figured that clouds parted for rescue missions. His story illustrates how a pilot's attitude can influence judgment. The right attitude in the wrong context too often leads to trouble.

A fairly new pilot who takes off on a weekend to practice landings certainly has the proper attitude; not when pride and complacency interfere, though.

●

It was October, and the coolness of autumn in central New York was upon us, along with what seemed like rain every weekend—weekends that I had previously spent flying about the beautiful Finger Lakes countryside. I have always considered myself a safe, careful pilot; I never enjoyed taking chances and have always scrupulously preflighted my aircraft, planned my courses carefully, and spent hours just practicing simple turns, flying omni radials and shooting touch-and-goes at local airports. In this way, I had accumulated about 300 hours of flight time, including about 15 hours with an instrument instructor.

My airplane, a Cherokee 180, is kept in top condition by two of my partners, who know considerably more about airplanes and engines than I. I have always rested comfortably in the knowledge that it was perfectly maintained. Later, I would only wish that I could have been as secure in my own knowledge and skill during the events that were to come to pass.

A light rain continued through Sunday morning and into the afternoon, but visibility seemed good. I was impatient with the drizzle and aching to get into the air again, so I decided to drop out to the airport and do a little flying as long as visibility held. Anyway, I wouldn't be wandering very far from home.

Taxiing out to the runway, I noticed the wind was out of the south—not blowing hard, but steadily. The small strip at which we keep our plane is exactly that: a small strip. It is a narrow, undulating ribbon on oil and stone that nicks the prop during run-up and defies a good landing in a gusty crosswind. It was built across a small valley in an east-west direction, and on the western end the runway is only a few feet wider than the wings of our plane. Because of this, I always practiced takeoffs and landings from a friend's grass field, about 12 miles away, and as I lifted from our own runway that Sunday afternoon, that's where I headed.

The light rain pattered gently on the Plexiglas, but visibility was good in all directions. In a matter of minutes, I was circling the 2,400-foot grass field for my first landing of the day.

I called on unicom and asked if there was any traffic in the area, or if the field was muddy from three days of rain.

"No traffic," my friend replied, "and the field is wet, but not soft."

By then, I was on downwind and beginning to turn on my base leg. I looked over the wing at the runway. I saw to my surprise that the south wind had been blowing harder than I realized; I was already almost in line with Runway 27, and hadn't yet turned final. I pulled the plane around in a tight turn to the left and angled in toward the runway.

Damn, I thought, now I'm too high!

Pulling full flaps, I dropped the nose and descended toward the runway, still fighting a steady crosswind. I neared the threshold—still high. I looked at the airspeed indicator, and it read about 15 mph too fast. I had to slow down to get this thing on the ground!

I pulled the nose up to slow the plane and begin a faster descent. The runway was running out on me, but I was almost down. I pushed in the carb heat and thought of going around. No! I knew there were people in the little shack near the end of the strip, and I knew how they joked after a botched approach. Besides, I had landed this far down the runway before, and I was positive I could brake to a quick stop.

I was positive, that is, until immediately after touchdown. As I felt the main gear hit, I lowered the nose, dumped the flaps and stepped on the toe brakes—but nothing happened. I didn't seem to be slowing at all. The wet grass! I continued sliding down the runway, at first pumping the brakes, and then, in desperation, I was practically standing on them. I began skidding to the left, off the edge of the runway, the airplane now turned sideways. I bounced down through a shallow, grass-covered ditch and out the other side. By now, I had turned completely around and was sliding backward. As the plane slowly continued turning, it came to rest just inches away from a car parked at the side of the field. I went limp in the cockpit, my feet still pressing the toe brakes.

Though damage to the airplane was relatively minor—the nosegear and left main were bent—I had ruined what should have been an accident-free record, and could have caused much more serious damage, all because I had neglected a few rules of common sense and good practice.

First, because practicing landings was something I did often, I had become complacent, neglecting the whole purpose of practicing them—to keep myself aware and accurate. I had allowed myself to drift much too close to the runway on downwind, my base leg had not been long enough to compensate for the drift and I found myself high and fast on final. The simple, basic landing pattern had not been used for its purpose—to adjust the final approach for a smooth landing.

Second, I knew I was too high and I knew I was too fast, and I knew I should have aborted and gone around, but pride, that little leprechaun in the back of my mind, helped me make the wrong decision.

Next, and an important lesson for me: I had landed long on the same runway in the past, and always managed to brake to a stop with room left at the end of the runway. However, wet grass is as slippery as ice at landing speeds, and should be approached with caution, room to spare and a light touch on the brakes.

●

Pride dented, gear bent, but unhurt at least, our hero found new meaning in patterns and in practicing. As usual, the most meaningful lessons are those that come hardest.

And having learned, is one insured against recurrence? No way. Robert Blodget's classic gear-up story really has two lessons in it.

●

One of aviation's most enduring folk sayings refers to gear-up landings. "There are those who have, and there are those who are going to." It has the weight of age and the ring of truth. Each pilot who starts flying retractables swears to himself that he is going to change things and confound his elders. He will, he is sure, be the first who hasn't, and who isn't gonna. Many have succeeded, so far.

While founding what may have been the first scheduled air-taxi service, some years ago, I bought a secondhand twin Cessna—a converted UC-78, sometimes called the Bamboo Bomber—and put it through annual inspection. The work was badly done and had to be done over again. I made one test flight, found a few squawks, and our chief mechanic worked them off. On the following flight, as I was turning from downwind to base, I saw another of my airplanes flying a head-on collision course with an airline DC-3. The airport had no control tower, and unicom hadn't been invented, so all I could do was watch. Both pilots saw the problem and took evasive action, and I don't suppose it could even be called a near-miss today. I turned final, and landed. I remember writing on my kneepad, while the dust was settling: "gear horn inop."

It's true what they say about belly landings in UC-78s: Just jack them up, drop the gear, put on new propellers and fly away. In my case, new tires were indicated, though neither had gone flat.

Our mechanic was distressed; said it was his fault, because the horn wasn't working. I didn't agree—and still don't—because I had plain forgot the gear. The near midair had interrupted my sequence. I decided that in the future, anytime any routine was broken, I would pull up and start again from the beginning. I did this, too, for the next 21 years, covering many hundreds of successful landings in a wide range of retractable singles and twins, mixed with thousands of fixed-gear landings.

Then, last March, I attended a soaring wave camp at Minden, Nevada. One of my friends took me for a wave ride in a Schweizer 2–32, and we reached nearly 22,000 feet before the downwind lenticular and the upwind cap cloud came close enough together to shut us off. This was a remarkable experience, and in return, I offered him a ride in my Beech Sierra. He wanted to photograph some of the outlying fields, so I put him in the left seat, where he could take pictures through the pilot's weather window. (This was doubly legal: Not only is there no law about where the pilot in command must sit, but I had had my instructor certificate renewed two months before.)

Coming back, we made a circuit around Carson City for more pictures, then returned to Minden, where I began planning my approach. Just as I was beginning my prelanding preparations, my companion asked if I could do a circuit around Minden, so that he could take pictures of the assembled sailplanes. Of course I did.

The landing was completely normal up to the time when the noise began, which was on ground contact. It turns out that the 1972 Beech Sierras also land beautifully with the gear up. The Sierra has cabin doors on both sides, and each door has its own entrance step. The result is that we landed on the two steps and the side of the nosewheel fork, grinding all three down some during the process. In the earlier models, the step on the right side would probably have caused the left wing to hit the ground, and that would have been an accident rather than an incident. Like the UC-78, all we had to do was hoist the Sierra, put the gear down, replace the propeller and fly home.

There were two things in common in both my gear-up landings: an interruption of routine, and a gear-warning horn that didn't work. In the later case, I had closed the throttle completely at 100 feet, and could easily have put the gear down or gone around if the horn had been doing its thing.

However, there was one additional factor. I was flying from the right seat, and our habit patterns are so delicate that it doesn't take much to cause a major upset in our responses.

A soaring pilot friend who flies big airplanes for United as a hobby tried to comfort me. He said, "As long as these machines are being flown by human beings, the human beings are going to make mistakes. The gear horn is there to help keep you from making a mistake; that's why it's required. If it isn't working, you don't have the system support you are supposed to have. That's why an airplane with the warning circuit inoperative isn't airworthy."

Well, thanks, captain. Nice try—but it's not enough, and I'll tell you why.

The head of the Reno General Aviation District Office came down to Minden and talked to me about the incident. He asked what I usually do before landing, and I told him that I usually put the wheels down first. He suggested that it might be a good idea to go back to the old military practice of checking the gear-warning horn in the prelanding sequence.

How right he was! This same airplane had had a previous warning-horn failure, found at the first hundred-hour inspection. That time, the bracket holding the switch had cracked. In my subconscious mind, I must have felt that fixed was fixed; and how many times can a warning system fail, for heaven's sake? But wouldn't you have thought, after my first experience, that I would thereafter have been as suspicious of warning-horn reliability as I am of the reliability of radios? Maybe not: If warning horns failed as often as radios, even I would suspect them. I do now, and my new standard procedure demands the throttle be closed enough to get the horn before I put the wheels down.

Finally, the old saying should be changed to: "There are those who have, and those who are going to, and those who are going to *again.*" After the first embarrassed shock faded, it slowly dawned on me—to my intense discomfort—that I had been taking *comfort* from the saying. I was one of those who *had,* therefore I wasn't *going to.* Like chicken pox, the measles, whooping cough and the mumps, I had had my gear-up landing, therefore that affliction couldn't strike me again.

Unfortunately, I have found that there is no such permanent inoculation against landings with the wheels in the wells, any more than there is a permanent prevention for the common cold or headache. You have to take a couple of pills each time, and the pills are contained in the prelanding checklist.

●

Then there is the hotshot, the show-off. He lurks in all of us, and all it takes is the temptation of a machine that presses pilot skills beyond the limit to confirm just how hazardous it can be to get in over your head.

A P-51 Mustang is the essence of such alluring airplanes. All pilots who have never flown one lust after the experience. Very few are born with the experience it takes to handle one, though. The war wasn't even over before one pilot had nearly bent himself on a solo "check ride" when he succumbed to the call of the P-51.

●

One sunny day late in World War II, I watched in awe as a badly shot-up P-51C sputtered onto the dirt-strip B-25 base where I was stationed on the east coast of Corsica. The -51 had been hit severely on a mission to southern France, and the wounded pilot was unable to make it back to his base in Italy.

The damaged fighter was turned over to our service group for repairs. I was then a 22-year-old B-25 pilot and, among other things, engineering test pilot for the group. I immediately began making quasi-legal plans to fly the ship when it was repaired. A quick look revealed that the checklist in the cockpit was torn in half—just below the takeoff data. The lower half was nowhere to be found, but as I checked the squadron bars, I uncovered one pilot who had flown the A-36 version of the Mustang. His only comment was, "Hell, just make your last turn like a B-25, at about 150, and you won't have any trouble." He seemed to feel that landing was the only important part of flying a P-51. There were no books in the aircraft, but to a 22-year-old this was not discouraging. I was amply confident; it had a stick and rudders, didn't it?

On the day of the flight, after dutifully buckling in, I taxied in sweeping S-turns to the end of the runway, checked the mags, dropped some flaps and cranked in five degrees of right rudder trim. I looked at the last remaining item on the checklist, which read, "takeoff power—61 inches." Now, to a B-25 pilot who got 44 inches at best out of his radial engines, a figure like 61 was hard to believe. I pushed the throttle to 45, then to 50 and finally locked it at 55.

Much of my anxiety prior to the flight had concerned torque (as it was known then), so I immediately stomped on the right rudder—which, of course, resulted in a 20-degree swerve to the right, followed by an instinctive opposite reaction that merely reversed the swerve. At this point, a still superbly unruffled, confident young pilot was covering 50 feet of runway laterally for every hundred forward. It dawned on me that I might be able to see better if I got the tail up, so a quick forward thrust of the stick popped the tail up so fast that the prop almost hit.

I snatched the stick back, and the cooperative bird tried to fly; alas, too soon, and it settled back. At this point, about halfway down the runway, a glance to the left disclosed the traffic controllers gathered on the tower balcony, roaring with unrestrained laughter. Angered at this disrespectful display, I wrenched the Mustang off the ground and began looking for the wheel handle, the location of which had slipped my mind during the events of the past few seconds.

With the eventual securing of the flaps and gear, and adjustment of the props and throttle to standard climb power, things began to look more normal. The confidence that had begun to wane slightly came flooding back. Now to get to the project of the day! The plan was to buzz the squadron area at treetop level, ending in a climbing roll. This would establish me as the hottest of the hot pilots.

First, however, I made the only intelligent move so far: The thought that it had been almost two years since flying a single-engine aircraft (an AT-6), and even longer since I'd tried a slow roll, suggested a practice roll. I quickly climbed to 4,000 feet (it should have been 15,000), leveled off, pulled the nose up, leaned on the left rudder and aileron and smoothly started to reverse the rudder as it passed the vertical. Suddenly, the blue Mediterranean was staring me in the face, and the increasing roar of the wind made it pretty clear that I was in the middle of a perfect split S. Chopping the throttle and sucking the stick back into my now-palpitating middle resulted in rounding out at about 800 feet, with the vibrating -51 indicating somewhere in the neighborhood of 380 mph.

A careful 10 seconds of analysis led me to the conclusion that I was applying no forward pressure. Now caution crept in. I climbed to 5,000, saying over and over to myself, "Watch the forward pressure." Again a fairly smooth entry, but this time, as the wings passed the vertical, I came through with ample forward pressure. Too ample, in fact, for the aircraft suddenly shuddered, did something resembling a half snap (I think) and turned right side up going in almost the opposite direction. The severe vibration aft during this maneuver was so bad that I looked back at the tail to be sure it was still there. (Later, I was told that the P-51 was firmly restricted against these tricks and had been known to separate at the tail when subjected to such stress.)

A bit shaken at this point, I decided to terminate today's practice session. The buzz job/slow roll would be postponed until tomorrow. Entering the pattern and lowering some flaps and the gear without incident, I made the last turn about where a B-25 turns final. During the turn, I lowered full flaps and rolled out rather smoothly. Everything looked lovely, except for one hitch: Bushes flashed past the window and I was still a hundred yards short of the runway.

At this point, the reason for the airplane's having a boosted MP of 61 inches of mercury became quite obvious: It took all of that to drag this unwilling aircraft to the runway. Over the fence at an elevation of three feet, I chopped the throttle, hit the ground with a thud and eased back in the seat as the ship slowed. The sigh of relief could be heard over the throb of the idling engine. "My God, the engine!" A huge cloud of black smoke now poured from the exhaust pipes, owing to the thoroughly fouled sparkplugs. That last act of stupidity earned the malice of the crew chief, who spent the next day replacing all 24 sparkplugs.

In retrospect, the hour-and-a-half ride (and all ensuing rides) in this magnificent airplane has remained etched in my memory —if only because it made me realize what my first flying instructor had meant when he said, "If you don't know, don't go."

●

Oh, how sly and malevolent is that urge to strut across the stage of air when the pilot knows there is an audience! Like the little devil perched on one shoulder in the cartoons, it whispers into the airman's ear, "Show 'em how it's done! You can do it!" The eyes narrow, a hint of a grin appears—and caution exits, bailing out while the going is good.

●

Most pilots at one time or another dream Walter Mitty dreams of flat-hatting a desert gunnery range at 600 knots in an F-4 Phantom, but the majority of us recognize the idiocy of attempting such antics without the proper training or equipment.

I, for one, was firmly convinced that buzzing was for birdbrains. Though tempted while a student pilot to take my rented Piper Colt over the sailboats in Los Angeles Harbor in a screaming, 110-mph low pass, the very real possibility of a judgment error, imaginary overwater downdrafts and the remote likelihood of a power failure kept me above 500 feet. Even then, I had the uncomfortable feeling that I shouldn't be flying that low, legal or not, and the urge to buzz remained rightfully repressed by common sense. My common sense, though, turned out to be a commodity of quite finite dimension.

My wife and I had nearly concluded a successful two-day cross-country trip from Los Angeles to Venice, Florida, a fast transit of nearly 2,300 miles in 13 hours. The winds at altitude had been howling out of the west as we departed Los Angeles, and these welcome tailwinds, reaching 50 knots on one leg across Texas, pushed us to northern Florida as if we had acquired an extra engine. Our Bellanca Cruisemaster normally clipped off the miles at 160 per, but these winds allowed us to bite off real estate in hourly 200-mile chunks.

We'd stopped at Fort Walton Beach, Florida, the second night and had added an extra coat of wax to the wings; that would impress the relatives we'd be meeting in Venice the following day.

Our trip down the peninsula was a short, smooth two and a half hours through broken blue skies dotted with puffy cumulus clouds. The turquoise waters of the Gulf of Mexico sparkled beneath our right wing in the early-morning sun. Cross City, Crystal River and Tampa drifted by below. As I pushed the Bellanca downhill over Sarasota, I began to wonder if perhaps a low pass might not be an appropriately spectacular way to arrive at Venice. My relatives would be waiting and watching for a blue-and-white triple-tail Bellanca that they'd never before seen—we had just bought it—and I decided to give them something to look at.

Five miles north of Venice, I dialed 122.8 and pushed the mike button.

"Venice Unicom, this is Bellanca 6586 November. Airport advisory, please."

After a short pause, the speaker above my head crackled back, "Bellanca Eight-Six November, Venice. Winds calm, using Runway 9. No reported traffic."

"Okay, Venice," I answered. "How about a low pass for the troops?"

"At your discretion, Eight-Six November," came the reply.

My wife expressed some halfhearted objections to the low pass, but I assured her I knew what I was doing, despite never having done it before.

I circled the airport at 1,500 feet and could see no other airplanes moving on the ground or in the air. Convinced that the pattern was clear, I swung back out over the water on a wide downwind and turned an extended base two miles from the runway.

The rationalizations were lined up back to back, and the pilot's brain was down and locked. Venice Airport was an uncontrolled field, so there was no tower to worry about. Even if it had been a controlled airport, my speed would be at or below the limit for an airport traffic area. The morning was winter-clear and dead calm. The approach to Runway 9 was an unobstructed overwater final that crossed a deserted beach and met the threshold a scant 100 yards from the Gulf of Mexico. I'd overflown the airport and had advised unicom of my intentions. They'd expressed no objections and confirmed by visual observation of "no reported traffic."

I rolled the Bellanca into an easy 30-degree bank to line up with the runway and pushed power and yoke forward simultaneously. The airspeed needle walked around the dial as the tach ran higher and settled on 2,550 rpm. Three hundred yards from the beach, I leveled the airplane at 100 feet altitude and watched the airspeed climb to 180 mph.

I saw the Cherokee coming straight at me as I flashed across the beach. The red-and-white 140 had just lifted off halfway down the runway and was spinner up and climbing. I was stupefied that I hadn't seen it taxiing out and that the pilot had apparently chosen to depart against traffic, but there wasn't time to argue right of way. Instinctively, I yanked the Bellanca into a steep right turn and watched the wing cross the tops of palm trees seemingly only inches away. The G force sucked me down into the seat as I mouthed silent obscenities at damn-fool Cherokee pilots and exhibitionist Bellanca owners. The Cherokee disappeared to my left, its pilot apparently oblivious to the near-midair we had collectively (or so I thought) perpetrated. When I was well clear of the airport and the offending Cherokee was out of sight, I pulled up to 1,000 feet and reentered the pattern for Runway 9.

My wife had remained silent during our misadventure, but her silence ended when we touched down and taxied past a windsock waving lazily *away* from us. Between my radio call and our low pass, a slight offshore breeze had drifted across the field. My landing and earlier ill-advised buzz job had been downwind. Though the Cherokee pilot had failed to advise unicom of his takeoff, he or she had selected the proper runway. Because of my ignorance, the Cherokee pilot had almost been dead right.

Fortunately, neither the expected relatives nor anyone else witnessed my abortive ego trip. The family was nowhere to be seen and the ramp deserted when we taxied in and shut down.

As I sat, trying to calm down and reconsider what had just occurred, I was grateful for the absence of an audience.

●

Sometimes showing off can take strange forms. An airline copilot who sat sweating through an eerie experience learned how dangerous it can be to impress others with how cool and calm you are when the chips are down. Was the Captain in this weird tale showing off, overconfident—or was he just hypnotized?

●

The needles lie almost horizontal. During my eight months of service as an airline copilot, I have never seen fuel gauges quite this low. My right hand, which holds the copilot's microphone, is soaked with perspiration. My eyes move slowly from the two fuel gauges to the outline of the man in the left seat. He sits as placid now as he did when it all began. Rain moves in small puddles across the windshield. The last grays of early evening melt into cold blackness. We begin another left turn.

Once again our aircraft is outbound in the holding pattern. Approach control originally promised a delay of less than 30 minutes before our turn to land. That promise is now one hour and 20 minutes old. The Captain reaches above his head to adjust the rheostat that controls cockpit lighting, and the lights bathing the flight instruments dim. The clouds disappear into the growing darkness outside, and all that remains in the windshield is the reflection of our own faces. The sound of the engines is steady, deep, solid.

The Captain is a man of middle age, average height and moderate weight. His face and stomach show the beginning of chubbiness. He has small fingers and wears a shirt that's too tight; it causes the skin on his neck to lap over the collar. His eyes are fixed on the instruments as he steers our Convair 440. He has both hands on the control column. The reflection of his face in the window is amazingly clear, and I can watch him without feeling conspicuous. Although his stare is both narrow and apparently concentrated, his attentions seem hypnotized;

no muscle strain, no lines of worry, none of the telltale movements of tension. If anything, he seems too calm, too serene, too unaffected. He sits as if he were in another world—as if the ticking clock and sinking fuel gauges didn't belong to our airplane, one he is both riding in and responsible for.

We are perilously low on fuel, and I am feeling a rattling of discomfort through my belly. "Should I get the latest weather?" I blurt in a voice that seems not my own. The question is more impulsive than logical, and I'm sorry I've spoken. Getting a weather report for this or any other facility would be a useless gesture. The opportunity to divert to an alternate has long since passed: We have already used so much fuel that we have barely enough to land at the airport below us.

Yet the Captain makes no move to inform anyone of our condition. Apparently, he has not heard my question, since he continues to sit in silence, his attention concentrated upon the flight instruments. Earlier, I had asked if I should tell approach control that we are low on fuel. "No, they'll get to us pretty soon," he said. I asked again later, after we had consumed even more of our remaining fuel. This time my question was ignored. He just sat there, as he sits now, wrapped in a wall of silence.

The thought of taking over has reluctantly occurred to me. For the first time, I understand what a tremendous step such an action requires. Sitting in an operations room crowded with copilots and bragging about telling off the captain is one matter; sitting in the right seat while the aircraft pitches and rolls through the heavy mist is quite another.

It seems unreal. The whole situation—the aircraft, the instruments, the weather—has become something other than what it was. I can understand the hypnotic condition of the Captain; I am almost in that state myself. There is, at this moment, no danger. We are quite comfortable, and the aircraft gently rocks us to sleep. We hold wheels and play with switches that are as familiar as home. We wrap the soothing engine sounds and the reassuring touch of our well-fitted cockpit around us. All is well because we are still comfortable. All is well, all is well.

The danger is in our imagination. It requires the efforts of imagination to push the fuel-gauge needles down to the very bottoms of the scales. By easing that thought from our minds, we remain comfortable. The airplane is, at this very moment, very comfortable.

But I must act. The pedestal, with its radio controls and engine levers, lies between us. I lean against it, and like a swimmer going upstream, I sense the force of the current. The words are in my throat. I take a deep breath.

I am saved from the struggle. The current has reversed. The cockpit speaker has announced, "Cleared for the approach." We begin a descent.

We review the approach plate. I emphasize field elevation once, then twice. There is no turning back; there remains no alternative. We must descend, if necessary, right to field elevation in an attempt to locate the airport. There is not enough fuel to do anything else.

The wipers beat up and down against the windshield. There is still nothing in the window but the reflections of our own faces. I tell myself it is still early on the approach. The weather is reported to be slightly above minimums.

Beacon inbound. Descend. Rain, and nothing else. "Go down a little lower!"

"A light!" No. Yes! A string of lights! The airport! "The runway, straight ahead," I announce, keeping myself from shouting only by the greatest of effort. We cross the threshold. We have saved ourselves.

"That sure took a long time," the Captain says—his only comment as we taxi in. We shut down at the gate and he hauls himself from his seat, leaves the airplane and walks into the terminal building. I sit alone, and the euphoria that filled me as we found the runway begins to fade. The fuel gauges persist like a bad dream. We have, at most, 15 minutes of flying remaining in the tanks.

"Where is the Captain?" comes a voice from behind. The stewardess. She has some minor problem that requires his attention. "Inside," I respond, more by pointing than speaking. "Oh, darn," she says in a tone of slight irritation. "Some captains are just never here when you need them!"

The needles move up almost imperceptibly as the fuel truck pumps gas on board for the next flight.

●

There is something very sinister about the force that urges the pilot to get there—and thereby ignore the known limits upon human performance and that of the airplane.

In this next hair-raising account, forgetting the human limits —in this case, the effect of high altitude with no oxygen—nearly led to the overstepping of the limit upon the airplane's range, namely, its usable fuel.

●

It was 2:25 P.M. Pacific Daylight Time and a beautiful autumn day when I lifted the nosewheel of the Cessna 175 off the runway at Marysville, California. I was on a flight plan from Marysville to Denver, Colorado, with a gas stop scheduled at Salt Lake City. During the preflight, I had made sure that the tanks were filled and found everything perfect at run-up. Furthermore, I felt fit and relaxed, the terminal and en-route weather was good, and an 8- to 10-knot tailwind was reported at 15,000 feet.

As we climbed out over Grass Valley, I thought of a conversation I'd had with my partner, a Navy jet pilot, about cruise control. He claimed that our airplane would burn 10 to 10.5 gallons per hour, whereas I claimed that I could get 7.5 gph without sacrificing speed. I decided this was the opportune time to prove my theory. The flight plan called for 15,500 feet, even though we had no oxygen system. I had flown without oxygen for as long as four hours at this altitude many times in my 25 years of flying, and I felt it would be no problem.

After leveling off at cruise altitude, I leaned the mixture to the optimum setting and computed my true airspeed to be 132 mph. Then I sat back to wait for my gas stop to show up. By the time I reached Elko, Nevada, I was certain I could make Rock Springs, Wyoming, with the fuel I had on board, and even Denver was a possibility. I could not compute exact fuel consumption, because the gas gauges were marked off in quarters, but I estimated a total available flying time of eight hours, or better than 1,000 miles' range.

Four hours after takeoff, Salt Lake City showed up on time. I was enjoying the last rays of the sun, while the city beneath me was already in the shadows and crisscrossed with lights. To the east, the sky was turning blue-black, and an occasional star was visible. At this point, the left tank finally went dry. I switched to the right tank, a little puzzled that I had gotten so far on 26 gallons of gas. My computer indicated that I had used about 6.5 gallons per hour. This was better than I had ever done, and I wondered about it. To keep ATC advised that I was changing my gas stop to Rock Springs, I notified Salt Lake Radio to change my flight plan accordingly.

As I passed over the Wasatch Range, the mountains were beautiful in the gathering darkness, especially since there were no rocks at my altitude. Over Fort Bridger I had a slightly uncomfortable feeling when I noticed that the needle of the right gas gauge was moving faster than the left had moved. However, I still had plenty of gas, and I had climbed to 17,500 feet to get over a little weather that I had encountered. By now it was truly dark, as the desolate country can easily get. Eventually, the lights of Rock Springs came into view and I began a descent. By the time I had dropped to 15,500 feet, I found I still had better than half a tank of gas. Boy, was I proving my theory about cruise control! I decided not to sacrifice the altitude by landing at Rock Springs, because I could let down more economically en route and not spoil my economy cruise. Having decided to go on, I radioed Rock Springs that I would gas up at Laramie. By eyeballing the gas gauge, I judged Laramie would be no problem, and that would be quite a distance nonstop.

Near Medicine Bow, still at 15,500 feet, and through scattered clouds, I could see the lights of Laramie. I homed on them, knowing the Medicine Bow mountains were to my right. This was truly a wonderful ride. Under me, the earth was completely black, and I shrugged off the problems that a forced landing might offer in this deserted, rugged area. I trimmed the airplane slightly nose-down. Arriving over Laramie, I still had a quarter of a tank of gas at about 14,000 feet. By this time I was considering the flight to Denver nonstop as a challenge, and I was reading the gas gauge every minute, leaning over to the right side of the cabin to eliminate parallax, using my flashlight to get an accurate reading. Highly pleased with the plane's performance to this point, and to prove my statements beyond a doubt, I decided, yes, I could make Denver nonstop from Marysville, California. I radioed Laramie that I was proceeding to Denver. Again I trimmed the airplane and eased back the throttle to get the best economy. By now I could see the glow of the Denver lights in the night sky on the horizon. As the airplane gradually lost altitude, I watched the lighted strip at Fort Collins, Colorado, creep by under me. Lighted strips are rare in this country. Everything was fine! I had one-eighth of a tank of gas and 12,000 feet. Denver nonstop would be nip-and-tuck, but I was proving my claim. Slightly apprehensive, I trimmed the airplane nose-down a little more, and this act probably was to save my life and the airplane.

Now I had a sixteenth of a tank of gas at 9,000 feet, and under me it was wall-to-wall black except for a few lights on the highway 10 miles or more away.

Suddenly I realized what was going on. Here I was, happily

running out of gas at night! My mouth became dry and the palms of my hands moist as I tried to figure out how I let myself get into this mess. Strangely enough, I was more concerned with my past than with my immediate future. By now I was listening for the engine to miss a beat, indicating the last of the gas supply, and I was carefully watching the gas gauge needle bump bottom. At the same time, I was looking for any lights that might be helpful in making a landing. Fort Collins was now too far behind me and Denver looked to be too far ahead. I thought of the Boulder Airport and decided to land there for gas no matter what. The thought struck me that it was entirely possible that I wouldn't make Boulder. Now I was nursing that throttle and counting the revolutions of the engine. Then I remembered I was close to Longmont; I was sure it had a lighted strip. In a couple of minutes that seemed like a week, the beautiful lights of the Longmont Airport appeared. I called Denver Radio and canceled my flight plan. Maintaining altitude until I had the runway made, I chopped the throttle and glided in for a landing. It was 9:15 P.M. Mountain Standard Time. The airport attendant and I put 49.5 gallons of gas in tanks that hold 52 gallons. According to my computer, I had 19 more minutes of flying left.

As it turned out, I would have made Jeffco Airport at Denver, but I probably would have had to push the airplane to the parking area. I was quite shaken. After two cups of coffee and 30 minutes to calm my jangled nerves, I took off from Longmont and about 15 minutes later touched down at Jeffco. I tied down, transferred my luggage to the car and drove home, pondering how I had gotten into such a tight fix, and just how tight it was.

Slowly, it dawned.

Many times I had been at that altitude for a four-hour period without oxygen, but never for a seven-hour period. I had covered 1,000 miles with an average speed of 133 miles per hour and a gas consumption of 7.4 gallons per hour. Great. But what about me? I had suffered from hypoxia, or lack of oxygen at altitude. Even after four hours, when the left tank went dry I should have known that my gas consumption was too low, which could only mean that gas from the full right tank was getting past the selector valve. After five hours at altitude, I had developed such a feeling of well-being that it was actually an amusing game to gamble on whether I could get to Denver nonstop. It wasn't until I reached 9,000 feet that I got enough oxygen in my blood to realize what a predicament I was in.

●

Fuel economy is an admirable goal, but to prove his point it certainly wasn't necessary to fly until the tanks were dry. Although all pilots are taught about the risks of hypoxia when they are beginning students, a surprising number feel they have to prove that their bodies are somehow immune to the need for oxygen.

At sea level, an oxygen shortage is no problem, but fatigue can still exert its pernicious influence; the results often mimic the symptoms of hypoxia. This harrowing account by a member of a helicopter crew describes eloquently a mission over water that led to vertigo. Ordinarily, a well-trained pilot recognizes vertigo and knows how to deal with it. In this case, fatigue overwhelmed the instincts of training in a crew that had been pushed beyond its limits.

●

There was a flap on. The squadron was preparing for a short at-sea training period, and the word had come down that we would run for 24 hours, and sharpen up on our primary antisubmarine-warfare mission and our secondary mission of air-sea rescue in order to make a good showing for the admiral. As a safety/survival instructor, I was somewhat concerned; I had only recently completed a series of lectures concerning "pushing" to our SH-3A Sea King helicopter crews. I had warned against "get-home-itis," making the days stretch, flying into marginal weather and accepting aircraft with minor deficiencies in order to meet a mission commitment or simply to arrive home in time for a party. Only half listening during the briefing and pondering the difference between mission, get-home-itis and hurry-up, I missed most of the weather and had to copy someone else's notes: No moon. Wind less than five knots. Sea slick. Caution—some advection-radiation fog along the coast. Should be able to get past it with no trouble. Keep your distance on the way out and there should be no problem.

The pilot was excellent, very qualified, and our copilot one of the more experienced junior men in the unit. My job was to evaluate a student crewman's ability, with both the electronic detection gear and the rescue hoist. My biggest concern was staying awake. Takeoff was 2 A.M.

"Whisper Five-Five to lift and depart the heliport; I have the numbers," the pilot called. The elements of the flight were to be spaced two minutes apart for separation.

"Five-Five, thank you."

The Sea King rose, hesitated at 15 feet. "Looks good," said the pilot. The copilot agreed.

We departed into the blackest night I've ever seen. The fog around Quonset Point diffused the light as soon as we passed over the edge of the sea wall. The pilot commented on the gloom as the helo rose smoothly to pass Fox Island at 200, the Jamestown Bridge at five, and proceeded level south to Point Judith on the right and Beavertail-Point, Conanicut Island, on the left. My student did the cabin check, returned to his seat and blew the verbal report with some sort of half-awake mishmash of words. He tried again and got it straight.

"Sonar," called the intercom, "stand by to mark dip."

"Standing by," my student replied, ready to drop the dome into the water. It was squadron procedure to check everything out just off Point Judith to avoid flying all the way out to the area and then discover that a piece of equipment that worked fine on the ground refused to perform aloft.

". . . cyclic coupler?" the pilot was calling.

"Set," the copilot replied. I realized that they were first going to attempt a Doppler radar automatic hover.

"Okay, be ready now," the pilot cautioned the copilot. "With a slick sea we have trouble getting a Doppler return. I want you to read my altitude off in 10-foot increments on the radalt, and if it looks like it isn't going to stop, I'll pickle the Doppler off and fly it out manually."

"Okay."

"Uh, sonar, we aren't going to dip this time, I just want to check the coupler. We'll drop it on the next one because I want to try an alternate also."

"Good enough," the student replied.

"Five-Five, marking dip."

"Coupler?"

"Engaged."

It was sick. The bottom fell out for the first 15 feet or so and the nose came up too rapidly. The pilot made the first mistake that made me decide that perhaps he hadn't had enough rest: he continued the approach.

"Forty (our hover altitude, where the helo should have stopped) . . . 30 . . . 20 . . ."

"I'm pickling." I breathed a sigh of relief as the Sea King rose. It was so dark we hadn't spotted the water, even that low.

"Okay, we'll try it once more before we head back," the pilot announced. Second mistake. Evidently command pressure had been heavy. Or else he was more tired than we thought. The student shot me a very odd look.

"Coupler?"

"Is engaged." The helo fell faster this time. The copilot's voice was pretty thin when he started calling off the altitude.

"Fifty . . . 40 . . . 30 . . . 20 . . ."

"I'm pickling."

The nose rose high and we slewed right. The aircraft seemed to be clawing for altitude. Instinct took over for a moment. I snapped the sonar off, determined not to be electrocuted should I live through impact. The student was now wide awake. In unison, we dropped our seats down and aft, locked our harnesses and threw arms over our faces. Meanwhile, the intercom conversation was terrifying.

"My God, I've got vertigo!" screamed the pilot. "Where's my nose? Where are the wings?"

"Okay," The copilot was on the case. "You got 15 degrees nose up, 10 degrees left wing down . . ."

I panicked. I was crammed into the right rear corner of my seat. He was calling the wrong wing down.

"I mean right wing . . . right wing . . ."

"What's my airspeed now?"

"Uh . . . 600 feet, zero airspeed, zero torque!"

We were falling straight out of the sky!

The Gs pulled at our faces, as the sound of aluminum hitting water filled our ears. Outside, I could see foam washing over the right sponson.

"Want me to take it?" The copilot's voice, a lot calmer.

"No." The pilot sounded drained. "I think I have it now." The nose was oscillating and the blades were making that peculiar whop-whop that goes with insufficient rotor speed.

"All right," said the copilot. "Get the nose over just a little more. Concentrate on your instruments. Don't move your head. Basic scan now. Keep the torque on it, damn it. You got altitude, wings are five right down. Don't overcorrect; *think* it level. That's good. I'm going to call Quonset."

"Quonset, Whisper Five-Five inbound from Point Judith for landing."

"Five-Five, maintain 600 feet over Jamestown Bridge, fly the right side, to clear the outbound helos, over," the tower replied.

"Negative, negative," the copilot shot back. "Have them

clear for us. Got an emergency. I want a straight-in to the heliport."

"Five-Five, roger as requested. What is your emergency?"

"Vertigo. Both pilots have vertigo."

I died.

"Break, break," another voice cut in. "Whisper One-Three, calling Five-Five. Turn off your bottom rotating beacon. Have a crewman do it. Don't turn your head."

My student unstrapped and reached the switch before I could move.

"Five-Five, One-Three, have you in sight. "We're rigged and following you in."

"Got it, thanks, Five-Five."

I dreaded the turn and climb we would have to make to get into Quonset. As we flew along, I began to wonder if the pilot, too, was sweating it out. We seemed to fly for too long a time, and I leaned out and up to see what was going on up front. Jamestown Bridge was straight ahead. We had, in addition to everything else, made a complete 180-degree turn!

"Five-Five, Fox with the gear," the pilot seemed to sigh on the radio.

"Roger, Five-Five. How you feeling now?" Tower came back.

"Pretty well now, thank you."

"Uh, roger, Five-Five. Want to cancel your emergency?"

"Uh, that's negative. I think I've pushed it far enough tonight."

7/FAR
OUT

Airplanes and people may have their limits, but there seems to be no limit on chance. Throw all the rules out the window and trash the training textbooks; when fate runs wild, it's like a crap game with three dice. This chapter deals with those one-of-a-kind tales that are so far out they absolutely, positively, without question could not happen again.

Well . . . probably not.

Most of them are so weird that they should not have happened at all. In that sense, one would have to admit that there is not much to be learned from them. Look again, though, and there is a lesson common to each and every story:

Pilots are, by nature, careful planners; if not by nature, then by training. To begin a flight without every contingency taken care of is to be sloppy in preparation, and there are rules against that. The rules make the pilot responsible for everything, in fact, and the fundamental assumption underlying all regulations is that the captain has the last word. (That's rather nice of the rule-makers, since they have made the captain responsible.) If there is a conflict between a traffic controller on the ground and the pilot in the air, it is the latter who holds sway. Sure, they may make life miserable for the poor wretch later if he or she should act contrary to the rules without a good reason, but no one would dare to question the prerogative of command while the aircraft is still airborne.

To be responsible is not always to be in control, however; that is the unique lesson offered by these wild and woolly happenings. Command is a heady sensation—until it comes up against the unanticipated freak occurrence. That's the moment when most airmen would gladly relinquish the left seat and let some other boob enjoy the privilege of figuring out what to do next.

This is, then, what it feels like to go from the modest but satisfying position of aircraft commander to that of test pilot— instantly.

●

It was one of those beautiful spring days that promise so much of summer and seem so especially wonderful coming fresh out of winter. I was at a small glider field just north of Pirmasens, Germany, flying a Sikorsky S-58 helicopter with another pilot and our crew chief in support of a military sky-diving club. We were providing a one-way elevator service, yo-yo-ing up and down with cargos of eager sky-divers.

This particular day I was flying for about 20 of them. They were a mixed group. Some were going up for the first time, while others had been jumping for 20 years. For one of the beginners, Gladys, a girl of about 20, I felt particularly sorry. It was obvious that she was scared to death. Her turn to go up was heralded by her lighting many cigarettes and then immediately stamping them out; quick, nervous knee bends and periods of rapid speech followed intervals of stricken silence. I expected her to faint when they gave her the nod that her turn had come.

One rule in sky-diving is that everyone is a volunteer. As a result, Gladys went up three times and came down with the helicopter three times. The day drew to a close without Gladys's joining the club.

The event of the day now approached. I was to take nine of the best jumpers up to 14,000 feet, where they would jump in groups and pass a baton from one to the other on the way down. Up to this point, my crew chief had had nothing to do. Supervision of all loading and unloading had been done by the jump master. When Gladys asked to go on the flight as crew chief to watch the jumpers, I agreed, never realizing the implications of my decision.

The S-58 is a powerful machine, but at 14,000 feet with 12 people aboard, the rotor blades stall at much lower indicated flight speeds, and the ship seems to wallow around like a drunken seal on a beachball.

I was much relieved when we finally reached the specified altitude and turned on course for the first jump. I followed the minute heading corrections repeated to me from below by my new crew chief and watched the first five jumpers get ready at the door. As the cross on the field far below appeared beneath us, all five pairs of boots turned sole upwards and fell away.

With this, my helicopter, like a seesaw when one occupant jumps off, turned on its tail and tried to become the first helicopter in orbit. Full forward control had little effect.

Without a crew chief to direct them otherwise, the jumpers in the rear of the ship had not moved forward from the tail. The five men who had jumped left us hopelessly out of balance, with nearly all the remaining passengers in the rear of the helicopter. We encountered unbelievable buffeting and audible flapping of the rotor blades. The helicopter wallowed from side to side, with every instrument on the panel swinging full range in both directions.

I hit the crew bailout alarm and prayed that those below could bail out before the helicopter broke up. The copilot and I had no parachutes. The helicopter gave every indication that it was going over on its back, which would have resulted in immediate collapse of the main rotor blades.

As quick as the situation had developed, it was over. The nose pitched down to a normal attitude, and we recovered control. I glanced down into the passenger compartment. There was no one to be seen. Where Gladys had stood minutes before, there swung only an empty headset.

We made a hurried descent, worrying about the condition of both our recent passengers and our badly stressed aircraft. On the ground we met a jubilant crowd of spectators who congratulated us on the most spectacular show they had ever seen.

Gladys was beside herself. She had made her first jump, and not just a 1,200-foot static-line jump at that, but an honest-to-goodness 14,000-foot free fall. As for me, I had learned a lesson I'll never forget. Fourteen thousand feet up is no place to shift cargo and retrim any aircraft. I decided then and there that I had left my crew chief on the ground for the last time.

How four people burdened with parachutes managed to climb up the inside of a near-vertical, thrashing fuselage, I'll never know, but I am eternally thankful for their dexterity. I owe another debt of gratitude to the Sikorsky company for building a most rugged helicopter. I am sure that I put mine into a flight configuration none of their engineers had imagined when they designed the aircraft.

●

Sure, it seems obvious in hindsight that if you place a loaded tray halfway onto a narrow shelf and then remove the shelf-side load, the remainder will come crashing down; but you don't necessarily think of those things when you have your hands full of helicopter.

Apocryphal tales abound of carrier pilots launching with the wings folded, but here's a real *one! It's a story that's almost worth carrying around with you for making bets at saloons.*

●

It was May in Korea, the birds were singing, the sun was shining—and I was sitting on a pile of dirt, watching my AD Skyraider burn to ashes. I had just qualified as one of the two aviators in the world who have flown a combat airplane with the wings folded.

It's hard to believe that an experienced aviator could be careless enough to take off in an airplane with its wings neatly folded overhead, and it's even more unbelievable that a bomb-loaded airplane could fly in that configuration. As an expert on the subject, let me tell you—it can be done!

When the Douglas Aircraft Company built the AD, they

turned out an aviator's dream. The plane can carry a tremendous bomb load for hundreds of miles and still fight its way out of a tight corner. Because of carrier landing requirements and the load that Navy bombers carry, Douglas built an extremely high lift factor into the wings. They also designed a scientifically safe cockpit in the Skyraider and included a large red-and-white-striped handle marked "wing fold," but even the most cautious aircraft designer never thought anyone would try to make a takeoff with the wings folded.

At the time of my "accident" I was flying Skyraiders from the U.S.S. *Princeton* with Air Group 19, specializing in night attack work. Our group had been in Korea for six months.

We had been pounding away for weeks, and everyone in the group was fagged. It was May 11, 1951, and I had gotten up at midnight to brief for a predawn heckler mission. There had been a lot of targets on the flight and the strain of making low-level attacks at night had tired all of us.

I groaned when we landed back aboard the carrier and saw the flight schedule. I was due for a bridge-busting strike near Pyŏngyang in another two hours. That meant a fast breakfast, an hour's briefing and back into the air again.

We were checking mags just before takeoff on the bridge strike when the squadron duty officer hopped up on my wing and cheerfully announced that I was scheduled for a third strike that day. An AD from a previous launch had aborted his mission and landed at Kangnŭng, the most forward airstrip in Korea. My orders were to fly the Pyŏngyang bridge strike, then drop out of the formation and fly to Kangnŭng. There I would pick up the unused bombs from the crippled Skyraider and go out on a close-air-support mission, returning to the carrier after the bombs had been dropped. Even my rear-seat radarman groaned when he heard the assignment.

Kangnŭng was a typical forward-area fighter strip. Its only runway consisted of 3,000 feet of pierced steel plank matting laid on the rice paddy. There was no tower—a radio-equipped jeep controlled traffic—and the course rules were "every man for himself."

It was a bright, sunny day when we pulled in over Kangnŭng. The bridge strike had gone well, and so far everything was going according to schedule. I looked down on the airfield and spotted the AD with my replacement bomb load. It was parked in the middle of a grass area, surrounded by Corsairs and Mustangs.

I pitched out over the end of the runway, landed and taxied over alongside the other AD. The area was crowded, so I raised my wings. Then complications set in. There was no ordnance crew available to transfer the bombs, so with the help of a few Marines and my radarman we shifted the bombs from one plane to the other. If you've ever had to load 250-pound bombs and five-inch rockets by hand, you'll know what I mean when I say we were tired.

We should have rested at that point, but I was eager to get back to the carrier. With my radarman in the back seat and a Marine to guide me out of the chocks, I began to taxi. There wasn't room for me to get past the plane we had just unloaded, so I left the wings folded and jockeyed around until we could pass. I taxied out to the end of the runway, ran up the engine and went over the checklist. I remember going over each of the items, carefully skipping the one that said "unfold wings," since that was so obvious. Who ever heard of anyone forgetting to unfold his wings!

When the checklist was completed, I taxied onto the runway. The tower jeep operator must have been manicuring his fingernails or absorbing the latest issue of *Thrilling Tales*, because he cleared me for takeoff without a qualm.

The runway was fairly short, so I put on the brakes, added throttle, then released the brakes. By the time the throttle was full on, we were scooting down the runway like a scalded cat. When half the runway had slipped under the wheels, I eased back on the stick—but the plane just sat there! The airspeed was well above what was needed for takeoff, so I two-blocked the throttle and began dropping flaps. Still no lift! I looked out to make sure the flaps were going down. NO WINGS!!!

The runway continued to flash past, and I could see a large, deep drainage ditch awaiting at the end. Instinctively I cut the throttle, then decided that it would be fatal to hit the ditch with the wheels down. The Skyraider is equipped with a solenoid to keep the pilot from raising the wheels when the plane's weight is still compressing the shock struts, so my first concern was with lifting the airplane off the struts. I slammed the throttle all the way forward and turned on the water injection in an attempt to get more lift. The airplane was just beginning to feel light when we unexpectedly hit a bump, and I was airborne.

If an airplane could ever talk, this one must have been cussing a blue streak as it hauled bombs, gasoline, passengers and all into the air. For a minute I was stupefied at the idea of flying without wings, then my reflexes took over. The ailerons were useless, but the airplane answered the rudders and elevator. I was about 150 feet in the air. The altimeter steadied for a few seconds, then began to dip downward. I kept the nose straight by kicking rudders, pointed the airplane at a clear spot ahead, chopped the throttle and eased down for a landing. At that point, my faithful Skyraider quit. With a dying wheeze she stalled out and fell in on a still-folded wing.

I came back to consciousness about 10 seconds later to find the cockpit sitting squarely in the middle of a bonfire. Thinking the obvious, I looked around for the man with the pitchfork and found that I was still at Kangnŭng. I hopped out and ran back to the rear compartment.

The radar compartment in an AD is built like an automobile, with doors on both sides. Since the plane was lying on its side, I climbed up on the fuselage and opened the door that was still usable.

My radarman was unhurt but was struggling with the opposite door and cussing fluently because it wouldn't open. I leaned in and said, "Are you all right?" He looked up, nodded and went right back to struggling frantically with the wrong door.

People were beginning to gather around the airplane, and two of them helped me retrieve the radarman. Suddenly someone shouted, "Look out for the bombs," and we found ourselves very much alone with the burning remains. We joined the others—rapidly!

Flying with the wings folded is definitely not recommended, but there are two major lessons to be learned from my fiasco. Never fly when you're tired; and most important, never take any item on the checklist for granted.

I have flown several different airplanes since then, and I use my checklist religiously whether I'm flying a fighter or a four-engine transport. You can bet there's one item that gets checked at least twice—"wings checked down and locked."

●

Of course it couldn't happen; everybody knows that. An airplane fly with its wings folded? That's about as likely as every airport on the Denver Sectional moving seven miles to the east.

●

We planned the 400-mile flight for no special reason, other than to see a chunk of the Southwest, which had been our home for a year. My passenger and I squatted in the shadow of the Tri-Pacer's wing and reviewed the trapezoidal course I had plotted, while my wife set up housekeeping in the back seat. The flight would begin and end at my tiedown spot on Senator Clarke Field in Gallup, New Mexico.

Although my friend had 750 hours as a B-29 tail gunner, this was to be his first lightplane ride. I had done a careful preflight, and I wanted to explain our route to him clearly. We would start by flying 125 miles northwest to Monument Valley, in northern Arizona. We intended to photograph Canyon De-Chelly and cruise among the stone monuments before heading northeast another 70 miles to Blanding, Utah, for a fuel stop. From there we would head southeast across the Four Corners area, where Arizona, Utah, Colorado and New Mexico meet, to Shiprock, New Mexico, and thence homeward almost due south. It would be a leisurely flight over wild and beautiful country, and although most of it was unfamiliar to me from the air, I felt well prepared by a recent vacation cross-country trip from western New Mexico to Ohio and back.

Visibility was good and rain showers were, as forecast, widely scattered, so it wasn't any trick to navigate to the prominent canyon and to the spirelike rock formations farther northwest. We had some difficulty spotting the dirt strips my new Denver Sectional showed along the way, but we chalked this up to the random nature of Navajo reservation roads and the natural brown-on-brown camouflage of desert airfields.

The northeastbound leg to Blanding was out of omni range for the Tri-Pacer's old Mark II, but it roughly followed a paved road, rare enough in that country to be reliable as a navaid. As the town of Blanding came up dead ahead, we began looking for the runway, which the chart showed to be seven miles east of the road. The closer we got, the more apparent it became that there was a concrete strip just *west* of the road straight south of the town. While my passenger and I kept looking for the field ahead and to the right, my wife was pounding me on the back and pointing down on the left side of the plane at "Blanding," painted in big letters right down the runway.

"Is this a new field?" I asked the fixed-base operator after we had landed. "The chart shows only one southeast of town."

"I'd like to see a chart like that," he replied, adding, "This is the only airport we have."

He pronounced my Denver Sectional a collector's item, showing me that it also placed the Cortez, Colorado, and Farmington, New Mexico, airports about seven-eighths of an inch east of their actual locations. Moreover, their omni stations had moved eastward with them. The same thing held true wherever he looked, whether an airport appeared in blue or red.

"It's as if they had moved all the airports," he said.

Since we had come about 200 miles on the misprinted chart, it seemed we could make the easier return leg without difficulty. With no thought of asking for another chart, we took off for Shiprock, to the southeast. The town is named for a nearby tower of stone, which Navajos see as a giant sailing ship in the desert. Visible for 35 miles that day, the rock and the prominent San Juan River along our course made this the simplest leg so far.

We circled the big rock, took our pictures and headed for home on what looked like an even easier run, a straight shot south along a well-defined paved highway, U.S. 666.

Only somehow we followed the wrong road. It quickly changed from a heading of 210 degrees to 240 and then almost straight west. With the sun in our eyes and the paved road giving way to dirt, I turned east. Immediately to the south was the northern end of the Chuska mountain chain, which stretched southward almost to our destination.

For a few minutes—it seemed longer than it probably was—we looked for the north-south highway, which on the chart appeared to run parallel to the mountains and east of them (and which, in fact, it does). Our recollections of that vicinity from surface travels were sketchy, and my mistrust of the misprinted chart was growing.

Our fuel stop had provided a comfortable reserve for sightseeing, but I did not want to waste any of it in aimless wandering. I could not trust the Cortez VOR to the north or the Farmington station east of me to give an accurate steer toward home. Recharting the omnis to plot an accurate course seemed beyond our cockpit capabilities in moderately bumpy air. And besides, what if the omni azimuth rosettes had been tilted as well as displaced on the undependable chart? We could not see a north-south road to the east, so I elected to return to the original road we had followed, climbing all the while.

We would give the road a few more minutes as we gained altitude. The Mark II was working fine, and I wanted to be well above the Chuskas' highest peak, 9,800 feet msl, and at the same time be high enough to pick up Gallup Vortac as soon as possible.

The road kept straying westward, so I headed south. In only four or five minutes, we reached 11,500 feet and heard the Gallup identification code loud and clear. We and our misleading road had wandered quite a distance west, for our heading to Gallup was 155 degrees.

There was Window Rock, Arizona, its airport still in place, the FAA sectional notwithstanding. Soon Gallup stretched before us along Interstate 40, its 6,300-foot runway paralleling the highway.

At the Gallup Flight Service Station, there was a great deal of head-scratching over the silly sectional. One of the FSS men unfolded the chart to its full length and discovered on the right-hand edge a white margin into which red and dark-blue markings overlapped.

Apparently all the brown and the light blue of lakes and rivers had been printed seven-eighths of an inch too far to the left on half the chart. (There is no green on that chart because of the high elevation.)

From the printing standpoint, the airports and omnis were where they belonged, but the ground was out of place. At any rate, the result was that all the airports and omnis were shown on the other side of town, on the opposite side of the highway or across the river from where they really are. Somehow, the chart had been sold instead of being destroyed.

Ordinarily, my goof in following the wrong highway could have been rectified immediately. Two omnis were close enough for triangulation, if that had become necessary, but I couldn't trust the chart. My biggest mistake was in not throwing it away and begging, borrowing or stealing another when I had the chance.

Now the first thing I do when I buy a chart is to unfold it completely and examine both sides, concentrating on the margins. If one or more colors are off register, the unevenness will show at the edges. I don't accept a chart on which the colors don't match up there.

A misplaced airport may be a little joke on a sunny day on the ramp, but in the air it loses its humor.

●

If that doesn't challenge the aircraft commander enough for you, try this one: What do you do when the airplane suddenly smells bad? The answer is not *"hold your nose."*

●

The airplane was spanking-new, of a type that shall be nameless because our misadventures were not the fault of the airframe but of the accessories. My father had flown it to Madison, Wisconsin, from Los Angeles to pick me up and take me back to the West Coast. I was looking forward to the return flight, since I would get to do all the flying and would, I hoped, squeeze in a little instrument time if we could dig up a cloud somewhere. The instrument schemes were frustrated from the first, since the radio turned out to be acting up—it would warm up and then the nav function would cut out. We figured that there was a voltage problem somewhere, but hadn't a clue what to do about it, and it was Sunday to boot. We stopped at Radio Ranch, at Polo, Illinois, where we understood that great wonders were often performed; but the guru was in Bermuda, and so we checked weather (all clear), drew a straight line on our sectionals from Polo to Kansas City and took off.

We tooled along monotonously at 10,500 for a couple of hours, pointing out to each other where we were on various sectionals and WAC charts. Everything was fine, we were right on course and less than an hour out of KC, when our respective noses puckered and sniffed, and we asked each other at once whether there wasn't an odd smell in the air.

There was definitely a slight but insistent odd smell. We sniffed like so many hounds, but could not quite pin it down. We thought of carbon monoxide right away, of course, but agreed that the smell was definitely something other than exhaust gases. There was a funny, pungent chemical quality about it that made me think, with a qualm, that some kind of miracle plastic insulation under the cowling was bungling its job.

The smell got stronger. We opened the gaspers—those airline-style ventilators that you turn to open—to see if the smell would go away, but it remained. I had a brainstorm: Perhaps we were flying through a mass of ozone-laden air created by some sort of inversion. The ozone theory sounded good for a while, but the odor got stronger and stronger, and it seemed as though that much ozone ought to make a noise hitting the plane.

We were getting a bit anxious. Everyone pretended to be very casual, but eye movements were becoming more rapid, and voice pitch had risen a quarter-tone or so. We were already at the point where it was not possible to take a deep breath without coughing, and the situation was worsening.

I then opened the vent window by my side with the notion that if the fumes were coming from the engine (which I was sure they were) we would notice them becoming stronger as some outside air swirled into the cockpit.

My theory seemed to be vindicated when, the instant I opened the window, the fumes doubled in intensity. Even normal breathing became uncomfortable, and a deep breath led to gagging. Now I was certain that we had an engine fire, and immediately chopped the power, pushed over the nose and brought the airspeed up to redline. My father was breathing through his shirt, and I through mine; our two rear-seat passengers—one an experienced private pilot and the other a first-(and perhaps last-) timer in the air—were presumably having a merry time repenting their sins.

We came down fast and headed for the nearest field. Once off the runway and shut down, we piled out and opened the cowlings, ready to snuff out the smoldering whatever-it-was with rags, grass and mud.

Nothing whatever: pristine, odorless perfection.

I walked around the plane and found a yellow liquid dripping out of the sheet seams on the right side of the plane. I opened the luggage compartment—and the stench nearly knocked me over.

My umpteenth incorrect surmise for the day was that someone was carrying a vial of an unidentified loathsome substance in his luggage, and that it had leaked out at altitude. All pleaded innocent, and finally we tracked the trouble to the batteries—or what was left of them.

They were boiling like mad, had altered strangely in shape and were giving off a gas of sulphurous odor that one could scarcely bear to inhale. We turned the plane so that the luggage door faced into the wind, and waited for things to air out and cool down while we discussed strategy. We decided that it would be possible to continue to Kansas City for repairs by leaving the electrical system shut off; and so we telephoned ahead to ask the tower for a no-radio approach, eventually propped the engine and set off for our destination.

Now the landing gear had to stay down because it was electrically operated; and the fuel gauges were out, along with a lot of the other instruments. Gear speed was about 100 mph, and we stuck to that, climbing fairly high to get the best TAS. We knew that the two tanks were each about quarter full, and that that would get us to KC—assuming that our fuel consumption was not too badly affected by the gear. We let one tank drain out completely, and when the engine quit over Richmond, we switched tanks with the *sangfroid* of habitually forgetful pilots.

When we landed, after a seemingly eternal flight, no fuel whatever could be seen in either tank, and the fuel bill was for 53 of the plane's advertised 55-gallon capacity.

The mechanic fished out the batteries, one of which was irreparably melted, the other only superficially. There was a short in one of them, he explained, which threw the voltage regulator out of operation and permitted the batteries to take full generator amperage continuously, eventually bringing the acid to a boil and giving off fumes that have been variously identified, but unanimously declared to be dangerous or even potentially fatal. My father said that he had noted the 40-amp positive charge indication on the ammeter, but had been unsure what it implied; I confessed that I had not noted it. I suppose that I checked it only on starting the engine, when at idle the indication had been closer to neutral.

The lessons of this little homily are numerous. One is that telltale signs that seem inconsequential in themselves—radios *kaput* and odd ammeter readings—may be the harbingers of bigger and more awful things. Another is that you have a potentially dangerous device right behind your cabin (in most aircraft) ready to wage gas warfare against you, but which you can outsmart (by shutting off the electrical system and opening only ventilators that force air into the cabin from the front)— if you can recognize it. Another is that a sense of triumph and relief at having successfully dealt with one emergency (fumes, in this case) may reduce one's alertness and concern with the next (running out of gas).

The most interesting and important lesson for me, however, was that I could not think very clearly under pressure. Whether my reactions would be typical of those of most nonprofessional pilots, and whether they were influenced by the altitude, I don't know. But I am surprised at the narrowness of my reasoning. It led me to jump to a false conclusion about the nature of the problem (engine fire) and then interpret all the symptoms— even contradictory ones—as supporting my analysis. I am, in retrospect, surprised at my slowness in starting down; and worse, at my failure to consider that opening the small side window did not bring outside air into the cockpit, but sucked inside air out—a fact that I could have told you any day of the week since I began to fly.

The point is that it pays to know the facts about possible emergencies, to have gone over them in one's mind and to have a complete acquaintance with the various parts of a plane and what can go wrong with them. Never skip a chance to read an accident report. I was lucky; there was an airfield nearby, it was daytime, things came on slowly and I had time to react. But suppose it had been nighttime over mountains or water—in a twin, if you like. We might have stopped the coughing the hard way, since it probably would not have occurred to me that I should start ventilating the cockpit by shutting off the electrics. Who would think of that—who, that is, but somebody who had thought about it in advance?

●

Everyone reacts with adequate speed—usually—when the emergency is something that was covered during training, but that pilot described perfectly the slow-motion lethargy which characterizes reaction to the unconventional.

Here's a lighthearted tale about a pilot flying in the fierce environs of Teterboro Airport in New Jersey, when his airplane started making like Gene Krupa. Like, man, there was this banging . . .

●

Three times I've gone to Teterboro and three times I've returned. Just the kind of round trips I like. But each time it's been rough.

Now Teterboro, New Jersey, has a great airport. If it could be lugged bodily about 15 miles west or north, it would be classified as a real great airport.

Like everyone else, I leave my airport to fly to Teterboro by following a 90-degree course, adding or subtracting a few degrees depending on whether the wind is north or south.

There are some people who fly right to Teterboro from home base without blinking an eye. These cats claim they can see Teterboro from 15 miles west. Not me. Every time I've made the trip and get to a point 15 miles west, I immediately penetrate a solid vertical wall of soot, gas fumes and coagulated essence of garbage, all lightly mixed with air. This night-at-noon always occurs just as the Teterboro Tower has given me landing instruction.

Like all good courageous pilots who have 125 hours' total time and know they know nothing about flying, I find this situation unnerving. Their nerve endings get an added tingle when the murky terrain below becomes a solid welter of factories, houses, highways and superhighways, intermixing like a potful of spaghetti. And all the important rivers have so many twists and turns as to be absolutely useless for navigation.

How do others handle this problem? Beats me. Stick with the compass, strain the eyeballs, swivel that neck!

Ah! Blessed relief when a pale-gray runway shows up.

Now let's compound the whole wretched business and discover how to lose 10 pounds instantly.

I'm a renter. Other cats own, fly in clubs, but me, I rent. I've got my reasons, although I don't know what they are. I feel the owner's plane deserves my care and attention. Because of this, I circle the aircraft in preflight, clutching the manual, and drawing out fluids like a leech on a sore. Because of the respect I have for the owner, man, I do everything. I told my wife and four children about this, and they all agreed that my respect for the owner was commendable and in the American Tradition of Respect for Private Property.

Well, sir, I had forethoughtedly arranged for a Cessna 172 to be available for the trip. Manual in hand, I completed the walk-around, climbed in and took off on trip number three to Teterboro, where I was to pick up an associate.

Friends of Teterboro will claim it enjoys perpetually fair weather except when it rains or snows, and it's true they have a very strong case. Every time I *drive* by, the weather is perfect, so sure enough, at the self-designated call-up point, over a golf course, there was my friendly wall of soot, gas, fumes and thick garbage odors waiting to clutch me and my 172.

Used to it from past experience, I got my nose, by stretching my neck, right up by the magnetic compass, kept rotating each eye 360 degrees in azimuth and elevation and became immediately aware that Teterboro Tower was talking to at least 10,000 High-Performance Aircraft, each a quarter of a mile from the other all around the field. The old nerve endings are tingling. This 15-minute trip in the logbook will represent 20 hours of flying anywhere else I go.

Instantly, with no warning, a great, loud hammering begins on the right side of the aircraft near the bottom of the door. In the identical instant, I am soaked in sweat, right down to my little toes. It warms my heart to realize that, 45 years old or not, all my sweat glands work. Disassociating this euphoria from present unbearable circumstances, I discover the aircraft is still flying and the great din is continuing.

Fortunately, I had had a great instructor whom I used to hate during each lesson. Automatically getting down to slow-flight speed, I would have, if I'd thought of it, kissed him on both cheeks if he were present. I'd have even given him the honor of taking over control. He knew what to do the time the cowling hinge pin pulled out on us . . . but that's another story.

Well, sir, what next? Is the right wheel—or something else equally essential to ground or air travel—coming off? Removing my nose and rotating eyeballs from the magnetic compass and twisting as far to the right as possible, I could see for an instant the strut and the wheel fairing, both right where they should be. Getting back to the attention position by the compass, I wedged the mike in between my mouth and the windshield to advise Teterboro Tower in calm, even tones that I was coming in for an emergency landing on any runway "because of a loud and unexplained noise on the right side of the aircraft."

Teterboro Tower allowed as how that was okay with them —they would take care of 10,000 High-Performance Aircraft still surrounding the field like a flock of starlings. Would I kindly advise them where I was?

Ah, that's the rub. Where in God's name was I? Logic said I was either west, north or south of the field. I wasn't east of it because if I had been, I'd have seen it pass under me, since it's too big to miss from directly overhead. I figured I should be nearly at the field, so I must be either north or south. Since I had allowed for a northerly wind, I should be south of the field. This was impeccable logic, and I didn't believe it. So I lied to the tower and said I was two miles south of the field.

Teterboro Tower swallowed this statement and asked was I inbound now? Consider my situation. I had already lied about my location. Soaking wet, I was descending through saturated air, surrounded by High-Performance Aircraft, like a pea in a bucket of ball bearings, and assailed by a banging that filled the aircraft with a noise like unto that in a foundry.

Someone up there at the aircraft owners' insurance company watches out for aircraft renters, because there, with all the glory of an increased paycheck, was the approach end of a runway.

In a palsied voice, but with some inner triumph, I advised Teterboro Tower that I was on short final. I subsequently made a lousy landing. Safely on the ground, I began telling the tower all about it in an excess of nervous tension.

The voice cut me short, told me to get off the runway and tell my story to ground control.

Ground control was pretty short with me too and ordered me to taxi to and park at the foot of the tower. Pulling into position, I was the center of attention of the occupants of three yellow cars, which crowded up close to the plane as I shut down.

Coming around the tail of the plane to the right side, I noticed lots of pointing and wide smiles.

Yeah, that's right. All of you who know better know what the trouble was. The seat belt was hanging out under the door. "It's better to be laughed at and safe," said the kindly old Port Authority man as he approached me for a $1.50 landing fee. Well said.

●

And that's no jive.

Sometimes a pilot has to pause and wonder if there isn't a better way to make a living. Earl Robinson was one of several early movie stunters who had strange experiences. He too heard a bang—a big one—but it was explosives, not a seat belt. It gives the expression "to be blown up" real meaning.

●

"You are only as good as the man on the ground." In no branch of aviation is this unwritten law more inflexible than in movie stunt flying. When we take off to perform a stunt that will leave the audience gasping, we leave our lives behind us in the hands of the ground crews. The penalty for a mistake is . . . well, there are only 12 of us left.

During the filming of *Dawn Patrol* in 1930, starring Richard Barthelmess and Douglas Fairbanks, Jr., there was a sequence in which the two heroes bombed a German airdrome and machine-gunned the ground personnel. If you didn't see the original picture, the 1938 issue of the film, starring Errol Flynn and David Niven, contains the same scenes. (Warner Brothers saved the expense of filming the dangerous flying sequences by lifting them bodily from the 1930 version.)

Leo Nomis (who was killed a year later during the filming of *Sky Bride* for Paramount) and I did the flying in the airdrome raid. To understand our task, you should know how the scene was made. A "location" airport complete with hangars, shops and officers' quarters, was built in a valley about 30 miles from Hollywood. On the field were several Jennys and other old planes painted with German insignia. Each was loaded with a charge of high explosive. Additional charges were planted on the field, in the buildings and at other points. Wires led from each charge to a button on a "powder table" out of camera range. Stationed at the table was a "powder man," supposedly an expert at placing the charges for the best pictorial effect and also supposedly a cool-headed technician who would set off the proper blasts a split second after Nomis and I passed over a given point in our roaring "attacks."

Director Howard Hawks, the powder man, Nomis and I went over the scene in advance. Nomis and I were to make a series of power dives and chandelles over the field from predetermined angles. Each dive would bring us above a row of dynamite charges. The powder man, with the whole layout of the airdrome on the table before him, would press the proper buttons a fraction of a second *after* the planes passed. The effect would be just as if the planes had actually bombed the row of airplanes, the hangars or whatever it was we had just swooped over.

Our conference with Director Hawks developed into a two-hour argument, which Nomis and I lost. Hawks had picked for a powder man a technician whom we did not know. Nomis and I had nothing against the man except that we had not worked with him before. We were afraid he might become excited at a critical moment. Our candidate for the powder-table job was another engineer working on this picture and in charge of all flying and field equipment.

We were flying two new Speedwing Travel Airs painted to resemble British pursuit ships and mounted with dummy machine guns. We took off after the charges all were planted, and circled out of camera range at about 5,000 feet until we received the signal to start diving.

The airport was built just under the brow of a low hill. Our first dive was to take us just behind the hill, with our pull-out timed so we could appear suddenly over the crest in a surprise attack. We were to come roaring across a small hangar and "bomb" a row of planes on the line in front of it.

Nomis led the attack. I came close behind and a little to one side in a standard two-plane formation. We came over the hangar less than 30 feet high at about 250 mph. The explosives expert set off his first blast behind Nomis—right in my face!

A Jenny wing crumpled against my landing gear. A strut shot up and tangled with the propeller. Bits of debris, rocks and chunks of wrecked airplane ripped through the wings and fuselage. The concussion made me black out; my last instinctive act was to haul back on the stick. "Get altitude . . . get altitude so you can bail out . . . get altitude!" my subconscious must have flashed to my hands and feet on the controls.

I recovered consciousness in a full-power stall at 1,700 feet with the motor vibrating so badly from the bent propeller that it threatened to shake itself loose from the plane. Dazed, I leveled off, eased back on the throttle and flipped the catch on my safety belt to free myself for a jump.

As my mind cleared, I gave myself an instant for a lightning estimate of my chances for saving the ship. The wings were in shreds, but the tail surfaces, miraculously, were intact. The ailerons were damaged, but there was enough surface left for control if . . . yes, a kick at the rudder and a joggle of the stick showed the control wires all still connected.

I decided then to try for a landing, and shoved the nose forward. I might make it, I thought, if the landing gear was still there. Trying to hold the ship in a flat glide revealed to me that most of my lifting surface was gone. I realized that I was in a sharp dive. Then it dawned upon me that I hadn't climbed to 1,700 feet after the explosion—not with most of my wings gone.

I had been blown up there!

Desperately I tried to kill my speed, then twice as desperately nosed down to pick it up again. If I slowed the plane any further, I was certain to spin to the ground—I could *feel* the ship nearing the stall point. Those tattered wings, from which shreds of fabric were tearing loose, just wouldn't hold me up. But by now I was too low to jump. I *had* to land . . .

Ahead of me was a wire fence and, beyond that, part of the runway of the airdrome. I saw that if I kicked enough rudder to angle safely over the fence, I would have only a few hundred feet of runway left—and at the end waited the flimsy hangars —a sure bet for a nasty fire. I didn't dare risk a turn to a more favorable spot. Grimly I settled deeper into my seat, lifted my goggles up from my eyes and waited for the crash.

The plane leveled out over the fence and groped for the ground, the airspeed showing more than 100 mph. The wheels hit and the plane lurched drunkenly. The landing gear *was* damaged! I fought for control as the hangars rushed at me. Gingerly I felt for the brakes; they held. I breathed a prayer of thanksgiving as I brought the crippled plane to a stop with a scant 20 feet to spare.

First to reach me were Hawks and the "expert."

"Are you hurt?" they chorused. I could only shake my head.

The director tottered around the corner of the hangar and was violently ill. The powder man went back to his table. Nomis, you see, was playing an aerial *Pagliacci*—finishing out the scene single-handed.

Two weeks later we moved to another location. The powder man and his son drove a truckload of explosives to the new field. I flew one of the ships over; just as I landed I heard a terrific explosion. The truck had gone up in a sheet of flame. They found the powder man and his son 150 feet away, bruised and burned. I walked over.

"Are you hurt?" I asked.

●

Too bad Earl Robinson hadn't heard of ejection seats. He would have loved the ride.

Bailing out is no answer, though, if your own airplane turns around and buzzes you. Try to imagine how this pilot felt as he hung from the parachute and watched the position lights of his Cessna—from which he had just jumped—approaching out of the gloom. Talk about wanting to trade places . . .

●

It was a rather routine instrument flight, as routine as one would expect during early February in the Mid-west. I was en route from Omaha to Fort Rucker, Alabama, flying alone in an Army TL-19D, similar to the Cessna 180. I landed at Fort Smith for fuel just as darkness was descending, and the field conditions were IFR.

My air traffic control clearance came through promptly and I was airborne once again shortly after six o'clock. I made my position reports to Fort Smith departure control as directed, and broke through the cloud decks at 6,000 feet. I continued climbing into the clear night sky to 7,500 feet, where I leveled off and picked up favorable tailwinds. I cruised along for perhaps 30 minutes and was not due to make another position report until I reached Little Rock, some 70 miles ahead.

Suddenly, there was a loud banging and clanging up front, accompanied by shuddering and vibration in the engine. It sounded like someone beating on a radiator with a ball-peen hammer. I immediately thought about carburetor icing, then remembered that I had applied full heat shortly after leaving Fort Smith, just as a precaution. The engine manifold pressure started to drop off rapidly, and the engine vibrations increased in severity. The vibrations were so intense that at one time my headset was shaken off my head.

I began jockeying the throttle, pumping the engine primer, changing gas tanks, and sweeping out the cockpit in general. In addition I tried to raise someone on the radio. I had no success with any of these actions. Then, just as suddenly as the knocking had begun, the engine stopped completely.

I have been flying for more than 12 years, as a military pilot, both fixed- and rotary-wing aircraft, with close to 5,000 hours, and I have never experienced the sensations that I felt at this time—and the others that were soon to follow. It is hard to describe the eerie quiet that descends upon the aviator, alone at night, 7,000 feet in the air in a dead airplane, with nothing but clouds and mountains beneath. I calculated my position and found that I was over the heart of the Ouachita Mountains. The closest airport with any navigational aids for an instrument letdown was Little Rock, still some 70 miles east. I was in a jam and I knew it.

For some reason I had been nervously checking the clock and my wristwatch every few seconds. Why, I don't know, but now talking aloud to myself, I said that time was no longer a factor in my predicament and that altitude was the thing I needed most to keep and preserve. My eyes flashed over to the altimeter; it registered approximately 6,500 feet.

Snatching my map off the floor where it had fallen during all this frenzied activity, I discovered that the highest mountains along my route were at 3,000 feet. Using my altimeter now as a clock, I quickly made a mental checklist of the items I was to accomplish at each thousand-foot level as the altimeter unwound.

Working from the lowest altitude, which I now knew to be 3,000, my checklist ran something like this: 4,000 feet, bail out; between 5,000 and 4,000, check and tighten parachute harness, jettison door; between 6,000 and 5,000 feet, try to restart engine. I now had a definite course of action to follow, and immediately noted that most of the fear and tension was gone as I started putting my checklist into effect.

The aircraft quietly glided into the clouds, and I had to devote some attention to the controls in order to keep straight and level. I was nearing the 5,000-foot mark, and all my attempts to start the engine were unsuccessful. At 5,000 feet, I ceased all efforts at restarting the aircraft and, according to plan, went to work on the parachute strapped to my back. I examined all the straps and harness, and reached back into the rear seat and retrieved my gloves, which I figured would be a big help in shielding my face against trees and branches. Then I jettisoned the door, to be free from all encumbrances when abandoning ship.

Having a few hundred feet left, I pondered the manner in which I was going to make this grand exit. Feet first? Head first? How? Looking back and out through the gap left by the missing door, I noted that the horizontal stabilizer was apparently much closer than I had ever thought it to be; in fact, I wondered if I had room to get out and under it. I decided that the best way would be to tumble out of the seat, head first, as if those clouds were a great big swimming pool.

The checklist was working right on schedule, and it almost seemed as if a giant alarm sounded when the altimeter reached 4,000 feet, the altitude I had set for the bailout. I didn't hesitate. I hit the cold, damp air, counted aloud, and on reaching three, pulled the ripcord. A second or so later the chute opened with a violent but heavenly jolt.

Everything was great at this point. I was happily thanking the Lord, congratulating myself on still being alive and praising that parachute packer as being the finest in the business. I was still in the dark gray-black clouds drifting earthward when suddenly the quiet bird returned. It was coming directly toward me through the clouds. Although there was no sound, other than a gentle whooshing noise, I could see the brilliant rotating anticollision light. At first the light appeared small and orange in color; but as the ship came closer, I could distinguish the wingtip lights. The pilotless plane passed a few feet overhead, while my heart pounded, and then just as abruptly, it disappeared.

I now started to breathe again and once more gave thanks to the heavenly guardian who was with me tonight. A few moments later I broke through the clouds and down into the clear

black night above the Ouachita Mountains, which could be seen
vaguely beneath. On the horizon all around were lights from
small Arkansas towns, with smaller, isolated lights scattered at
frequent intervals a few miles around me. Now I noticed that
a strong wind was drifting me along sideways at a rather brisk
clip. I wasn't thinking about anything in particular at this point,
merely drinking in the wonders of floating downward at night
over rather rugged terrain, and wondering when all this would
come to an end.

Then, there it was again. The airplane, which had supposedly
headed toward Little Rock, descended out of the clouds in front
of me, in a gentle right bank. I later surmised that this was
because I had used only fuel from the left wing tank, thereby
making the right wing heavier. Also, I had jettisoned the door
on the right side. The slipstream, passing the right side of the
fuselage and entering the opening where the door was, pushed
against the rear of the aircraft. This forced the tail to the left
and the nose to the right, a position the plane was loath to leave.

I watched, fascinated, relieved that it was going away from
me. This was short-lived, however, for just as abruptly as it
appeared, it turned and was now in a wide-ranging arc on a
collision course with me. If I panicked at all, it was during those
next few moments. I started, or rather tried, to climb up the
nylon risers, only to have the parachute collapse on that side
each time I pulled them down. I drew my feet up and even
shouted curses, alternating with prayers, that the thing would
go away. It did, finally, passing about a hundred feet in front
of me. I still have a vivid recollection that I could read the
instrument panel as it flew by, but of course this was just
hysterical imagination. Once again, I started to breathe and
relax, more or less, when darned if it didn't make a grand orbit
about half a mile in front and start back toward me again. It
was porpoising, sometimes above and sometimes below me, but
still in that gentle turn. The second passing was just as anxious
as the first. This time my dead bird passed behind me. My head

and eyes had remained glued to it, and it was made even more ominous-looking by that brilliant anticollision light that was flicking its eerie beam. I was a nervous wreck at this point and was vociferously calling on my Maker for help.

As I watched, unable to look or think about anything else except this crazy, mixed-up airplane, it suddenly crashed into the ground with a ripping, tearing noise. I then realized that I too must be near the ground and should start making preparations for landing. I was there. I had time only to think: relax. I was drawing up my legs when I plummeted to the ground. Being relaxed, I tumbled forward toward the chute, which was lodged against a tree on the side of what I later discovered to be Mount Chickalah. Rolling and tumbling uphill, I finally came to rest enmeshed in the shroud lines, upside down, and feet grotesquely entwined.

Taking a fast physical inventory, I found that I was in relatively serviceable condition. Except for soreness and bruises, I had escaped unharmed. I made my way through the woods and climbed to the top, where I found the farm of a friendly but bewildered Arkansas mountaineer.

I have relived this flight a hundred times or more, weighing each step that I took and the order in which the events occurred. So far, in hindsight, there is no action that I think I would change. The one main item which I should like to pass on for what it's worth to other pilots who may someday find themselves in a similar predicament, is this: Don't panic! You really have more time than you think, especially if you trim the aircraft for a shallow glide. Then formulate a plan or sequence of events that you want to try to accomplish, using the altimeter as your stopwatch. Plan these actions from the lowest level that will assure you plenty of time to get the chute open. Allow at least 1,000 feet, and fix that altitude firmly in your mind. When you reach it, GO. Don't wait around and reminisce. If you are not well versed in parachute landing techniques, don't worry;

if you will just force yourself to relax and draw your feet up slightly, you can't miss.

As for the quiet bird, I can only suggest you trim it full down just before you leave it, and keep your fingers crossed.

●

Of course, the odds were against the plane's doing that. Pilots are always playing the odds, which may account for why odd things keep happening to them. Given the entire country of Ecuador in which to fly, what odds might one give that a pilot who spiraled down through a hole in the clouds would end up in the cone of a volcano?

●

In the days before omnirange radio replaced over-the-top navigation and before aircraft radio was in general use, navigation and flying were largely guesswork. Couple this with mountain ranges rising to 21,000 feet, the aircraft engines rated at 3,500 feet—toss in an absence of accurate maps—and you have a picture of what it was like to fly in Ecuador 17 years ago.

Now reduce your flight instruments to a magnetic compass (which functions like a directional gyro in the absence of turning error and dip at the Equator), an airspeed indicator, an altimeter, turn-and-bank and a clock, and you can visualize the setting for the most surprising navigational boner I experienced in 27 years of flying.

During the rainy season, the coastal plains of Ecuador are covered by a solid overcast 4,000 or 5,000 feet thick, which normally is broken only by early afternoon. The Alto Plano, a valley 10,000 feet above sea level in which Quito nestles, lies just to the east of the principal ridge of the Andes. Here the weather is normally reversed, with broken clouds in the morning going to solid in the afternoon. The ridge separating the Alto Plano from the Occidental, or coastal plains, is from 12,000 to 21,000 feet high.

I took off from Guayaquil one morning in a Curtiss Osprey on one of my frequent flights to Quito. The weather was normal, so I followed my customary procedure of staying under the overcast up to Santo Domingo de los Colorados, nearly due west of Quito, then turning west, away from the mountains, and climbing above the overcast. There the course would be reversed 180 degrees, and I would climb up to 15,000 feet to clear the ridge between Santo Domingo and Quito.

From this point on, the procedure was routine. It was necessary to find a hole large enough for a letdown. On this particular trip, all went well. I found a hole which would accommodate a comfortable spiral. Beneath the hole, and several hundred feet below the clouds, was a large lake, obviously the lake near Otovallo, just a few miles north of Quito. Though I couldn't see the shoreline for positive identification, it had to be the lake near Quito, as there were no others of that size in the area.

Ahead of schedule and in a relaxed mood, I decided upon a comfortable letdown, instead of diving through as I had done occasionally. I spiraled down leisurely from 18,000 feet and emerged below the clouds.

Then procedure went to hell in a hurry. From the clouds to the water were sheer vertical rock walls. I had scored a bull's-eye on a lake in an extinct volcano crater not shown on any map!

I held the airplane in a steep turn to look the would-be graveyard over, and it was immediately apparent that the only way out was up. The hole through which I had let down was rapidly drifting past the crater. I couldn't gaze at the scenery any longer, as I had to reverse the spiral to as fast a climb as possible. I wanted to get out while the getting was good.

During the brief survey, I noticed that the lake was a little over 14,000 feet up, 4,000 feet higher than the lake I was seeking. I also noted that it becomes mighty cold when you perspire freely at that altitude.

The holes I afterwards chose to spiral down through showed glimpses of cultivated land or villages at 10,000 feet. Or else I passed them by. That remote and beautiful crater lake is now on the maps in an unmistakable shade of blue. Pilots in Ecuador no longer have to discover it for themselves.

●

Note that down in the portion of your training notes labeled "volcano flying." You never know when it might turn up on an FAA exam.

The rules and regs cover a lot, but nowhere—absolutely no-where—does it say what you're supposed to do when you find yourself with a couple of bees for passengers. But don't worry; you won't be the first. Another pilot has already covered that contingency in this hilarious account.

●

Pilots take themselves too seriously. Doesn't anything funny ever happen to pilots? I know that some of my own I-learned-about-flying experiences have been more hysterical than terrifying—but then, maybe I haven't learned much.

Ridiculous things can happen when you least expect them. It was a beautiful, smooth CAVU day and I leveled off at 8,500, cranked the trim, settled back and opened a stick of chewing gum. It was all very peaceful, but while part of the gum was sticking out of my mouth, a bee landed on it.

I exploded the gum as far as the windshield. This must have put the bee in a bad mood, because he did an Immelmann and came at me out of the sun. As soon as he got me in his sights, he was joined by another bee.

I made a rather haphazard attack with a folded low-level

chart, but the situation deteriorated when the bees made a flank attack up my trouser leg.

By this time, I imagined I was sitting on a whole nest of bees and began looking for an airport. In answer to my screaming into the mike, a pedantic voice told me wind direction and velocity, barometric pressure, runway, and then asked me to report downwind. I was hoping for a straight-in approach, so I began to shout about bees.

Of course, the tower said, "Repeat."

I suppose it sounded something like: "Blah blah blah, Comanche, two bees . . ."

"Comanche Bravo Bravo, go ahead."

"Negative Bravo Bravo. Bees, I've got two bees."

"You've got to what?"

"Seven-Five Pop has got two bees!"

The tower somehow got the idea that I wanted to use the facilities, and cleared me straight in. I went literally buzzing up to the wire fence beside the terminal, leaped madly out on the wing and took off my pants. Not until there was a burst of applause from a Girl Scout troop did I realize how totally I had been routed by the emergency.

Now bees are part of my checklist.

●

And now a story about a Girl Scout trapped at an airport while a pilot taxied up and took his pants off right in front of her . . .

Just kidding, actually. Something like that would be too far out.

8/LEARNING
TO LOVE IT

f this book were to end here, it would be an injustice to the art and science of flying aircraft.

Although those grim moments when pilots are under great pressure often seem to reveal great truths, they are not the *only* source of such revelations. It is sometimes too easy to see truth within those fleeting glimpses of danger. There are other great moments: moments of reflection, rewarding hours when an insight is gained in the quiet *after* a flight, experiences that bring home for once and always the warming fraternity of airmen doing what they love to do best.

An airplane makes demands, certainly, but the rewards it can offer are without measure. For those few moments when a pilot is caught in the vise of fear, there is the overwhelming balance of many hours of lofty pleasure. Against the grim times, pilots counter with the humorous ones. The busy seconds when everything goes to hell are far outweighed by the meditative aeon of a full-moon night flight.

Most rewarding of all is the triumphant time when you sit back in the pilot's seat and realize that the airplane has just taught you something about yourself that you never knew before. Flying can find inner dimensions, unexplored realms of the true person within the body that flinches, sweats, jiggles the mixture—or *smiles.*

Just as the airplane teaches the pilot, so do pilots teach one another. This final collection of stories are the kind that are too good to go without sharing. In that, they are a little like flying itself. All the tales have in common an affection for aviation; some show it through humor and others with a very special eloquence; all of them reach inside the writer and find the unique satisfaction each derives from time spent up in the sky.

Colby Blodget, an instructor, wrote this clever tale about the quintessential dud student—Jules; if Blodget is complaining, he is also laughing all the way.

●

Jules sits in the left seat of his trusty, rented Cessna 150, diligently chasing the rate-of-climb indicator with the elevator, oblivious to the fact that he is 300 feet above his assigned altitude. He has also turned 110 degrees since he began to level off, but he has no time to consider such trivia, since the most important instrument in the airplane is, after all, the rate-of-climb indicator. He finally stabilizes the needle 150 feet per minute too high and sits back satisfied.

I clear my throat. "Jules," I say carefully, "I would like you to perform a departure stall in a left turn, please."

Jules responds to my request by punching the throttle all the way forward. Now everybody knows departure stalls are done at full power, and everybody knows that if you don't look at the rpm indicator, the engine won't go over redline. Now for that stall: *Boom!* Lots of left rudder; got to coordinate those ailerons. Clank! The ball hits the end of the race. Got to get that nose up. Keep that left rudder in there to take care of the torque . . . or is that right rudder? Never mind, keep the nose coming up. There, that's about a 60-degree angle; more right aileron, more back pressure. Why is the prop making those outboard-motor noises? No time to worry about it, airspeed's almost down . . . uh-oh. For the sixth time, Jules has just demonstrated his expertise at entering power-on spins.

I look at Jules. He is staring, fascinated, at the spectacle of the Pacific Ocean and the California coastline spinning around in front of his windshield. All thought of stall recovery is forgotten with the rediscovery of this ultimate thrill.

"Jules," I ask patiently, "what are you going to do now?"

He doesn't answer. The wheel is held firmly back, and his left leg is ramrod-stiff, planted solidly on the rudder pedal, as if to prevent it from taking any unilateral action to save him. I am losing my patience, but I speak calmly. "Jules, do you think it is a good idea to be spinning down through the practice area like this? After all, you're making it extremely difficult for other aircraft to see you, coming down from this angle."

Slowly he turns to look at me, grins and asks, "Huh?"

Jules is definitely a challenge. I bite my lip and decide he deserves one more chance. After all, of the approximately 400 stalls he's done, he's only spun 87 times. "Now, Jules," I plead, "I'd really rather not go below 1,500 feet . . ."

No reaction. Then, finally, my tone of voice—not the meaning of my words—gets to him and *wham,* aside from that .87 Mach pull-out, Jules makes a rather nice recovery.

Although Jules is by no means an average student, he is representative of the kind who force many an instructor into early retirement. He is also the cause of many of the problems that you have with your instructor. A Jules is anyone who has scared the living hell out of him, and you should do everything in your power to keep from becoming one. Remember those times when your instructor grabbed the controls for no apparent reason, or when, tight-jawed and sweating, he told you to do something you were just about to do? These reactions come from a Jules in his past, and you should try to bear this in mind the next time he seems to be an overbearing, overpaid, arrogant *prima donna.*

My very first Jules was a Mr. Dunley, who tried to get me to fly a glider through a barbed-wire fence. Picture the airport: It has one tree, one hangar, one trailer, assorted gliders and towplanes, and three-fourths of a runway, the approach end of which coincides with the end of a drag strip. The runway gradually tapers from normal width to nothing, causing many pilots to assume it's not there at all. It is a beautiful day, the sky is cobalt blue, with fluffy, white cumulus clouds everywhere, promising a good soaring flight.

Enter Dunley, a 747 copilot with a spectacular female in tow. This jet jock is also a commercial glider pilot and wishes to soar aloft.

"Have you flown here before?"

Negative.

"Are you current?"

Additional negative.

"Well, you'll have to check out with one of our instructors and get current."

Roger.

"Let's see. Colby? Would you like to give Mr. Dunley here a field check?"

"Let's take 81W there, Mr. Dunley."

Dunley says, "I'd like to fly from the back seat, if it's all right with you. I used to be an instructor."

"Sure." My opinion of Dunley rises a notch. Every glider instructor knows that he or she has better control in the rear seat. Since he is about three inches farther back from the stick, he can utilize full aileron and elevator travel. Up front, you keep running into your legs and crotch while vainly trying to duplicate the maneuvers he demonstrates.

By the time we reach 1,000 feet, I know that Dunley is going to be no problem. Flying tow brings out a pilot's worst, and Dunley's worst is not bad at all. We release at 2,000 feet, and after a few stalls and steep turns, he wants to try some soaring. Fine. He stumbles into a thermal immediately and soon is at 4,500 feet, sniffing and poking among the clouds, exploring their potential. By this time I'm so confident about him that I'm practically asleep. He soon decides he'd better head back to the airport to get current in takeoffs and landings. I agree and go back to sleep.

Suddenly Dunley snaps me back to reality. He has the spoilers out, and a casual glance at the airport reveals that we are now quite low. Since adding power is frowned upon in gliding, I am interested to see how he is going to get himself out of this mess. To my surprise, he flies on obliviously, sinking lower and lower. I can see the duck ponds smiling in anticipation. I sit on my hands, not wanting to preempt him until it's absolutely necessary. He begins to turn final much too early, and he now has my complete attention. Unbelievably, he pulls on full spoilers and begins a slip. A thought suddenly occurs to me: "Where are you going to land?"

"On the runway."

"Point to it."

Dunley points to the drag strip.

"I've got it." I slam the spoilers shut and turn toward the airport.

Dunley emits an embarrassed "Oh . . ." from the back seat. In all his years of flying the big jobs, he has gotten into the habit of lining his airplane up with a runway just before he lands. This is an admirable trait, to be sure, but it has not prepared him to consider our airport's collage of gravel, ruts, dirt and tar for a runway when there's 3,000 feet of beautifully paved blacktop right next door.

I am now faced with the classic low-and-slow situation. A common, though thoroughly disapproved, method for curing students of landing long is to take them around the pattern and line them up on final one mile out at 150 feet above ground level, then dive down to ground level, trading altitude for airspeed, and float up to the fence in ground effect, effortlessly vaulting it at the last moment and making a normal landing. This method occurs to me now, and I only wish I had 150 feet instead of my miserable 50.

The airspeed is relentlessly bleeding off, and the fence is getting closer. It appears that I'm going to stall coincidentally with striking the fence, which, should I survive, will require quite a bit of explaining.

The fence looms closer, in curious slow motion. I dare not look at the airspeed indicator. I wait until the last second, take a deep breath and yank the stick all the way back. To my amazement, 81W rears up, hesitates, shudders and stalls with a resounding bang into the weeds on the other side of the fence.

As the dust slowly drifts away, Dunley clears his throat. "Sorry . . ."

I'll admit that I should have known better than to trust Dunley, but his flying and his ATR lulled me into complacency. I learned from him to be suspicious of *any* pilot I haven't flown with before, and if that makes you high-time guys uncomfortable, I'm sorry.

Sometimes a pilot you know quite well can turn into a Jules. That he and his flying habits are familiar merely assures that the change will be quick and unexpected. Sam is an excellent pilot, the best I've ever flown with. He is working on his flight instructor certificate and can do all the standard maneuvers better than I can. I am brushing him up on the things he has not practiced in 10 years, and soon he will be ready to meet his local Fed for the check ride.

This particular evening, we are running through the stall series. Sam has done impeccable power-on and -off stalls, departure stalls, approach stalls and a series of accelerated stalls. I am satisfied and tell him to hurry down to the Long Beach breakwater before it gets dark, so we can do a few pylon eights.

Sam obediently begins to descend, and as we pass through 2,000 feet, he asks, "Is that how you're supposed to do accelerated stalls?"

"Yes, why?"

"Well, I just couldn't seem to get a real stall break banked 45 degrees like that."

I assume my most professorial tone. "Of course not, Sam. You are working with a limited amount of elevator travel whenever you do a stall, and a 45-degree bank in level flight uses up almost all of it, leaving you with very little power to exceed the critical angle of attack. You'll find that if you try to stall power off in a 60-degree bank, you can't stall at all. You just go around in circles until somebody throws up."

Sam nods politely but remains unconvinced. He adds power at 1,200 feet and levels off, saying, "I'm going to try one more." Now all pilots know it is idiotic to do stalls at 1,200 feet. They are right. Regardless, Sam rolls into a 45-degree bank, stabilizes the airspeed and begins to haul back. As before, full back elevator merely produces a little extra G and a spasmodic shuddering. Sam frowns and rolls out slightly. Picking up some airspeed, he rolls back in with an extra measure of rudder, and yanks the wheel all the way back.

Sam, who is pretty unflappable, exhales quietly and shakes his head. Then he smiles shyly and says, "Well, that's one way to get down to pivotal altitude."

Next time you're out at the airport with nothing to do, buy your instructor a cup of coffee and ask him about his experiences. He'll probably be more than happy to tell you, and you're sure to learn something. If he's not there, wait around for a while. He's probably just out spinning with Jules.

●

Jules was lucky. He didn't have this next instructor. If he had, he might have found himself learning spin recoveries all by himself. Witness the exquisite guilt in this man's recollection of almost soloing the wrong *student.*

●

In aviation lore, it is a maxim that a pilot will regard his first solo as the most memorable episode in his log. Risking the charge of heresy, I must confess that this event long ago drifted into the more clouded area of my memory.

There is, however, one solo flight that remains crystal clear, despite frequent efforts to forget it. This experience relates not to a solo I made, but to one I gave.

My first position of gainful employment in aviation was as the only flight instructor for the flying club of a small state college. The club was surprisingly active, and after only one week of recruiting, I found myself inundated with 17 nondescript characters corralled from every stratum of rural society —each eager to make like an eagle.

Regrettably, I had discovered that the greatest hazard faced by a professional pilot is starvation, and had realized that a flight instructor's fiscal rewards can only be economic disaster. Because of this, I was most pleased by the crowded daily schedule of dual periods. In the beginning, I looked forward to those busy days, but by the end of the first month, the monotony of primary instruction was dulling my enthusiasm. Each day, each hour and, finally, each student was much like the one before. To relieve the tedium, I invented any number of diversions from the approved curriculum. Although I made an honest effort to impart the required skills, the addition of an occasional spin, loop, or forced landing followed through to actual touchdown on a deserted road or closely cropped alfalfa field did much to stimulate my ego and the student's interest.

By the end of the fifth week, six of my most persistent students had logged almost 10 hours and were nearing solo. During this time, three members who had dropped out were quickly replaced from the names on a lengthy waiting list. This meant that I had students at almost every stage of the presolo course; some were ready to solo, while others were just at the introductory lesson. These circumstances, plus my lack of interest in the students as individuals, set the stage for a strange situation.

To relieve my pressing schedule, I decided to solo as rapidly as possible those students who were ready. Actually, I was looking forward to the first, as it would be my initial student solo—a clear milestone in any instructor's life.

After one particularly busy morning, I returned late from a rushed lunch break and noticed that a student was already preflighting our elderly J-3. On my way through the office, I glanced at the schedule and saw the name "Morris" in the block for that time period. Good: I had flown with this one the day before, and he was ready to leave the nest. A few quick touch-

and-goes, and I could jump out and let my digestive juices function while I relaxed to savor my accomplishments . . . and his.

The student was seated in the aircraft as I approached, and without bothering to look at him, I called out the starting procedure and propped the engine to life. Crawling into the cramped familiarity of the front seat, I told him to taxi out and take off, but to remain in the traffic pattern.

During taxi, I made my displeasure at his sudden clumsiness evident and loudly criticized his obvious oversights in the run-up procedure.

The takeoff was passable. The first turn to base was atrocious and was followed by a maneuver to final that was downright ridiculous. Angrily, I grabbed the stick, righted the aircraft and made the first landing.

For the subsequent 30 minutes, we circuited the airport, following a pattern known only to God and my student. No two landings were alike, and most could only be described as catastrophic. I was totally disillusioned. Here was a student who could easily have soloed the day before, now unable to fly straight and level.

Finally, after endless agony, a pattern and landing were achieved with only minor infractions. I relaxed as we took off again, rationalizing that the painful performance was more the result of presolo jitters than lack of ability. Morris must realize that solo was near. The second landing was equally good, and as we rolled out, I released my belt and turned to tell the student to taxi to the ramp: The time had come.

At this instant, there commenced a series of aeronautical calisthenics I considered impossible for any aircraft with its wheels on the ground to perform. The wild gyrations were punctuated by screeching tires, desperate applications of full power followed by chugging idle throttle. During this time, both the student and myself fought the Cub and each other for control. At last, the torture ceased; we came to rest some 30 feet from any man-made surface; civilization lay beyond the field of mature barley that surrounded us. I slowly surveyed the green world around me and moaned to the petrified student that the instruction period had ended. His only response was a long sigh of relief that sounded much like a leaky tire. As I began the safari back to the airport, he remained motionless in the aircraft.

The half-mile walk to the flight office did not diminish my irritation. Storming through the door, I angrily told the scheduling girl that Morris needed at least 10 more hours and even then would probably never solo. She gave me a confused smile, examined the schedule and said, "Morris isn't scheduled today . . . Oh, you mean *Norris,* the new one."

At first, the degree of my misdeed didn't register. Then, after the full impact of what might have happened filtered into my brain, I realized how terribly close I'd come to soloing the wrong student. Norris was of a personality that required him to do exactly as instructed—without question. He had logged a total of only three hours, but was an excellent student. For the better part of an hour, I had verbally mauled him into a degree of superficial ability that I had considered safe for solo flight. Had he not ground-looped on that final landing . . . I shuddered at the probability.

During the days that followed, I wallowed in an abyss of self-degradation and pity. What madness had led me to consider myself capable of teaching people to fly? I found myself avoiding those students with more than eight hours, and canceled schedules without notice or reason. When forced to fly the advanced students, I concentrated on high work or maneuvers well away from the airport. Touch-and-go landings were all but dropped from the curriculum.

More than two weeks had gone by, when I heard rumors that many students were bitterly complaining that I was not soloing anyone because I wanted to boost my income with more dual time. By now, at least 12 were ready, and even the obedient

Norris had overcome his trauma and was approaching the big day.

With each flight, the pressure grew. Time and again, I began a training period determined to solo the student; but when the hour ended, I would still be in the aircraft. Often, the decision would be only a landing away, when the student would commit a minor infraction, reminding me of that life-saving ground loop.

Finally, I realized the decision had to be made. I was tormented by the two alternatives. If I continued to delay, my job would be lost and another instructor would judge my questionable ability; or I could solo a student, and if he crashed, I would probably lose my treasured certificates as well as face charges of negligent homicide.

Slowly, an idea began to take form. The airport was four miles from town in a totally uninhabited area. The field was always deserted from sunset until eight each morning. Sunrise occurred at 6:15, so for at least an hour and a half there would be no witnesses to what happened.

With the meticulous care of a professional assassin, I made my dark plan. The student would meet me at the airport at 6:30, we'd shoot a few landings to make it look good and then I'd get out to let him try three alone. I'd drive my car to the far end of the field. If he made it, I'd drive back to the office while he taxied in; if not, steer for home and go to bed. Later, when learning of the unfortunate tragedy, I'd be shocked that a student would steal an aircraft and try to fly it solo when he obviously wasn't qualified.

Now all that remained was to choose my victim. Fate would have a definite influence in his selection. Certain requirements had to be met. He must live alone, off campus, and have a car. I couldn't take the risk of his telling a roommate of the dual flight or of having someone bring him to the airport.

Several students met these demands, but one in particular seemed most likely. His name was Dobbs. He was a senior and a loner. He was one of the noisier critics of my delayed solo policy. Dobbs did not fit the physical appearance one normally expects of a pilot. He inhabited a large, angular body with short legs and hairy arms that extended well below his waist. His stoop-shouldered, flat-footed, clomping walk gave him the distinct characteristics of an orangutan. After a summer of employment as a lifeguard, he had a face the color and texture of walnuts. The ideal candidate.

It was now Sunday. The schedule showed that Dobbs had reserved a dual period Monday afternoon at three. Late that night, I called his number. A sleepy voice answered, "Hullo?"

"Dobbs? Did I wake you?"

"Uh-huh."

"Say, I can't make your flight tomorrow at three; I have a dental appointment."

"Oh, okay." He was disappointed.

"But so you won't lose the time, how about meeting me at the field at 6:30 in the morning? I know it's awfully early, but the wind is calm and it's a great time to fly."

"Sure, that'd be swell." The voice was considerably brighter.

"Fine, see you at 6:30. Don't be late." I hung up.

I spent a long, sleepless night in the company of a painful conscience. At last, the hour arrived and I drove to the field. Dobbs was already waiting in his car and was alone. As he preflighted the aircraft, I paced nervously nearby, looking furtively over my shoulder, fearing the sudden appearance of an unwanted visitor to ruin my careful scheme.

The Cub climbed easily in the crisp morning air, but my attention was focused on the roads leading to the airport rather than on the weather or my student's performance. Based largely on his grim appearance and my dislike for him, I had already presumed Dobbs's fate. I suffered through the time needed to make three landings without being aware of the skill demonstrated. After this, I crawled quickly out of the aircraft and waved my surprised student on to his doom with the optimistic statement, "Shoot three and come back to the ramp." He was grinning broadly as he taxied away.

Goodbye, Dobbs.

Quickly, I drove to where I could see the drama about to unfold. When I got into position, the Cub was already climbing on crosswind. I felt a final wave of remorse for poor Dobbs as the tiny bird turned onto a wobbly final.

The main gear touched the runway first, and then the aircraft rolled out as the tail settled gently. Before I could fully absorb the event, there was the sound of full throttle and the Cub was airborne again. I stifled a feeling of encouragement and waited for the inevitable finale.

The next landing began with a resounding thud as the main gear struck the runway hard. The aircraft bounced high. I groaned as the crash approached. He'd probably survive this one. Then came a short burst of power, and I watched a text-book recovery followed by a smooth landing. One more to go —if Dobbs's luck would only last. I began to allow myself the luxury of hope.

During the final pattern and landing, I witnessed a near-perfect exhibition. Unbelievably, the aircraft slid onto the runway and rolled out precisely down the centerline. Almost in shock, I hurried back to congratulate the grateful, jubilant student.

During the next three days, 11 more students soloed as I rode the wave of enthusiasm and confidence resulting from Dobbs's unexpected survival. On Friday morning, my original nemesis, Norris, was ready. After the customary three dual landings, we taxied to the ramp and I sent him out alone. As I stood watching, the college A&P instructor approached: "That makes an even dozen in less than a week. How in the world do you know when they're ready?"

With a slight twinge of conscience, I replied, "You just make a good plan and follow it through."

●

Sometimes the monkey on the aviator's back has a more complex nature, as with the next pilot, whose father had lost his life in an airplane.

●

On a sunny, pleasant afternoon in early August 1928, a sleek, all-black Waco "Ten" stalled on final approach and crashed in a grassy meadow adjacent to New Jersey's now-defunct Hadley Field. The aircraft was destroyed and the student pilot, my father, was decapitated, as was his instructor, a German World War I ace.

My father's death in his twenty-eighth year did not come before he had instilled in me, then a boy of four, a deep fascination for flying, but it was to be many years before I could resolve the emotional conflicts with which his premature demise confronted me to the point where I could undertake an uninterrupted course of flight instruction without feeling that somehow I was signing my own death warrant. Throughout those years, I heard countless stories of bold pilots who would never become old pilots, and I often reflected upon the circumstances of my father's crash: attempting to stretch a glide with a rough engine that just wouldn't pull him through. I promised myself that if ever I became a pilot, I was going to be a prudent, cautious, safe one. As a result, after a virtual lifetime of exposure to control tower yarns, I began to develop a kind of false, neurotic self-confidence born of the belief that because I had heard so many stories about them, certainly my knowledge of the pitfalls of flying would protect me. If ever I did begin to fly, I would have the necessary judgment already built in, just waiting to be applied.

So it was that I presented myself to the flight school at Monmouth County Airport in New Jersey, and thereby set in motion a chain of events that, some 30 months later, would see me putting my precious store of secondhand experience to the very test from which I had hoped it would protect me. After what seemed like an interminable student apprenticeship, my instructor finally decided that I could go up for examination. Curiously, for all my earlier hang-ups, I was full of confidence that day, and my self-evaluation was justified, I thought, when the examiner told me to return to the ramp after a mere 30 minutes' air work and one landing. Far from washing out, I had passed the exam with flying colors.

From then on, I seemed unable to resist any excuse to fly, however illogical the rationale. Only occasionally, such as upon a niggling, minor lapse in proficiency, would I be reminded that I did not want to follow my father's example. If the old fears did begin to rise, I stifled them, certain that no matter what the tragedies of the past, I was not going to repeat them—I was too smart for that. Then two events occurred in quick succession that brought all my old conflicts to the fore. In December 1970, I was copilot in a Beech Baron on an ILS approach to Runway 15 at Burlington, Vermont. I was monitoring the approach plate and providing the pilot with the information he requested relating to the approach. During the approach, we were advised of falling snow and four-foot snowbanks on either side of the runway. The tower also said that the runway had been cleared to its full width.

The instrument portion of our descent was uneventful. Visual contact was hampered, however, by an accumulation of ice on the windshield, and I knew from having flown the plane straight and level minutes before that we had ice—a lot of it—on our wings. Still, as I cramped my head against the side window for a glimpse of the runway, I felt little apprehension. The pilot—a seasoned, lifetime lightplane pro—had more than 18,000 hours laid down in his logbook, all without incident. In his hands, the effect of the ice load seemed minimal except that the runway was difficult to see. He sideslipped from time to time to improve his vision out the side. Another moment or two and we would be down.

Our touchdown was hard, a consequence of the load of ice we were carrying, and the pilot applied power. At that very instant, with our airspeed still well over 100 knots, the plane seemed to be inexorably drawn to the left, and finally rotated fully to the left, caroming down the runway tail-first as runway lights zoomed by from the rear with bewildering speed. I could hear the landing gear tearing loose, while on either side the propellers flailed the runway like triphammers. Meanwhile the baggage door behind me ruptured inward and snow spumed into the cockpit. We were covered from head to foot.

At last the plane came to rest, tail-first and nose-down. Only then did we realize that we had struck one of the "four-foot snowbanks." (As we later observed, the runway had not been cleared to "full width," advisory to the contrary notwithstanding.)

Fearful of fire, I wasted not an instant evacuating the cockpit while the pilot remained behind to deactivate fuel and electrical systems. I eased my mortification over my glaring predilection for self-preservation with mental assurances that next time I would exercise better discipline over my own actions.

More to the point of this narrative, however, is the fact that as I became more aware of the totality of what had happened, I could almost feel my long-stifled fear of emulating my father melt away. It was as though I had become lightened of a burden I had borne for so long that I had become unaware of it. Now suddenly, perversely, I was free: I had had *my* crash, *my* crisis, and unless the law of averages took an even more perverse turn, I would, I told myself, probably never again experience such a harrowing episode—not with today's planes. And most assuredly, not with my attitude about safety.

Fate didn't withhold its judgment long. A mere six days after my Burlington sleigh ride, I went to the Oneida County Airport in New York for a weather briefing for a flight between Oneida County and Monmouth County Airport in New Jersey. I examined the most recent satellite photo and discussed its significance with the FAA advisor on duty. His evaluation was that while the local area was occluded, the photo seemed to show that VFR conditions might be expected at my intended destination. The 1400Z terminal forecast had not yet come in, so we reviewed the prior summary, which indicated that adequate ceiling and visibility conditions prevailed between Newark and Philadelphia. I interpreted the report to mean that comparable conditions would also prevail over the Monmouth County area, which lies between these two points.

The summary also showed that various points en route would be below VFR minimums, but the advisor suggested that I could probably undertake the trip if I could get on top, then indicated to be about 4,000 feet msl. Local conditions, however, suggested that this might not be feasible—no openings in the overcast existed. During the discussion, the 1400Z report came in. It indicated a potentially deteriorating condition to the south, the direction of my destination. It was apparent that if I did not leave immediately, the weather near Monmouth would move in before I could get there.

As we spoke, the skies overhead cleared, and I decided that I could very easily get on top and reach Monmouth before the weather fell below VFR minimums. Accordingly, I departed from the airport at 0945 local time, flew eastward a few miles to where there was no overcast whatsoever, and proceeded to climb on top as planned. I had purposely delayed in filing my flight plan until I was certain that I could actually execute it. This was my first attempt at VFR on top, and I became so engrossed in the actual flying aspects of the flight that only later, when it was altogether too late, did I realize that I had neglected to file.

Nevertheless, conditions, at least initially, were quite favorable, and for a while I experienced no problems other than a feeling of awe at being on top and seeing my options disappear behind me. The first inkling that VFR on top might not be a panacea came when I realized that both tanks were half empty. According to my careful preflight plan, this should not have occurred until I was within minutes of my destination. With four hours of fuel aboard, I had estimated my time of arrival to be some two hours and 15 minutes after departure. It is now approaching noon, yet my VOR fixes seemed to indicate that at my present rate of progress I had more than an hour's flying time ahead of me.

At the same time, it became apparent that an overcast—above the one over which I was flying—was emerging in my direction of flight. Suddenly intensely alert, I began listening for FSS and tower advisories at every station and airport in range. Happily, while the weather was not going to hold as long as I had hoped it would, VFR conditions seemed to prevail throughout the area. The unanswered question was: Were there breaks in the overcast through which I could descend?

Ill at ease, I considered returning to Oneida County or possibly landing at the first field along the way. One look at the overcast below resolved the debate: There were no openings that I could see, and to attempt to return to Oneida would put me in an even more critical fuel condition over mountainous terrain with no assurance that there would be a break in the overcast when I got there. On the other hand, if I could reach the vicinity of Monmouth, I knew that the terrain was but a hundred feet or so above sea level and virtually flat. If it was going to come to that, I could at least make a slow descent through the murk with more than an even chance of breaking out before encountering a solid object.

As I pondered these things, my environment evolved into an overcast above and an overcast below. Ahead, the two cloud layers converged into a solid wall of ugly gray. An Eastern Electra added to my concern as it suddenly emerged nearby from the clouds above and just as suddenly disappeared into those beneath me. I now realized that I was penetrating the peripheries of Metroplex, for in my anxiety to shorten my remaining trip, I had taken a direct heading for the Colts Neck VOR instead of the circuitous route originally planned. Yet if I could only reach Colts Neck, my worries would be over, I thought, for I recalled one of my instructors having said that most ATC routings via Colts Neck are above 6,000 feet msl, whereas I was at 4,000 feet. I tried to assure myself that this was solid fact. Soon I became aware that the two overcasts converged at almost the precise point where in my mind's eye I perceived the Colts Neck VOR to be.

I began making radio calls to Teterboro FSS, Monmouth Unicom, Newark Tower, LaGuardia, Kennedy and almost all the stations within reasonable distance. No response. The radio had been having a crystal seating problem. All the evidence suggested that the problem was recurring at this very moment. I found myself unconsciously easing away from where the two overcasts blended into a solid wall, and I was making little headway.

I estimated that I was within eight miles of the Colts Neck VOR and less than 20 miles from my destination. By this time, I had begun to accept the fact that I would not get there. My mind raced through a score of alternatives, finally settling on one: I would try to raise Newark or Teterboro in the hope of obtaining a radar vector for a GCA approach at Newark or to a break in the overcast.

I tried to position the dial in such a way as to seat the crystal properly, but the results were the same as before. In the interim, the convergence of the two overcasts had spread to all directions but the east, cutting off my route back to New York. A glance at my fuel gauges showed the left tank empty; a mere five gallons remained in the right. It occurred to me that this might be a good opportunity to explore the practical applications of slow flight, and I added about 10 degrees of flaps, eased the throttle back to 2,000 rpm and trimmed to maintain altitude.

I decided that the only remaining chance I had was to head toward the ocean in the fanciful hope that the disparity in temperature between land and sea would produce a cloud break. I could recall numerous occasions when I had observed that the cloud cover seemed to match the contours of the shoreline perfectly.

The results were almost immediate. The overcast below took on a darker hue, and moments later I perceived the welcome shapes of buildings, fields and streets through a mantle of snow.

Eagerly, I nosed the plane sharply down and plunged through the opening. Below me loomed an estuary, yet as familiar as I thought myself to be with my native New Jersey, I could not place it. With so little fuel, I had scant time left for orientation. My attention was instantly diverted by the realization that I had entered a driving rain, but still more disconcerting, it was adhering to the windshield. Visions of our ice-encrusted landing less than a week before at Burlington loomed before me, but with one significant difference: This ice was building up fast, and I had no deicers. I knew, too, that if it was building up on the windshield, it was building up all over. Already the controls were more sluggish than they had been six days earlier. I considered climbing back up on top, but then, remembering my critical fuel predicament, I added more flap and scanned the snow-covered earth below. Ahead, the estuary led into a bay whipped with frothy whitecaps. As the driving, freezing rain obscured more and more of the windshield, I turned into the wind and began to formulate a plan for ditching: I would attempt a very nose-high, full-flap, full-stall landing as close to the shore as I could get without risking hitting bottom.

As I began my descent (I was now at 1,500 feet), I saw what seemed to be an unencumbered stretch of beach to my left. Perhaps the dry beach would be better than cold water. Adding a little left rudder and aileron, I continued my descent, hoping that on touchdown I could keep from nosing over.

At possibly seven or eight hundred feet, my eyes were diverted by a movement to my left. A car was pulling away from a large, flat, snow-covered surface which I recognized as an empty parking lot. Adding more left rudder and aileron, I knew that I was perfectly set up to make this new-found landing site. A recollection of my father's overstretched glide more than 40 years earlier flashed to mind, but I knew I had this one made. I added full flaps, cut the throttle and flared out an instant after clearing the low fence that bounded the lot. The roll-out left me with room to spare. I had made the first landing of record at Great Kills Park on Staten Island.

Now, a year later, my sense of elation at having survived two critical incidents within a week has given way to disgust and self-contempt. I had taken off under predicted marginal conditions at my destination. Knowing about the radio problem, I should have determined beyond doubt that it had been restored to full operating dependability; clearly this called for more than my cursory radio check and tower clearance. If I had remembered to file a flight plan, perhaps I would have perceived the problem before my troubles had begun to compound. Beyond failing to file, I had failed to monitor my progress adequately, and at no time had I specifically evolved a plan of alternative action. If I had remained more alert to the subtle changes in the weather environment, I could possibly have forestalled the crisis. Last, by taking off in unsettled local weather, I effectively eliminated any options for terminating the flight once I was above the overcast.

If any good has come out of these events, it is the much-needed realization that there never was and never will be any relationship between my father's accident and my own flying skills. Incidents which have befallen others will never protect me from duplicating their errors. Secondhand experience, no matter what its source, is of no value.

In the year since, I have logged an additional 75 hours of flight time. One of my most enthusiastic passengers is my four-year-old son, who, if the flight is too long, tends to fall asleep.

I know I have made a good landing if I can taxi back to the ramp without awakening him.

●

For that pilot, the battle was with himself. For others, the test is one of learning to adapt to the system; that means accommodating the vagaries of other people. It is romantic to be up there all alone, but flying on instruments, one doesn't want to be too much alone.

●

As an Air Force pilot, just out of cadet training and gunnery school, I had no use for people who didn't fly airplanes. Tower operators were there to help me get an ATC clearance; when they cleared me onto the runway for takeoff, I'd be sure to look around for myself, not as a double check, but because I just didn't trust their word that the way was clear. Flight maintenance crews were people who left wrenches and screwdrivers in the air intake of the engine and rarely knew much more than I did about repairing an airplane.

The air traffic control system was a stone's throw from worthless and far too wound up in its own little world to realize it. I once waited an hour and a half to be cleared on a 20-minute hop because someone along the line was confused about ADIZ procedures. At the end of one cross-country, with fuel down to 20 minutes, I had a traffic controller insist on keeping me in the holding pattern so that he could bring in a C-124 that had been waiting to land for 10 minutes. I had to declare an emergency to make him realize that my single turbine just wasn't going to run much longer and that I was not looking forward to a flameout in the weather. I landed with 30 gallons of fuel remaining, enough for another four minutes of flight. With the exception of some always-sharp GCA units, I felt that I was pretty much on my own from the time I fired up the engine until the time I shut it down. I changed.

The sky as I took off had a high overcast that Weather told me would lower as I neared Riverside, California's March AFB, but that March would be carrying 1,200 broken by the time I got there. No problem. I was alone in a T-33 jet trainer and had flown the penetration at March before, so I didn't feel that there would be too much that was unfamiliar for me to do. ATC, for once, was prompt, and my wheels folded into the well five minutes before estimated takeoff time. I turned out of the pattern at Stead AFB, Nevada, and flew a standard departure route over Reno.

"Report over Bakersfield to Oakland Center," Reno Approach Control said. "Have a good trip."

"Wilco, and thank you, Reno," I called, and settled into a climb on course.

At 25,000 feet the bottom of the overcast was flicking the top of my canopy, and in a second I was on instruments. The cloud was still thick as I pulled the throttle back to cruise power and leveled at 35,000 feet. Smooth air, easy flying.

Then it started. A red light flashed at the lower-right side of the instrument panel, over a placard that said "inverter out warning." The inverter supplies all the power to the radio navigation instruments, the heading indicator and the attitude indicator. I'd have a hard time letting down at March without those needles showing me where to go and when to turn in the penetration. Fortunately, the Lockheed people had installed a spare inverter, and I flicked the switch from "main" to "spare." The light went out. This must be the fifth inverter to go out on this airplane in the last month, I thought. If I were a mechanic . . .

The light came on again; the spare inverter had burned out. I flicked the switch back to "main," and the light went out for a minute, then flickered on again.

"The things are overheating," I said to myself. If I give them a chance to cool, maybe I can make one last long enough to get me far enough through the letdown to break out of the weather.

If I could get into the clear, there would be no problem, but here in the weather on instruments and entering the high-density area above Los Angeles, I needed inverters.

I turned the inverter switch off and the little "off" alarm flags dropped into place in the omni course indicator and the attitude indicator. This meant flying partial-panel instruments, something I hadn't done since primary flight training a year earlier. The low-frequency radio compass was useless. I had heard for a long time that the bird dog was fine in clear weather, but hopeless in the soup. This was a typical example: static in the earphones, and no matter how finely I tried to tune it, the needle simply would not point to any radio station. It wandered 50 degrees on either side of the nose, and occasionally even swung around to point behind the tail. I figured that I was still five minutes from Bakersfield, if the winds at altitude were what the weatherman predicted. I flew by the magnetic compass, mounted directly over a placard saying "caution—magnetic compass may be as much as 10 degrees in error with heater-blower operating." With the outside air temperature at minus 55° C., the heater-blower was working overtime, and in the maze of airways over Los Angeles, I simply could not afford to be 10 degrees off course. I called for assistance.

"Bakersfield Radio, this is Air Force Jet 29159, over." All I heard was the quiet crackle of static in the earphones of my helmet. "Bakersfield Radio, Bakersfield Radio, Air Force Jet Two Niner One Five Niner, how do you read? Over." Nothing. "Any radio facility reading Air Force Jet Two Niner One Five Niner, give a call on three zero one point four, over." Good grief, I thought, don't tell me my radio's out, too!

A faint voice sounded through the static. ". . . Five-Niner, this is Shady Lady on Guard, can we be of assistance?"

A flood of relief swept through me as I spun the channel selector of the radio to the emergency channel. Shady Lady is a GCI site, I thought happily, they'll have radar that can steer me to Bakersfield, or maybe even March!

"Roger, Shady Lady, One-Five-Niner at angels three-five, navigation instruments out and in the weather. Request assistance to letdown at March AFB."

Static. I called again, but heard no reply. I had lost contact with Shady Lady. This was not good. If the winds were right, I should have been over Bakersfield, and I turned to the heading for Los Angeles, my next checkpoint. The mag compass bobbled and swung in its case, and I may easily have been 20 degrees off course. With civilian airliners crowding the airways beneath me, I couldn't dive down to get under the weather. It was also possible that the ceiling had lowered during my flight, and there wouldn't *be* any "under the weather." I had only one card left to play. The inverter switch went back to "main," and the red light reluctantly went out. The ghostly voice of a forgotten instructor in cadets rang in my mind. "If you ever get in trouble, don't hesitate to turn that dial on your IFF set to 'emergency.' It gives a mayday pattern on the GCI radar screens that can't be missed. They'll drop everything to help you."

The inverters on this plane also gave power to the IFF equipment, and I prayed that there would be enough life in the main inverter to get a distress signal on somebody's radar. There was. As soon as the selector dial stopped at "emergency," a calm voice came clearly in the earphones, as if the man were in the back seat of my plane talking to me.

"Aircraft squawking mayday, this is March Rapcon. Can we be of assistance?"

I pressed the mike button.

"Roger, March Rapcon, Air Force Jet 29159 at angels three-five, approximately over Los Angeles omni in the weather, all navigation instruments out. Request vector to March and a GCA pickup."

"Roger, Five-Niner," he answered, "we have a target over the ocean 15 miles west of Catalina Island. Turn to heading 080 degrees, begin descent to angels two-five." The voice was calm and nonchalant. I continued my left turn around to the general direction of 080, and started to let down through the featureless world of gray.

"March Rapcon, be advised Five-Niner has negative directional indicator, requests no-gyro letdown and GCA to full stop at March, over."

"Roger," came the unruffled voice. "Roll out . . . now, call passing angels two-seven."

I was elated and felt as secure as if I were already in the chocks. I followed his directions as he led me through the tangle of airways and traffic in the Los Angeles sky. It was simple. It was ridiculously easy. In a minute he was saying, "You are now turning to a seven-mile final for GCA no-gyro approach. Complete your prelanding check and contact the final controller on 363.8 megacycles."

In 40 seconds I was looking down to 13,000 feet of white concrete; in 40 more my wheels spun on that huge runway and a school of fire trucks raced along at my side, their red lights flashing. I don't think I've ever smiled so broadly in my life.

I don't have to say that my opinion of the value of the man on the ground took an abrupt about-face; in fact, it turned into sheer admiration when the calm voice said, "Five-Niner, you have a follow-me truck waiting at the end of the runway. You can park to the east of the tower."

●

The young Air Force pilot signed his byline Richard Bach, and some of the sentiments he wrote about then found their way into other writings later. More than any other aviation writer around, Bach has told most stirringly of his own introspective moments around airplanes.

It's hard to pin down why it is so hard for pilots to learn their way into the system; it is one of the first hurdles for the new pilot to overcome. A woman learning to fly at a busy airport described the time when she finally managed to get past that haunting fear that she had no business being there.

●

I learned to fly at Honolulu International Airport, a facility that sees just about every type of flying machine there is. If you're one of those people who tends to avoid airliners and military jets, you'll sympathize with the fact that my who-goes-first priorities were: first, the largest; second, the fastest; third, those who knew what they were doing; fourth, me. My instructor had other priorities, however—and, I'm now convinced, a more realistic attitude. "You have as much right to be here as anyone else," he insisted. I doubted it, but with the innocent cooperation of our tower controllers, he finally persuaded me.

One bright morning, my instructor said, "Jack seems a little worried about your flying in and out of this airport. I noticed he was pretty tense in the back seat yesterday afternoon."

"He's not the only one, Jim," I said. "It's an ordeal every time." I toted up a short, ugly list of reasons why it was such an ordeal. There was self-consciousness—all those monsters on five-mile final, just waiting for me to get my tail down. And there was a lack of confidence in my own ability to make the plane do what I was told to do with it.

"Well," said Jim, "today we're going to do some touch-and-goes right here at the airport instead of wasting our time flying over to Dillingham."

I had trouble getting out of my chair. My ankles had turned to *poi.*

"No, don't get up yet," he said. "First, I'm going to show you all the possible instructions the tower might give you in the pattern."

At the blackboard, with a piece of chalk and his most non-chalant radio voice, he took me through a dizzying series of approach variations from all legs of the pattern. "Seven-Four November, make a 360 to the right. Start your base. Square your pattern. Make a 270." (A 270?) "Seven-Four, lengthen your downwind. Turn final *now.* Change to 4 Right, November. Expedite! You're number three. Follow the 727. Hold your altitude. Caution, wake turbulence. Runways 22 and 26 now in use." (A *kona* wind.) "Make a left 360." And so on. Jim concluded, "You see, there are only so many things he can say, so just be prepared." I was only partly reassured. Whenever I got in the air, they invented something new.

We took off, somehow, and I asked permission for a right turnout. The approach end of Runway 4 Right has a short length marked on it; small planes making touch-and-goes are supposed to use this length, taking off before reaching a white stripe. Jim requested permission to use it, and it was granted. I was horrified. Why, I kept asking him, should the controllers have to be bothered with me, smack in the middle of the prime tourist-arrival time? I would scare everyone to death. But all he said was, "Call in. You're on your downwind already and he doesn't even know you're there."

I didn't even have time to yell help! From then on, it was just the controller and me. Seven-Four November flew itself. I did all the variations on the blackboard as the controller wove me in and out of heavy incoming traffic. Sure enough, there were a few new phrases—personal favorites of this controller—now they're as clear and vivid as the old standards. Jim insisted that I confirm each instruction from the tower, even if only a word, if at all possible. "Extending. Right. Final. Expediting. I have him. Following." Somehow, I heard it all and said it all and did it all, and it was one of the most exhilarating half hours of my life.

Jim finally requested a full stop, and then said, "There. Now you and Jack can quit worrying."

As we rolled down the runway to our intersection, Jim thanked the controller, who replied, to my astonishment, "Glad to oblige. As long as you stay below that white stripe, we can keep it up all day."

The second step in the education of a flying mouse had to do with Runway 8. That's the longest runway, the one pointed more directly out to sea, and to my mind, it was a big-jet preserve. When 747s were first doing trial runs to Honolulu, I saw one take off on Runway 8. I had never been given an approach to 8.

My instructor assumed correctly that I had not yet been fully divested of my mistaken notions. One day, coming in over Pearl City, we listened to the ATIS reporting a wind straight down Runway 4, a common situation. With all my concentration devoted to holding my altitude over Pearl Harbor, I barely heard Jim say, "Request Runway 8. We'll do a cross-wind landing." I took up the mike routinely, but the words had begun to penetrate. "Eight? Why do we need 8? We've been doing crosswind landings for an hour at Dillingham. Did you say 8?"

Jim said, "Yes," and casually stubbed out a cigarette.

I honestly didn't think I'd find my voice, feeling such an utter lack of conviction, and my breath was somewhere under the seat belt, strapped in. "I want you to request 8," said my favorite block of granite.

I requested 8.

"Uh, Seven-Four November, you're cleared for 8," said the tower, quite tentatively, I thought. "Lengthen your downwind and square your pattern."

I obliged, more or less.

A deep, sexy voice boomed up. "Continental, ready for ta-keoff on Runway 8."

I directed a few pertinent thoughts to my instructor, who seemed to be looking at the scenery. We were cautioned about wake turbulence, and then, by golly, we landed on Runway 8.

Said Jim, "There's nothing sacred about his runway. If he can fit you in, he'll do it. If for some reason he can't, he'll request that you accept an alternative. All he has to worry about is speed and maneuverability, not the hotel situation in Waikiki."

Logic, and now experience, told me he was right. And then,

one solo day, a happy thing occurred. I had given myself a good maneuvers workout over Kunia Road, and with precision on my mind, was doing a fairly creditable approach to Honolulu.

"Seven-Four November, you're cleared for Runway 4 Left. There's a 747 on 10-mile final for 4 Right."

Well, heck, I'll be at the gas pump by then. He must be saying that as a reminder to himself.

I took my time and did everything carefully.

"Northwest Niner, cleared for 4 Right. There's a Cherokee letting down on your left."

Well, all right, all right, I'll be long gone.

I raised my line of sight off the nose to where it should be and settled onto the runway. Leaning over to let down the flap handle, I caught sight of Northwest Niner. It filled the sky and the earth on my right side.

And yet, there was something polite and modest about its aspect.

"Seven-Four November, turn left at the next intersection and contact ground control. Uh, 747, follow that Cherokee."

●

It's true; we're all in this together: controllers, other pilots—even passengers, as this next airman found out when his young daughter sounded a timely alarm on a poor approach.

●

Approaching New York on your way home from Atlantic City that Sunday was supposed to be fun. For the first time, my 10-year-old daughter, Dana, would see the Manhattan skyline glowing in the late-afternoon sun, from 2,000 feet up. She would enjoy it all the more, I had thought, because she had at last cured herself of an ever-threatening queasiness that had led to many an unscheduled landing. Now, however, she sat beside me in our Arrow, glumly watching the skyline disappear behind a deepening grayness. Somewhere to the west, something had jarred loose, and a winter storm was beginning to move in, causing us to dash for Westchester County Airport, our home base, in hopes of reaching it before it went IFR.

Some buffets again turned my attention toward Dana, who was becoming a telltale pale. My flight bag contained some plastic sacks, but my main concern was that her new-found confidence in her airworthiness would be spoiled.

We descended to 2,500 feet to get well below the New York TCA and headed north, toward the Sparta Vortac. Flight service reported Teterboro Airport still VFR, with Westchester, 24 statute miles farther to the northeast, still marginal but worsening. At Teterboro, the situation was normal for a late weekend afternoon: "Stay out of the control zone. We have your number. We'll call you," was the controller's warning to everyone wanting to land. He sounded as if he were talking to unqualified supplicants for jobs. A pilot could end up circling outside the control zone for 30 or 40 minutes before his number came up and he was cleared into the pattern. Who needs it, I thought. Besides, my car was at Westchester; it would be damned inconvenient not to land at Westchester. So much for Teterboro as an alternate. Press on, I said to myself, swinging to the northeast and staring Westchesterward into a mass of crud.

"Why don't we land?" Dana said.

"Feeling queasy?"

"Even if I didn't, it looks awful there."

"You don't want to stay up here waiting to get into Teterboro, do you?"

"I don't know. What about that airport we flew over a while ago?"

She meant Morristown, which was but 15 minutes away, uncongested and definitely VFR.

"You mean spend the night in Morristown, when we're so close to home? Come on, Dana, the car's at Westchester."

"Well, Dad, I'm a little scared."

"We'll be okay. This is just some haze," I said testily as the Cherokee answered to a sharp, sudden gust. Her reply was a doubting look.

I had aimed for the Tappan Zee Bridge, which spans the Hudson River and is a good reporting point for Westchester Tower. I thought it was still somewhere up ahead. On the ground, lights were dimly appearing, blinking in the gathering haze. Behind us, the sun was setting.

Where was the bridge? Irritated by the distraction, I turned down the radio volume, barely noticing that I was still tuned to the tense chatter at Teterboro.

Five minutes passed. The ground was now almost impossible to read. Desperately, I switched to Westchester Tower and reported myself near the Tappan Zee.

From the tower: "Cherokee 1621 Quebec, do you have information Sierra?"

Good grief. "No, I don't."

"Are you IFR or VFR?"

"I'm VFR."

"Sir, Westchester is currently IFR."

"Any . . . is there any chance for special VFR?"

"Sir, our visibility is one-half mile. No special VFR."

Dana was now hunched over, resting her face in her cupped hands. Her body remained motionless as I turned 180 degrees back into New Jersey. How much longer could she hold out? Could I still find Teterboro? How about the fuel? How long would Teterboro hold me outside the zone, and would the field go IFR?

The fuel gauges were reassuring, but the visibility was not. I switched back to the Teterboro frequency. Nestled amid the haze-swollen lights of the cluttered area, Teterboro was still VFR but lost to me in the dusk. The sun was gone.

"Dad—"

"It's okay. We're going to Teterboro."

"I think I'm going to be—"

"No! Don't! We'll be okay." My voice had become harsh, and she looked at me again in that doubting way.

"Just hang on," I said, as my eyeglasses began to mist.

As I called Teterboro, I prepared a stabbing estimate of my position. But I caught sight of the lights of the George Washington Bridge, about five miles from the airport. I dreaded Teterboro's reply.

"Cherokee 1621 Quebec, we have your number. Stay out of the control zone until we call you. Cessna Three-Two November, do you read?"

"Three-Two November ready and waiting."

"Three-Two November, report downwind for Runway 1."

"About time."

"Three-Two November, just report. We've got enough to do here."

To my right, a sick girl was fading fast. Her eyes were closed, as if she were trying to sleep or faint or be anywhere but where she was. As I began to circle just outside the control zone, trying not to lose the lights of the bridge, I felt an urge to break into the stream of requests, denials, reprieves and general hassles to say, "Look, I've got an ailing passenger here, and it's getting harder to see. Please, please clear me in." But I could just hear the controller asking, with a threat in his voice, "Are you declaring an emergency?" And I could visualize the climb up to the tower, the explanations, the chewing out ("Hell, *that's* no emergency"), the forms to be filled out, and who knew what else. So I held my peace, feeling the ominous passage of time, watching the bridge lights and thinking, Lord, keep me legal, keep me legal.

At last, out of the jumble of numbers and instructions, of remarks and chastisements, came my number. I responded hoarsely and received the welcome order to report downwind for Runway 1.

As I reported, Dana stared ahead, as if helplessly awaiting the inevitable. I kept my eyes fixed on the runway lights, turned base and went through my landing checklist for the third time —one notch of flaps to go. I was still completing the turn to final when I again glanced over to Dana. She was hunched over, trembling.

"You want the bag? You need the bag?" I asked urgently.

"Cherokee Two-One Quebec, cleared to land," squawked the radio speaker.

"Dana? Here—here's a bag," and I reached behind her seat, knocking over my flight kit as I did.

"Dad!" she yelled, "You're supposed to fly the plane!"

My face suddenly chilled as I snapped back to the situation: short final, lights coming up, airplane low, airspeed high, pilot paralyzed.

My adjustments were enough to let us get down with only two bounces. As we turned off the runway, I avoided Dana's eyes.

Only 10 years old, she had perhaps just saved us by being more mature than I. Sick, scared and untrained, she had known instinctively the essential thing: Fly the plane, first things first —indulge yourself later. Throughout the homeward flight, I had indulged myself, coddling my convenience, pressing the situation, creating unnecessary pressures and so working myself up that I had completely lost my poise and almost my control of the airplane at the crucial moment.

Dana and I have flown together often since then, and we are able to laugh now about "that landing," as we politely call it. She intends to become a pilot, and she'll be a good one. After all, she's already taught one pilot a lot about flying.

●

When the pilot makes a mistake, it is no fun at the time; however, the discomfort during the instant when the mistake is being made is nothing compared with the agony of self-recrimination that follows. There's another side to it, though; most airmen seem to grow a little as a result of these experiences. Few put that into words better than this down-south duster pilot who had a feeling he was jinxed.

●

Moisture condensing from the tips of the prop swirled by the Stearman cockpit. The penciled sketch and notes for the morning's dusting were barely visible in the Mississippi dawn.

There were two fields, one large and simple, the other small and difficult. I intended to take the worse first. The small field supported a stand of cypress trees.

The trees had no limbs near the ground, and the tops were tight knots towering above dusting altitude. From still higher, where I circled a few minutes after takeoff, the trees appeared closer together than from the ground the day before. But I was hooked; I flew seriously and tried to do a thorough job. The farmer had hired me instead of the other dusters around for this very reason.

Using the sketch, I confirmed the tree avenue with the most wingtip clearance, flew it just above the treetops, then swung way out for a long approach to the low dusting run. Once among the trees, I tried slight control movements to discover how critical the act of flying would be in such close quarters. There was no problem. In the still air, controlling the ship was the same as driving a car down a narrow road.

The straightaway lanes were soon exhausted. I tried a run with a gradual turn. It could be done, so I hit that cypress patch from every direction. There were several hard-to-reach areas, but each time after circling above for a look I could see a way. It was a point of honor with me that the farmer wouldn't have to take a tractor in to clean up my leftovers.

After I landed, the farmer lighted my cigarette. "The hands

figure you fly through the trees, not between them." I used the cigarette to hide the twitch in my smile.

The big field promised to be a lead-pipe cinch for several reasons. The only obstacle was a lone, dead chinaberry tree in the center. The limbs were gray and stood out in contrast to the green of the cotton. At 12 1/2 cents an acre, this field would be putting money in my pocket fast.

Moreover, the farmer liked the field dusted low, with wheels tickling the cottontops. This is easier dusting than five feet up, as the book calls for. You can feel the cottontops and know exactly where you are; holding five feet higher is much harder.

The farmer liked low dusting for another reason. The triangle formed by the landing gear strut and the oleo scissors collected a neat pyramid of cotton bolls, which he inspected during each refill stop. He could tell where the weevils had been busy.

The large field went along well. The dollar in my pocket every three minutes was sweet. I began using the chinaberry tree to check mid-field dust swathe spacing. Soon I flared out onto the run in direct line with the distant tree.

It grew larger. I jerked back on the stick.

The Stearman "rotated" well, but with a full hopper and the usual slow dusting speed, it mushed instead of climbing. I popped the stick forward to take the tree dead-on, but too late. There was a sharp explosive crash. Something popped me—not too hard—on the side of my head. The Stearman slammed to a halt, or so it seemed. It bounced once, heavy, then flew out. I couldn't believe it. The urge was strong to chop the throttle and flatten some cotton. But I didn't know where the potholes might be in the soft Mississippi Delta soil, and the dust hopper was full. Sulphur dust burns well.

The ship vibrated under full throttle. I cut it a bit; the vibration lessened. The stick had a little slop, but we were a going concern.

Looking astern, I noticed that there was no tree in the field. I couldn't see even where it might have been. As for where it was at the moment, the answer was easy. Tangled in the wing wires, snagged in the fabric and flapping in the airstream was a substantial collection of kindling wood and branches. Thankfully, the tree had been dead and splintery. The fuel tank, in the upper-wing center section, was intact. The propeller was to be commended for clearing the way.

I dragged the strip until my fellow duster—also my boss—got the message to look my gear over. The Stearman was heavy, so I set it down hot and used up the whole strip.

"Gawdamn!" he exploded. (The Stearman was part of his fleet; I was on his payroll.) He tore into the tangle of wood and rigging. Things looked a sorry mess. The prop tips were bent, the front ignition harness flapped loose from broken plugs. The agitator prop was a splintered hub, and the lower half of the dusting venturi was dangling. The entire undersurface of the bird was riddled with rips. The left half of the horizontal stabilizer possessed an inverted V to a depth of several inches.

Still, the Stearman was all there; no large chunks of canvas were missing. It was battered a bit, that's all.

The boss ordered, "Spread the rest of the dust and take her over to Greenwood. We'll put her back together there."

No, thank you, I told him. (If I had used my head, I would have dumped the dust on the way to the strip.) I wasn't about to fly it anywhere with a full hopper. Despite a guilty feeling, I dug up enough courage to say, "You want the dust flown out, you fly it yourself. I'll take your ship. Fair enough?" This stopped him; we dumped the dust.

There was no dope at Greenwood to match the Stearman's wartime yellow, only clear stuff. With white canvas, the poor airplane soon sported a healthy crop of freckles—162 that I counted in disgust halfway through the job.

The farmer later reported that the chinaberry was splintered off just above the cottontops.

I told myself, ramming trees is something I just don't do.

This can't be; I was better trained than *that!* I approached an old-time duster pilot for perspective on my problem.

"How long you been dusting?" he asked.

"Little under two months."

"What you worrying about? You're doing better than most. We figure to hit something or other maybe once a month."

This was incredible. "You mean you keep flying, figuring to bust up a tree?"

"Or a piece of one, or a fence," he said. "Been doing it since before you were born, I bet. Look, you didn't get hurt. Your birdcage has a case of measles, is all."

The Stearman and I returned to battle the bugs. I was going to be doubly careful. The old pilot's fatalism was not for me.

The next farm had a wire patch, another challenge for me. I looked the place over from the ground. The four powerlines met in a common center near the farm buildings. The wires were high enough to fly under, for the most part. Near the center I intended to use pull-ups rather than dodging poles and guy wires.

The perimeter work went fast. There was plenty of room to line up between poles, hug the cottontops under the wires and make one continuous pass across the field. This went on for better than an hour.

Near the center, I stopped the underflying and began pull-ups, something I never liked at all. Wires and skinny poles don't provide much in the way of cues for pull-ups. This time, because of the star-shaped arrangement, I resorted to flying in toward the center, parallel to one of the radial powerlines, and beginning the pull-up at a preselected post alongside. This worked well for the first three quadrants, and the last one should have been equally successful. But I must have allowed my vision to skip a few posts.

Wires directly ahead caught my peripheral vision as I concentrated on that wrong post. Too close, I hauled back hard.

This time, the Stearman was light and lifted at the first touch. It almost cleared. It slewed to the right, with a sharp snap.

Full left rudder brought it out, and a fire-walled throttle lifted it on the step, but it was sluggish. I leaned over the side of the cockpit. A bar-taut, thin bundle of wires streamed from under the wing. A gentle bank revealed a long line curving down to the cottontops.

I stayed high and turned tight onto final, watching the wire ends to see that they cleared the fence before letting the bottom fall out for the short strip. The curious farmer later measured the wire. It wasn't a mile long as I thought; only 980-odd feet.

My resolution was made then and there. There may be some hardy souls who accept the probability of flying their planes into objects. Not me. I flipped in the half-hitches, tucking the Stearman into her mooring, and paid lip service to my boss's encouragement: "Hell, you're doing fine. The farmers like your work. They'd rather you dusted them than me . . ."

The next Greyhound out of the little Mississippi town had me aboard. The highway passed close to our strip, and I squelched a bitter tear during the last look at the freckled Stearman. If "quitter" was my name, I would have to wear it.

It was a year later—I had even begun to hate the sight of a Stearman—before an incident happened to help trigger a more mature look at myself and at flying. An eager-beaver colonel took our full squadron of National Guard F-47s under cables across a lake—no warning, just, "Tighten up, everybody."

Idiot, I thought to myself, suppose one of your tail-end Charlies had been flying close and hard during the earlier part of the flight, and slipped up a little when called on to tighten up? There was room under the cable, but not an awful lot.

In time, I applied the same reasoning to my crop-dusting shame. I had pushed too hard, too long, for a perfect job. Today, if a farmer planted cotton in a cypress-tree patch and asked me if I thought I could dust it, I would smile a polite "no" and help him drink his local moonshine while the hired hand drove the tractor through.

●

Sometimes a pilot needs the comfort and counsel of another's opinion to help him get his wings level. It's a bit like visiting the chaplain, and it usually helps.

●

A blinding snowstorm caught us at dusk. First the ground disappeared, then nothing was left but the glow of instruments and a white blur of driving snow in front of the landing lights. A VFR pilot is lucky to last five minutes under these menacing conditions, but an hour and a half later, we were guided to a safe landing, thanks to a Mohawk Airlines captain.

For 250 miles, my wife and I wove our way through a continuous field of small black clouds, each supported on a column of snow. Their comfortable spacing left plenty of time to absorb the beauty of this strange world. Fascinated by these delightful surroundings, we flew blindly into trouble. Our Binghamton destination forecast was 2,500 broken, with occasional light snow showers. Fifteen miles from home, we saw the big one: snowfall for 20 miles north and 20 miles south.

I tried to fly around that mess, but there was no end to it. The cloud seemed to expand in all directions until it surrounded us. As I wasted precious time looking for a hole, the snowfall thickened and the hills below merged into a white nothingness. For a fellow who has abandoned planes all over New York, I don't know why I didn't run while I could.

An anxious appeal to flight service brought no answer. The Binghamton Tower did respond, but while we were talking, the airport closed. Binghamton routed us to Oneonta via Rockdale Vortac. On the way to Rockdale, the sun set and darkness closed in. ATC told us that Mohawk Flight 368 was diverting itself to aid us, but I was too busy even to wonder how they could help. As we reached the vortac, however, two white eyes pierced the snow above us. Ten seconds later, they were gone, and we saw no more of Mohawk for quite some time. Somewhere in the darkness above us, the airliner captain radioed me a heading and the distance to the Rockdale Airport, but my timing was off and we ended up circling the dim city lights.

Those two welcome white eyes appeared again, and he gave me a new heading out into the blackness. Thirty seconds later, we broke out of the snow to see the world's most beautiful runway lights: Oneonta Airport.

It would be unfair to continue without giving credit to the others who contributed their fine efforts, but my main purpose is to share with you a letter I got from that airline captain:

Dear Ed,

I'm sorry I didn't get your first name when we were talking over the radio—but now that I know it, I hope you won't mind proceeding on that basis.

Ed, my friend, there is a great service you can do for your fellow pilots. That is to tell them of the things you did right. Perhaps you are aware of the number of aircraft lost every year. If they had sought help in time, their fate might have been different.

Your story of what you did right might save a life. Such as:

1/Having sufficient instrument training to enable a pilot to retain control of the aircraft under adverse conditions. The point? No one can fly an airplane from the ground or from another airplane.

2/Letting someone know that assistance is necessary. This must be done before adverse weather can force the aircraft to too low an altitude, where blocked line-of-sight VHF communications become impossible. If you're too low for someone to hear you, no one can help you.

3/Making the decision to request aid at a time when

enough fuel still remains to give people time to help. It will almost always take at least 30 minutes to become oriented and to fly to a prepared landing site.

This is just a suggestion, but it might say the right things to someone who will one day find himself in trouble. As an ex-flight instructor looking back over 11,000 hours, I know there are only two kinds of pilots: those who have been lost and those who will be lost.

All pilots should have the opportunity to learn from other pilots' mistakes, because they'll never live long enough to make them all themselves.

●

There is comfort in that, whether you are a pilot or not, for the underlying message in that captain's letter is that flying brings out the best in people. There is a certain equality among those who dare to rise from the ground; it brings people together, and when you can understand that, you learn to love it, too.